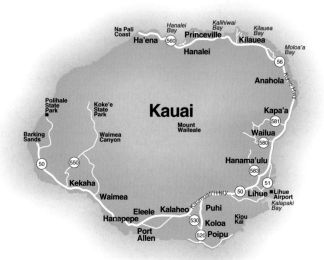

Na Pali
Coast

Hanalei
Bay

Kalihiwai
Bay

Kilauea
Bay

Ha'ena

560

Princeville

Kilauea

Hanalei

Moloa'a
Bay

56

Anahola

Polihale
State
Park

Koke'e
State
Park

Kauai

Kapa'a

581

Mount
Waialeale

Wailua

580

Barking
Sands

Waimea
Canyon

Hanama'ulu

583

50

550

51

Kekaha

50

Lihue

Lihue
Airport

Waimea

Kalapaki
Bay

Eleele

Kalaheo

Puhi

Hanapepe

530

Koloa

Kipu
Kai

Port
Allen

520

Poipu

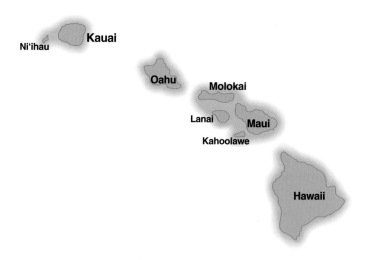

Ni'ihau

Kauai

Oahu

Molokai

Lanai

Maui

Kahoolawe

Hawaii

Kauai Underground Guide

Lenore & Mirah Horowitz

Papaloa Press

18th edition

First edition:	1980
Second edition:	1981
Third Edition:	1982
Fourth edition:	1983
Fifth edition:	1984
Sixth edition:	1985
Seventh edition:	1986
Eighth edition:	1987
Ninth edition:	1988
Tenth edition:	1989
Eleventh edition:	1990
Twelfth edition:	1992
Thirteenth edition:	1995
Fourteenth edition:	1996
2nd printing	1997
Fifteenth edition:	1998
Sixteenth edition:	2000
2nd printing	2002
3rd printing	2003
Seventeenth edition	2004
Eighteenth edition	June, 2007

ISBN-13: 978-0-9745956-1-0
ISBN-10: 0-9745956-1-6
ISSN 1045-1358
Library of Congress Catalog card 82-643643

Original Line Drawings by Lauren, Mirah, Jeremy,
& Mike Horowitz, Devon Davey & Tara French
Historic Petroglyph Drawings by Likeke R. McBride
Photographs by Lenore W. Horowitz

Special thanks to Jeremy, Mike, Lauren, & Larry
for their help with the research, writing, and design of this 18th edition
& mahalo nui loa to Keali'i & Fred
& special thanks to Andy, Peter, Rockie, Marvis, Megan,
John Edmark & his Design Class at Stanford University
and in fond remembrance of John Akana

Printed in Canada
by Kromar Printing, Winnipeg, Canada

Contents

Exploring Kauai

Eastside Beach Adventures, 27

North Shore Beach Adventures, 41

Restaurants, 147

Definitely Don't Miss on Kauai!

* **Discover our favorite north shore beaches**: *Hanalei Bay* for incredible beachwalks, calm summertime swimming, and challenging winter surf breaks; *Kalihiwai* for family fun, with firm, level sand perfect for running, and river kayaking (in summer, you can kayak in the bay itself); *Secret Beach* for quiet seclusion, accessible only down a cliffside trail; *Larsen's* for lazy afternoons of beachcombing; or *Tunnels* for amazing snorkeling, best in summer or on calm winter days.

* **Drive to the end of the road on the north shore.** From *Hanalei* to *Ha'ena* and then on to *Ke'e Beach*, you will wind along a narrow road, at times crossing one lane bridges, at times hugging the cliff, or perched next to the sea. At road's end, Ke'e Beach is a great spot for summertime snorkeling, and is also the trailhead for the Kalalau trail.

* **Tour the Na Pali Coast.** This spectacular wilderness area is one of the most beautiful places in the world – huge waves crash against jagged cliffs, and waterfalls plunge into the cobalt sea. See the whole Na Pali coast either by *boat* or *helicopter.* One gives you a bird's eye view; the other takes you up close into sea caves and under sparkling waterfalls. If possible, try both.

* **Hike the Kalalau Trail** even if only for the first quarter mile. Experience the amazing Na Pali cliffs from a narrow footpath winding through tropical trees and streams along the coastline. Seasoned hikers can forge ahead to *Hanakapi'ai Beach, Hanakapi'ai Falls,* or beyond.

* **Snorkel with Kauai's fish**: *Poipu Beach* on the south, *Lydgate Park* on the east, and on the north, *Tunnels* (best in summer or calm winter days) and *Ke'e Beach* (summer only). Or try scuba diving. Gregg Winston at Watersports Adventures, an excellent scuba teacher and pro guide, can coax even the most timid first-timers into the water and on to adventure.

* **Escape to a hidden beach**, perhaps *Secret Beach, Larsen's,* or *Kilauea* (north shore); *Maha'ulepu Beach* (south shore); the long beach walk south of *Lydgate Park* (eastside); or *Pakala's* (also called *Infinities)* (westside).

* **Sunrise, sunset**: In summer, head north to one of our favorite beach overlooks, or visit the *Princeville Hotel,* watch the sun set into the ocean (summer) before a leisurely dinner in Hanalei. In winter, try *Beach House Restaurant* in Poipu, or drive father west to the beach at Kekaha. At sunrise, walk the beach south of *Lydgate Park* on the eastside.

* **Drive to the end of the road on the westside.** See spectacular *Polihale Beach,* miles of white sand and a limitless horizon against tall cliffs.

* **Taste local Kauai**. Try a restaurant that has been serving meals on the island for more than 70 years: *Haimura's Saimin, Barbecue Inn,* or *Tip Top* (Lihue); and *Hanama'ulu Café & Tea House* (Hanama'ulu). Here you can find authentic Kauai!

* **Sample Kauai treats**: *lilikoi chiffon pie, Taro-Ka Chips, shave ice,* and home-made *ice cream.*

* **Meet local farmers at farmers' markets**. On different days in different parts of the island, you can sample wonderful fruits and vegetables from the back of pick up trucks and on folding card tables – mangoes, papayas, tasty bananas and star fruit, as well as beautiful flowers. You will be tempted to cook eggplant and stringbeans – even if you're on vacation!

* **Try Kauai's fresh catch**: Local fish markets sell fish off the boat: *Ara Sushi Market* (Hanama'ulu), *Fish Express* (Lihue), and *Pono Market* (Kapa'a) which has what many consider the island's best poki (sashimi grade fish with seasoning and onions). For a terrific lunch or cook-your-own filets, try *Kilauea Fish Market* (north shore) or *Koloa Fish Market* (south shore). Or hook your own dinner on a fishing charter.

* **Zipline** over Kauai's valleys and streams on a Kipu adventure.

* **Drive Waimea and hike Koke'e**. The *Waimea Canyon* is Kauai's own miniature version of the Grand Canyon. At road's end, hiking trails in *Koke'e* can show you gorgeous forest scenery entirely different from coast and beach.

* **Take the kids to great family beaches**: *Kalihiwai* (north shore), *Lydgate Beach Park* or *Hanama'ulu Bay* (eastside), *Poipu Beach* (south shore), and *Salt Pond Beach* (westside). The *Kamalani Playground* at Lydgate has something special for kids of all ages.

* **See the privately-owned island of Ni'ihau,** off limits to all but native Hawaiians (in order to preserve Hawaiian culture). *Holo Holo Charters* and *Blue Dolphin Charters* take snorkeling trips to the reefs off Ni'ihau; *Seasport Divers* has an all-day three-tank scuba boat dive for certified divers. *Ni'ihau Helicopters* (operated by the Robinson family) offers an air tour with a beach and picnic stop.

Preface

Kauai is a very different island than the one we wrote about in our first *Kauai Underground Guide* in 1980, when sixteen typewritten pages were enough to give advice on what to do and see. Today, you can still enjoy the Hanama'ulu Tea House, Barbecue Inn, Hanalei Dolphin, Kountry Kitchen, Bull Shed, Beach House – but the island has changed dramatically. And so has our Guide, growing into a full color book with a great website, packed with an exclusive music CD by Keali'i Reichel, Hawaii's foremost singing star. With Keali'i as our partner, the *Kauai Underground Guide 'Campaign for Kids,'* which is funded by our book's profits, has already helped Kauai's children in health and welfare, education, literacy, and the arts (for a listing of the non-profits we are proud to assist, see page 238).

We've been writing *The Kauai Underground Guide* for more than twenty years, through two hurricanes and dramatic changes, as tourism replaces sugar in driving the economy. Coffee, macadamia nuts, and vacation homes are growing up on land once used for sugar cane. Starbucks has arrived, and so have Home Depot, Wal-Mart, KMart, and Costco.

You can still find that rare and special Kauai we love so much, and we want to share with you our favorite adventures at the beaches, in restaurants, on tours and expeditions. We do not describe every restaurant or tour, only those we have tried, and our opinions are shaped by a preference for peace and quiet, privacy and natural beauty.

In many ways our *Guide* is unique. As a family of six, we can offer lots of advice on beaches and activities for children of all ages. For adventurers, we describe the most exciting and challenging things to do and see. Even a single year brings dramatic change, and our working vacations keep us busy tracking what's new, what's different, and what's still as lovely as ever. You may find in some cases that prices, policies, even managements may be changed, so do your research carefully when making decisions and keep us posted about what you find out. It's been great fun hearing from people all over the world who have explored Kauai with our *Guide,* and want to help update the next one.

So as we go to press with this 18th edition, we want to thank all the friends and readers who have helped make our *Guide* a storybook success. Who would have thought that our first edition would grow into a book which has sold more than 225,000 copies! Like an old friend, Kauai gets better with each visit. We hope you will feel the same way about this special place and return again soon.

Lumahai Beach on the spectacular north shore

Planning your ideal Kauai vacation

Where to Stay: location, location, & location

Kauai has a little of everything. Like an America in miniature, it has rolling hills and valleys to the east, sun-warmed beaches to the south, and majestic coastal mountains to the north and west. Such variety is rare, particularly on an island only 44 miles in diameter, but it can make deciding where to stay and what to do a bit difficult. Luckily, there is no wrong answer, and planning the perfect vacation is definitely part of the fun.

Almost circular in shape, Kauai has three main tourist areas: Princeville & Hanalei to the north, Poipu to the south, and the 'Coconut Coast' between Lihue and Kapaʻa to the east. Choosing your home-base depends on what you want to see and do. Families with limited mobility might prefer the gentle surf and primarily pleasant weather of the south shore. Adventurers on the other hand may want to head north to gorgeous cliffside beaches where hiking and camping offer chances to see unparalleled, unspoiled beauty, but where the weather is more variable. Those who locate on the eastside – like our family – can access both: from the eastside you can drive north or south in a little less than an hour, depending (increasingly) on traffic. The towns of Kapaʻa and Wailua sit about midway in the road system that goes almost all the way around the island's perimeter, with the Na Pali cliffs of the northwest quadrant off limits to wheeled vehicles.

Before you go: Request a free *Kauai Vacation Planner* (800-262-1400; kauaidiscovery.com). Visit kauai-hawaii.com for helpful info about attractions, calendars, point to point driving tips, parks, recreation, culture. Get up to speed on local news at *The Garden Island* newspaper (kauaiworld.com).

The North Shore

With by far the most spectacular landscape, the north shore combines rugged mountains with beautiful beaches and green vistas – the Kauai of postcards. As the windward shore, the north also gets the most rainfall, particularly in winter months when surf at the beaches is also larger and more unpredictable. No matter the season, many people love the north shore for its rural tranquility and magnificent beauty, and come here to 'get away from it all,' to wind down to 'island time' in an area made remote by one lane bridges occasionally washed out in winter storms.

The major resort area on the north shore is *Princeville*, perched high on an ocean bluff overlooking Hanalei Bay. Princeville includes private homes and condos, two championship golf courses, and the 5-star *Princeville Hotel*, with elegant rooms and service, gourmet dining, and a stunning cliffside setting. A small beach at the base of the cliff, reached by the hotel's elevator, offers marvelous views and, when seas are calm, swimming and snorkeling. From $400/night plus $15/day for parking (Starwood Hotels: 826-9644; 800-826-4400; princeville.com).

Spectacular Hanalei Bay in summer, from the terrace, Princeville Resort. In winter, surf can reach twenty feet, and boats take shelter in the south.

Princeville Resort overlooks Hanalei Bay

Nearby, the *Hanalei Bay Resort* combines the conveniences of a condominium with hotel amenities. From $205/night/room and $370/night/suite (Quintus Hotels: 826-6522; 800-827-4427; hanaleibayresort.com.)

Surrounding Princeville's golf courses are a host of condos and private homes offering gorgeous ocean views, particularly at sunset. Getting to the beach requires a hike down the cliff to one of the small beaches (hotel guests have elevator privileges). For listings, see kauaidiscovery.com.

Outside Princeville, you can get closer to the ocean, for example in the town of Hanalei, near one of Kauai's finest beaches at Hanalei Bay. You'll also find privacy on or near the beach in the lovely residential areas of Kalihiwai and Anini (east of Hanalei) and Wainiha and Ha'ena (west of Hanalei). The *Hanalei Colony Resort* in Ha'ena offers beachfront condos from $230/night (826-6235; 800-628-3004; hcr.com).

The South Shore

The south shore, at Poipu, on the island's leeward side, has drier weather and generally calm year-round swimming conditions. It's also flatter, with dryer vegetation than the north shore. For swimming, there is wonderful Poipu Beach, and for sheer beauty, Maha'ulepu.

You have many choices for lodgings, including two resort hotels – the *Grand Hyatt Resort* and the *Sheraton Kauai*. The *Grand Hyatt* offers 600

*At the Grand Hyatt in Poipu,
a popular waterway complex
features a salt water lagoon
and a 150-ft waterslide.*

spacious rooms and elegant dining in an architecturally beautiful resort. Because the beach has strong surf and intimidating currents, the Hyatt offers guests an elaborate swimming complex, with river pools, waterfalls, a 150 foot waterslide, as well as a 5 acre meandering saltwater lagoon with islands. From $340/night plus $15/night resort fee (724-1234; 800-233-1234; kauai-hyatt.com).

Poipu Beach

Nearby, the *Sheraton Kauai* has 413 rooms located right on beautiful Poipu Beach, great for swimming in all seasons. From $390/night, plus $16/night resort fee (742-1661; 800-782-9488; sheraton-kauai.com). The most famous south shore hotel, the *Waiohai,* is now a Marriott resort timeshare, with 238 two-BR villas. From $390/night (246-1401; 800-742-4400; marriott.com).

Beachfront at its best? The best location on Poipu Beach is the *Kiahuna.* Only a few buildings are directly on the beach; most are set back, several next to the road. Three competing companies manage the property: Outrigger's *Kiahuna Plantation* (115 units from $265/night. 742-6411; 800-688-7444; outrigger.com); *Castle Resorts* (95 units from $235/night. 742-2200; 800-367-5004; castleresorts.com); and *Kiahuna Beachfront* – the best beachfront units (only 13) – from $325/night (800-937-6642; kiahuna.com).

Poipu Kai, set farther back, walking distance from the beach, starts at $128/night, managed by ResortQuest (742-7424; 877-997-6667; resortquesthawaii.com) and Suite Paradise (742-7400; 800-367-8020; suiteparadise.com).

Kauai Marriott–great location on Kalapaki Beach

The *Poipu Point Resort* has luxurious suites, but fronts a beach too rough for easy swimming. From $200/night/1BR suite (877-696-6284; sunterrakauai.com).

Choose from condos and B&B's, many close to Poipu Beach Park, which has excellent protected swimming and snorkeling all year round. For more information: Poipu Beach Resort Association (742-7444; poipu-beach.org).

The Eastside

The eastside, from Lihue (where the airport is located) to Wailua and Kapa'a – the Coconut Coast– has convenient location as its main advantage. It's about midway between Poipu and Hanalei and about a 40 minute drive from each, so you can explore the island with ease in either direction, depending on the weather and your inclinations.

You'll find hotels, condos and B & B's, many of which can accurately be described as 'beachfront.' You should ask careful questions, however, because eastern shore beaches can have tricky currents, and swimmers must be very cautious. *Beachfront at its best?* The *Kauai Marriott* fronts the magnificent sandy swimming beach at Kalapaki Bay in Lihue, with a circular pool ringed by five jacuzzis, one of the state's largest. On more than 880 acres of golf courses and waterways, it has rooms that may be smaller

The Kauai Marriott pool

than the Hyatt's, but you can't beat the beach. From $370/night (245-5050; 800-220-2925; marriotthotels.com).

The *Coconut Coast* near Wailua offers a host of moderately priced hotels, condo resorts, and B & B's. Some excellent beachfront condos include *Lae Nani* (822-4938; 877-523-6264), *Wailua Bay View* (800-882-9007), *Lanikai* (822-7700), *Kapa'a Sands* (800-222-4901), and *Kapa'a Shores* (822-3055).

The newest complex, the enormous *Waipouli Beach Resort* features a swimming complex with waterslide to compensate for a modest beach. From $200 (822-6000; waipoulibeachresort.com or outrigger.com). Moderately priced hotels (about $200/night or less) include a great location for families, the *Aloha Beach Resort Kauai*, only a short walk to Lydgate Park's wonderful rock-rimmed pools and Kamalani playground. From $135/night (888-823-5111; alohabeachresortkauai.com). The Kauai Beach Resort has had a facelift and is now a *Hilton*; a sand pool and waterslide make up for a beach with currents too strong for safe swimming (245-1955; hilton.com).

Some hotels turned timeshares (suites with mini kitchens) include (for under $200) *Islander on the Beach* (877-997-6667; resortquesthawaii.com) and *Kauai Coast Resort at the Beachboy* (822-3441; 877-977-4355; kauaicoastresort.com).

The recently renovated *ResortQuest Kauai Beach at Makaiwa* (822-3455; 866-774-2924; resortquesthawaii.com) puts a new face on the old Sheraton. On a budget? Try the remodeled beachfront bargain, *Hotel Coral Reef* (800-843-4659; hotelcoralreefresort.com).

The Westside

Largely undeveloped, the west side is still 'local' Kauai. The weather is sunny, dry, even arid, which you'll appreciate when other parts of the island have rain. Just west of Poipu and Koloa, you'll come to the town of *Hanapepe*, with art galleries, a swinging bridge, and an authentic taro chip factory. *Salt Pond Beach Park* is nearby, a beautiful spot enjoyed primarily by local people. Further west, you'll love the long, sandy beach at *Kekaha*, great for swimming, surfing, and beachwalking. Beyond that is the awesome expanse of sand and cliffs at *Polihale*. Choose from vacation homes, apartments, and B & B's in the towns of Kekaha and Waimea. *Waimea Plantation Cottages* offers hotel services with old-style charm in vintage plantation cottages with free wireless internet access (From $150/night; 800-9-WAIMEA; waimea-plantation.com or resortquesthawaii.com). The best swimming beach, however, is at Kekaha.

Finding Home Base: hotels, condos & homes

Beachfront & oceanfront: the truth & the lingo

If you want to be located on or close to a swimming beach, consider these words carefully: 'ocean front' probably means a rocky place, or at least marginal swimming, but even 'beachfront' can be a misleading term. The so-called 'beach' could be rocky or unswimmable due to dangerous currents and strong surf. A property as a whole may be accurately described as 'beachfront,' but actually be shaped like a pie wedge, with the tip on the beach and the wide end (where *you* may end up being situated) back on the road. Or it may be technically adjacent to a beach, but with a building, a swimming pool (or even a road) in between.

Key questions: What will I see when I open up my sliding glass door? How far do I have to walk (or drive) to get to the nearest sandy swimming beach? If you have children, ask about the closest 'child-friendly' swimming beach. Swimming pools vary in size and location, and yours may end up being a tiny kidney next to the parking lot, so ask how far you have to walk to reach it— a key point if you have toddlers and all their paraphernalia to carry.

Renting condos and homes

New condo developments are going up all over the island, the result of accumulated building permits issued before Hurricane Iniki struck in 1992. New luxury complexes with high density and expensive interiors now compete with older, smaller developments in better locations but showing their age. New vs old: that's your first choice. The second is whether to rent direct from an owner or through an agency. Owners give better rates but obviously will have less flexibility to deal with changes in your vacation plans, and are less likely than agencies to refund your money if you are unhappy. If you decide to go owner-direct, one of the largest listings is *Vacation Rentals by Owner* (VRBO.com). *Tripadvisor.com* keeps up with changing opinions, and *The Kauai Vacation Planner* lists the operators for each condo complex (800-262-1400; kauaidiscovery.com). Check the classifieds in mags like *Hawaii Magazine* or *Sunset Magazine*, and contact resort associations in each area: South shore: P.O. Box 730, Koloa, HI 96756; 742-7444; poipu-beach.org. North shore: princeville.com.

For a human voice, try *Kauai Vacation Rentals* (800-367-5025; KauaiVacationRentals.com), a well-established agency offering personal-ized advice on rentals island-wide; *Garden Island Properties* (800-801-0378; kauaiproperties.com); or *Prosser Realty* (800-767-4707; prosser-realty.com). Some agencies specialize. SOUTH SHORE: *Grantham Resorts* (800-325-5701; grantham-resorts.com), *R & R Realty* (800-367-8022; R7R. com), *Poipu Connection* (800-742-2260; poipuconnection.com) *Garden Island Rentals* (800-247-5599; kauairentals.com), *Suite Paradise* (800-367-8020; suite-paradise.com).

NORTH SHORE: *Na Pali Properties* (800-715-7273; napaliprop.com), *North Shore Properties* (800-488-3336; kauai-vacation-rentals.com), *Harrington's Paradise Properties* (888-826-9655; oceanfrontkauai.com), *Hanalei Aloha Management* (800-487-9833; 800hawaii.com), *Oceanfront Realty* (800-222-5541; oceanfrontrealty.com). Expect to pay at least $140/night ($180/night for a condo at or near a swimming beach). Advance deposits and one week minimum stays are usual. Popular months (December–March; August) require advance reservations. Cancellation policies vary from two days to a month.

Renting bed & breakfasts

B & B's are plentiful on Kauai and come in all varieties and prices, from a beachfront cottage to the spare room-with-bath in a home with a gregarious host). Some owners list in the *Kauai Vacation Planner.*

Two agencies on Kauai represent many individual owners, as well as small hotels, inns and condos. *Bed & Breakfast Hawaii* (800-733-1632; bandb-hawaii.com) has listings on all the islands, and *Bed & Breakfast Kauai* (800-822-1176; BnBKauai.com) has an exclusive focus on Kauai.

Questions to ask: What's for breakfast (continental, full meal, or stocked kitchen)? What kind of beds (length, width)? What degree of interaction with host and other guests (How friendly or private do you want to be?)

Most require a deposit and a minimum stay. Ask about cancellation policy. Many are booked 2 to 3 months in advance, so plan ahead.

Renting rustic

If you like hiking and camping (yet amid relative comfort), you can rent cabins in some of Kauai's loveliest wilderness areas. In the Koke'e forest region, you can rent a cabin with stove, refrigerator, hot shower, cooking and eating utensils, linens, bedding, and wood burning stove at bargain rates, only $35-$45/night (maximum stay of 5 nights during a 30 day period). *Koke'e Aloha Lodge*, Box 819, Waimea HI 96796 (335-6061). Also in Koke'e, *YWCA Camp Sloggett* offers hostel accommodations ($20/pp/night) and platforms for tent camping ($10/pp). YWCA Kauai, 3094 Elua St, Lihue HI 96766. (245-5959; campingkauai.com).

On the north shore, *YMCA Camp Naue* in Ha'ena offers beachfront camping in bunk houses (or your own tent) $12/night. YMCA of Kauai, Box 1786, Lihue HI 96766 (246-9090).

Kapa'a's International Hostel has beds for $25/night/bunk; internet available (823-6142; hostels.com).

Getting There

What to pack — how not to lose it

If you travel only with carry-on bags, you avoid the risk of losing checked luggage on connecting flights, especially when changing carriers. Here are some tips (learned the hard way) for checking luggage: We pack a change of clothes and a bathing suit for each family member, as well as any prescription drugs in a carry-on bag just in case someone's suitcase is lost temporarily. We also distribute everybody's belongings in every suitcase, so that no one person is left without clothes if a suitcase is lost permanently. And we label each bag clearly *inside* where the label can't be accidentally detached.

A replacement-cost rider on your Homeowner's insurance policy may turn out to be a wise investment, for the airline's insurance limit is $1,850 per passenger. Airlines typically subtract 10% of the purchase price for each year you have owned an item, exclude cameras and jewelry, and may take up to six months to process a claim. If your luggage is missing or damaged, save all baggage-claim stubs, boarding passes, and tickets, and be sure to fill out an official claim form at the baggage supervisor's office *before* you leave the airport. Most clearly tagged luggage makes its way to the owner within 24 hours (and they deliver). Call daily for an update.

Vacation days are too precious to spend on line in stores. We try to cut down on clothes (except for swim suits and T-shirts) and use space for other essentials – beach sandals, walking or hiking shoes, snorkel gear, sunscreen, hat with brim, sunglasses, beach bag or back pack, frisbee, tennis ball, or beach ball. Island restaurants are informal – no tie or jacket, but bring long pants. A light sweater in winter is a good idea.

Flying to Kauai: it's all in your connections

The typical travel plan involves a flight first to Honolulu International Airport on Oahu and then a connecting flight to Kauai's Lihue Airport. This route can turn into a full day of travel, particularly on the return trip to the mainland, when the clock can move 3 (or even more) hours ahead of you. Consider paying a premium for a non-stop flight on United, American, Delta or ATA (from Los Angeles, San Francisco, or Phoenix). Charter discount fares may save you money, but can also cost you frustration: if there's a problem with your flight, you'll have no way to change carriers. Major airlines with frequent daily flights give you more options in case someone gets sick, or you need to go home earlier, or (even better) later!

Hawaiian, Aloha, and Go! Airlines fly the twenty-minute flight from Honolulu to Kauai. Airline regulations require a minimum 70 minute layover in Honolulu to allow passengers and baggage to be transferred to inter-island connecting flights. However, if you travel only with carry-on luggage, you might be able to catch an earlier flight to Lihue, if you are willing to take your chances as a stand-by. (The computer data is often wrong, and stand-bys can often get seats). Ever vigilant for a profit stream, Hawaiian and Aloha now charge a change fee, but instead of paying, you can try this: go directly to the gate and socialize with the attendant who might just want to put you on that earlier flight to clear the gate area. On your inter-island flight, you may be asked to check your carry-on luggage because of size, as some inter-island aircraft have small overhead bins. Keep your jewelry, camera, prescription drugs, and favorite stuffed animals in a small bag you can pull out of that carry on, if necessary.

Hawaiian Airlines	835-3700; 800-367-5320	hawaiianair.com
Aloha Airlines	484-1111; 800-367-5250	alohaair.com
GO! Airlines	888-IFLYGO2	iflygo.com

Traveling with kids

If you are traveling with babies or toddlers, you can request bulkhead seating (but not exit rows, which can be assigned only to adults) in advance. Be sure to get an assigned seat in the computer in advance too, so that your seats have priority if the flight is overbooked. Enroll in the airline's Frequent Flyer Program – the kids too.

You should bring along your child's car seat, which can go into the baggage compartment, as Hawaii state law requires them for children under three. Airlines now permit use of the child's restraint seat on board the aircraft, but that requires the child to have a paid seat on crowded flights. Staying a week or more? Save money and help kids. The YWCA (245-6362) can help you buy a car seat to use on Kauai, have it ready for you at your rental car then pick it up as a tax-deductible donation when you leave.

Families who fly to Kauai from the east coast might consider staying overnight in California to help children make the difficult time adjustment

Kite flying at Hanalei Bay

in stages, particularly on the long trip home. After flying from Kauai to California, the kids can run around the hotel, have ice cream, and stay up late in order to push their body clocks ahead 3 hours while they sleep. If you book a late morning flight out of California the next day, the kids can sleep late in the morning, and if you're lucky, wake up fresh for the second day's flight, ready to adjust their body clocks through another time zone.

On that journey home, if bad weather threatens to delay your connecting flight from Lihue to Honolulu, consider taking an earlier flight, before the inter-island flights get backed up. In fact, it's a good idea to get on any earlier flight to Honolulu once you're in the Lihue airport.

To amuse the kids during the long flight, you can pack small toys, crayons, books, paper dolls, and an 'airplane present' to be unwrapped when the seatbelt sign goes off. Ask the cabin attendants for 'kiddie packs' or cards right away as supplies are often limited. Snacks and a secret toy can save the day in those awful moments when one child spills coke on another. Keep chewing gum handy to help children relieve the ear-clogging which can be so uncomfortable, even painful, during the last twenty minutes of the descent when cabin pressure changes. Sucking on a bottle will help a baby or toddler cope with altitude adjustment.

To save shopping time, we stuff as many beach and swimming toys into suitcase corners as possible. 'Swimmies' (arm floats) are great for small children to use in the pool, as are goggles and masks, toy trucks for sand-dozing, frisbees, inflatable beach balls, and floats. Boogie boards, by far the best swimming toy, can be brought home in the baggage compartment after your vacation (packed in a pillowcase). Best choices are at the M. Miura store (Kapa'a), Progressive Expressions (Koloa), or even K-Mart, Wal-Mart, or Costco (Lihue). Boogie boards are better balanced than the cheaper imitations. Caution: they can be hazardous in a pool; a small child who tips over in deep water can be trapped underneath.

Rent children's equipment at *Ready Rentals* (823-8008; 800-599-8008; readyrentals.com). $20 delivery. To protect a baby's delicate skin, bring a hat with a large brim, socks for feet, and a strong, waterproof sunblock (re-apply frequently).

Tips for visitors with disabilities

Kauai County provides a 'Landeez' all-terrain wheelchair at lifeguard stations at Poipu Beach Park, Lydgate Park, and Salt Pond Beach Park. These parks, and Kalapaki Beach (for parking directions, see p 31) have the most accessible facilities and pathways. At Kalihiwai and Anini Beach (north shore) and Hanama'ulu Beach (eastside), parking is flat and close to the water. Some companies make a special effort to help: Gregg Winston at *Watersports Adventures,* whose efforts were much appreciated by 8-year-old Jeffrey Barrett (821-1599); Chuck Blay of *Kauai Nature Tours* (888-233-8365), and Debra Hookano at *Liko Kauai Cruises* (888-sea-liko). For rental of equipment 24/7, including Landeez chairs and ramps, and helpful island advice, call *Gammie Home Care* (632-2333; gammie.com). For help, contact the ADA Office (mayorsada@kauaigov.com; 241-6203 V/TTY). For non-hotel lodging options: *Bed and Breakfast Hawaii* (800-733-1632) or *Bed and Breakfast Kauai* (800-822-1176). For transportation, call ahead to the *Kauai Bus* (241-6410; kauai.gov), and be sure to bring your valid ADA paratransit ID card and parking placard for accessible parking stalls.

Getting Around: It's a two–lane lifestyle

No matter where you decide to stay, you can easily explore the rest of the island by car. Except for the wilderness area in the northwest quadrant, Kauai is nearly encircled by a main two-lane highway, with sequentially numbered 'mile markers' to make tracking easy. You can drive from Lihue to Kapaʻa in about 10 minutes, from Kapaʻa to Hanalei in about 30 minutes, from Lihue to Poipu in about 20 minutes, and from Poipu to Polihale in about 35 minutes.

The best places to explore on Kauai are accessible by either paved roads or established dirt roads in the cane fields which are maintained as 'rights of way' to the beaches. So pack a picnic lunch and some beach mats, sunscreen, your guidebook, a good novel, and your Kealiʻi Reichel music CD, and explore some of the island's most beautiful hidden beaches. Plan your adventures according to the weather and the season. In winter, the surf is more unpredictable and dangerous on the beaches to the north and northeast, while the best and safest swimming is on the south shore. In summer, the surf may be up on the south and west, with north shore beaches beautiful for swimming. Whatever the season, follow this simple rule for swimming safety: don't swim alone or too far out at any beach whose currents are unfamiliar to you. Read *Beach Safety* carefully (p 80). When you park, lock up and store valuables in the trunk, as you would at home.

Kauai is still rural in infrastructure – just two-lanes, pretty much all around the island. Traffic has led to establishing contra flow on Rt 56 between Hanamaʻulu and Wailua during rush hour, and 4 'bypass roads.' You'll see the first one, Rt 51, as you leave the airport; it merges with Rt 56 (Kuhio Highway, the main north/south road) near Hanamaʻulu. Maps 1, 2

Northbound traffic moves easily until you reach Wailua, where three little traffic lights can cause unbelievable congestion during rush hour. *The Wailua bypass* winds through cane fields, then comes out near the center of Kapaʻa, offering you a view of sugar cane rather than the rear bumper of the car in front of you. You'll see the turnoff to the west, just north of the traffic light at Wailua Family Restaurant and just south of the Coconut Plantation Marketplace. It brings you to the center of Kapaʻa about two blocks behind the ABC Store. Maps 1, 3, 4

The Koloa bypass avoids the center of Koloa town and ends at the Hyatt Resort. Turn left off Rt 520 (Maluhia Rd) just before Koloa (the left turn will be very well marked), and follow signs to Poipu. Maps 6, 7

The Lihue bypass: Take Niumali Rd in Nawiliwili near the small boat harbor to Halemalu Rd, and follow it past the Menehune Fish Pond to Puhi

Rd which then connects with Rt 50, and from there you continue on to Koloa and Poipu. This bypass skirts the traffic on Rt 56 as you pass Kukui Grove. Map 2

While driving your rental car on Kauai, keep this in mind: speed limits and seat belt laws are strictly enforced. It's illegal to make a U-turn in a 'business district,' even if it doesn't look like much of a business district.

On Kauai, it's a two-lane lifestyle. So polish your left hand turn skills, avoid driving between 4pm and 6:30pm, load your Keali'i Reichel CD into your car's stereo, and be patient. Remember, you're on vacation!

Best of virtual Kauai

Feeling awash in Kauai-related websites? Here are some of the best – with the most useful information and few ads.

First stops	kauaidiscovery.com
	kauai.gov
	kauai-hawaii.com
Garden Island Newspaper	kauaiworld.com
Beaches and Surf	kauaiexplorer.com
Kauai calendar	kauaiworld.com/calendar
	kauaiexplorer.com/guides/cool_happenings.php
Kauai sites of interest	hawaiiweb.com/kauai/html/sites
	wikitravel.org/en/kauai
All-island calendars	calendar.gohawaii.com
Kauai Yellow Pages	htyellowpages.com
Local Kauai links	trykauai.com/Lilikoi_Links.htm
Poipu Beach	poipu-beach.org
B & B's, condo rentals	kauaivacationrentals.com
	vrbo.com
Hawaiian music	mele.com
Keali'i Reichel MP3s	kealiireichel.com
Hawaiian language	hawaiianlanguage.com
Kauai hiking	hawaiitrails.org
	kokee.org
Kauai Gardens	ntbg.org
	naainakai.org
Kauai camping	campingkauai.com

Managing Kauai's weather: chasing the sun

If you dial 245-6001 for the weather report on Kauai, you will probably hear this 'forecast': "Mostly fair today, with occasional windward and mauka (mountain) showers. Tonight, mostly fair, with showers varying from time to time and from place to place." Except for storms, Kauai's normal weather pattern is mostly sunny, with showers passing over the ocean, crossing the coastline and backing up against the island's mountainous interior.

Like all the Hawaiian islands, Kauai's sunny side varies with the winds. Normal trade winds from the north and northeast bring rainfall to these 'windward' shores and create the 'lee' of the island in the south, at Poipu, and west, at Kekaha and Polihale. When the clouds back up against the mountains and bring showers to the north shore beaches, Poipu and Salt Pond may have sunny skies. However, when the winds blow from south and west, called 'Kona winds,' the lee is in the north and northeast. The north shore may be spectacular while the eastern and southern shores have rain.

Planning can make the most of any weather, since Kauai has 'micro climates' and a 20 minute drive may take you from rain to sun. Be prepared to drive to the sun – all the way west to Polihale if necessary. If it's clear up north, visit the north shore, for these beaches are by far the most spectacular, and if your stay is only for a few days, you may not get another chance. Rain outside? Drive south to Poipu or west to Salt Pond or Kekaha, where it's usually drier. With heavy rain, Polihale might be your best option.

Only an island-wide storm should send you indoors to rent a movie, so check the weather and surf report before deciding whether to go north to Hanalei, south to Poipu, or west to Kekaha. Call 245-6001, try kauaiworld. com/weather, or call these friendly merchants who have agreed to be your weather tipsters: *Nukumoi Beach Center,* Poipu (742-8019*); Wrangler's Steak House,* Waimea (328-1218); *Pedal & Paddle,* Hanalei (826-9069).

Weather patterns vary with the seasons. Showers are more frequent in winter and spring, while summer months are warmer and more humid, fall months clearer and more dry. Temperatures range between 60's at night & mid-80's most days, and in summer can reach the low 90's.

The beaches also change their moods with the seasons. In summer, the water may be calm and clear, but winter surf at the same beach can foam and crash like thunder. Some north shore beaches disappear entirely under winter surf, and may officially close for safety.

Eastside Beach Adventures

Kalapaki Beach, a family favorite for swimming & playing frisbee – and exploring the Marriott Hotel afterwards

Lydgate's rock pools, great for family swimming

Beaches

Hotels

Anahola Bay is great for beachwalks and family fun

For island tastes, visit farmers' markets in Lihue and Kapa'a, 96

Scuba anyone? Lessons are fun and can begin a great adventure, 130

Wailua River, Kauai's only navigable waterway: try kayak explorations, 120 & water-skiing, 142

Zipline, 145
Tubing, 140

Lydgate Park has snorkeling and rafting for the whole family

Long beachwalks along Wailua Beach south of Lydgate Park

Kauai's main traveled roads:
Rt 56 (Kuhio Hwy) travels north from Lihue to Wailua, Kapa'a and Anahola.
Rt 56 then curves to the west towards Kilauea, then Princeville, Hanalei, Ha'ena.

Rt 56 also connects in Lihue with Rt 50 heading west towards Poipu (via Rt 520), then Hanapepe, Port Allen, and Waimea.

Kayaking on the Hule'ia River and Alakoko (Menehune) Fish Pond, 120

Map 1
Eastside

Eastern Shore
Kauai

Secret Beach

Kilauea Lighthouse

Crater Hill

Kahili ("Rock Quarry") Beach

Kilauea Bay

Beach access

Kilauea Rd

Kolo Rd

Wailapa Rd

North Wailakalua Rd

To Princeville

Pila'a Beach

Larsen's Beach

Ko Ōolau Rd

Beach access

Moloa'a Bay

56

Moloa'a

Kuhio Hwy

Moloa'a Stream

Papa'a Stream

Aliomanu Beach

Anahola Beach Park

Aliomanu Rd

Anahola Bay

Kahala Point

Anahola

Anahola Stream

3

Anahola Rd

Kahena Rd

Kealia Rd

Kealia Stream

Kealia Rd

Donkey Beach

Kawaihau Rd

Mailihuna Rd

Kealia Beach

Kaehulua Rd

Kapuna Rd

Kapa'a

4

To Keahua Arboretum

5

Kapa'a Shopping Center

6

Kapa'a Farmers Market

Kauai Village Shopping Center

7

8

Kapa'a Beach Park

Kamalu Rd

580

581

9

Waipouli Town Center

10

11

12

A

Kuamōō Rd

Kapa'a Bypass Rd

Waipouli Beach

13

B

14

Coconut Plantation Marketplace

Wailua

C

Wailua Bay

15

D

Fern Grotto

Leho Rd

Rock Pool

Wailua Falls

Wailua River

Lydgate State Park

Nukolii Beach

583

Ma'alo Rd

Wailua Golf Course

Hanama'ulu Stream

56

E

16

Hanama'ulu

Hanama'ulu Beach

Hanama'ulu Bay

51

Ahukini Landing

Grove Farm Plantation

Ahukini Rd

Lihue Airport

22

Kaumuali'i Hwy

50

Lihue

17

Lihue Farmers Market

Rice St

20

Nawiliwili Rd

21

19

Kauai Lagoons Golf Course

To Poipu

Kukui Grove Shopping Center

18

F

Kalapaki Bay

Ninini Point & Lighthouse

Hulemalu Rd

Huleia River & Wildlife Preserve

Menehune Fishpond

Kalapaki Beach

Kalapaki Beach

N

0   1   2
Miles

Activities

Family Fun

Tours

The beautiful Wailua coastline along the 'coconut coast'

Restaurants

Kilauea

1	Lighthouse Bistro	203
2	Kilauea Bakery	200
	Pau Hana Pizza	200
	Kilauea Fish Market	201

Anahola

3	Ono Char Burger	181

Kapa'a

5	Kountry Kitchen	173
	Small Town Coffee	94
	Wasabi's	187
	Blossoming Lotus	154
6	El Café	178
	Ono Family Rest	180
	Lotus Root	155
	Mermaids Café	176
7	Sukothai	183

Wailua

8	Kauai Pasta	170
9	King & I	171
10	Waipouli Deli	186
	Coconuts	158
	Lemongrass	175

	Papaya's Café	182
	La Playita Azul	174
12	Bull Shed	155
14	Hukilau Lanai	166
	Mema Thai Cuisine	176
	Caffé Coco	156
13	Kintaro	172
	Monico's	177
15	Wailua Marina	185

Hanama'ulu

16	Hanama'ulu Tea House	164

Lihue

17	Okazu Hale	179
18	Duke's	159
	JJ's Broiler	168
	Kalapaki Beach Hut	168
	Portofino Café	157
	Tokyo Lobby	184
19	Garden Island BBQ	161
	Barbecue Inn	153
	Ma's Family Inc	176
	Hamura's Saimin	163
20	Oki Diner	179
21	Deli & Bread Connection	190
	La Bamba	173
22	Gaylord's at Kilohana	156

Favorite Eastside Beaches

• Our favorite swimming beach is *Kalapaki Beach*, wonderful for swimming, skim boarding, and when the surf is right, boogie boards. The sand is perfect for playing volleyball or frisbee, running, or simply sunning. Rent a catamaran or kayak if surf conditions are calm.

• *Lydgate Park* in Wailua is perfect for families – an enormous lava rock-rimmed pool offers wonderful swimming and snorkeling, with a smaller rock-rimmed pool just right for toddlers. Beyond the pools, the beach is great for long walks. Lydgate also offers the best playground on

Kauai, the Kamalani Playground, for the climbing and swinging set, and the beach is a great spot to watch glorious golden sunrises.

• For water activities, *Wailua Beach* is popular with local surfers. On the Wailua River, you can water ski or explore upstream by kayak (130).

• Surfers will love *Kealia Beach*, where wonderful, even rollers can give great rides when conditions are right.

• For picnics and beach walks, visit beautiful *Anahola Bay*.

• Hungry? For inexpensive lunch try *Hamura's Saimin, Barbecue Inn* or *Kalapaki Beach Hut* (Lihue), *Monico's* or *Caffé Coco* (Wailua) or *Mermaid's* and *Lotus Root* (Kapa'a). Spend a bit more and enjoy *Duke's Barefoot Bar* or *Gaylord's* (Lihue) or *Blossoming Lotus* (Kapa'a).

Eastside ins & outs

Most visits to Kauai begin (and end) on the east side, at the Lihue airport, the centerpoint of the driveable roads on the island. When you leave the airport in your rental car, you can head north along the eastern shore to Wailua and Kapa'a, then on to Princeville, Hanalei and Ha'ena. Or you can head west to Poipu, Kalaheo, and Waimea. *Lihue*, the county seat, sits on the right angle of Rt 56 going north and Rt 50 going west. It's home to many of Kauai's original family businesses, the *Kauai Museum,* and the *Kauai Lagoons Marriott Resort.* Just outside of town, as you head west toward Poipu on Rt 50, is *Kukui Grove Center* (Borders, Kauai Products Store, Starbucks, Quiznos, Wal-Mart, KMart, Costco and Home Depot).

Great Days on the Eastside

Day 1: WAILUA/KAPA'A: Breakfast at *Kountry Kitchen* (p 173) or *Ono Family Restaurant* (p 180). Morning: water-ski (p 142) or kayak on the Wailua River (p 120), or hike Sleeping Giant Mountain (p 115). Lunch *Monico's* (p 177) or *Caffé Coco* (p 156). Afternoon at *Lydgate Park*, great for family fun and long beachwalks (p 32). Dinner *Hukilau Lanai* (166), *Kintaro* (p 172), or *Blossoming Lotus* (p 154).

Day 2: LIHUE: Breakfast at *Tip Top* (p 184). Morning: kayak trip up the Hule'ia River (p 120), tour *Grove Farm Plantation* (p 123), or try a *zipline* (p 145) or *tubing* (p 141) adventure. Lunch at *Kalapaki Beach Hut* (p 168) or *Hamura's Saimin* (p 163). Afternoon: relax or sail at Kalapaki Beach. Dinner *Bull Shed* (p 155) or *Duke's* (p 159).

Heading north along the eastern shore takes you to the towns of *Wailua* and *Kapaʻa*. You will drive on Rt 56, Kuhio Highway, the most traveled of Kauai's three main roads. You'll come to Wailua as you cross the Wailua River, the only navigable river on Kauai, as it flows into Wailua Bay, a popular local spot for surfing and beachwalking. *Caffé Coco* (west side of Rt 56) and *Monico's* in Kinipopo Center (east side of Rt 56) offer tasty, inexpensive meals. Next door, browse *Goldsmith's Gallery* for exquisite jewelry by island goldsmiths and designers. About a mile north, *Coconut Plantation Marketplace* is a tourist-style shopping center with clothing stores, fast food, movie theater, and souvenir shops.

Continue north to *Kapaʻa* for small art galleries (*Kela Glass*), specialty shops, and great food (*Blossoming Lotus*). Take out a picnic lunch from *Lotus Root* or *Mermaids* and head just north of town to *Kealia Beach* (mile marker 10), a favorite surfing spot. Walk the long sandy beach, or explore the bike/walk improved pathway north around the rocky point to *Donkey Beach*.

Anahola, at mile marker 13, is a quiet residential area designated by law for families of Hawaiian descent. Anahola Beach is peaceful, great for a family picnic or a long, relaxing beach walk. Take out a picnic from *Ono Char Burger*. Beyond Anahola, the road curves towards Kilauea and the north shore.

Sail a catamaran on Kalapaki Bay

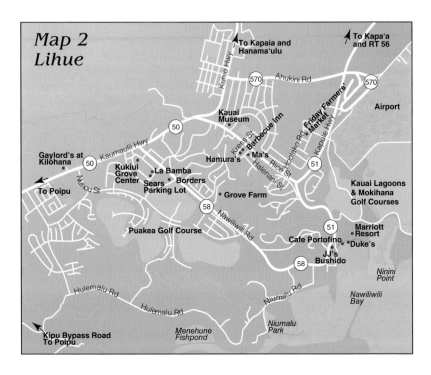

Map 2 Lihue

Eastside Beaches

Lihue Area Beaches: Kalapaki Beach

Kalapaki Bay is unforgettably beautiful. Almost enclosed by craggy green hillsides, this natural harbor has a wide sandy beach with some of the best swimming on the island. The waves roll to shore in long, even swells and break in shining white crests which are usually great for swimming and rafting. At times, surf is very rough, but even if you can't swim, you can enjoy beautiful views. Green mountains with the contours of a giant animal sleeping in the sun face houses on stilts perched precariously on the sheer cliff.

Fronting this beach is the spectacular Marriott Resort at Kauai Lagoons, a headline-maker from the time it opened in the late '80's as a Westin Hotel because of its lavish design, elaborate collection of far eastern art, and mini zoo of tropical birds and animals. Today you'll still find Kauai's largest swimming pool, its tallest high-rise (set into the cliff, it is technically still 'no higher than a coconut tree'), and its only two-storey escalator.

Kalapaki Beach is a favorite family spot. The firm sand is perfect for games and hard running, and the waves can at times break perfectly for boogie boards. Build sandcastles, play beach volleyball, rent a kayak or catamaran, or try your hand at windsurfing. Heed high surf warnings, however, for in winter months, the waves can break straight down with enormous force, and every so often a really big wave seems to come up out of nowhere to smash unwary swimmers.

Directions: Take Rice St through Lihue, and turn left into the main entrance of the Kauai Marriott. Pass the main lobby, and turn right at the first street, follow it down the hill to the beach access parking lot. The hotel maintains an accessible restroom for people with disabilities. Maps 1, 2

Ninini Beach

The drive to this tiny beach, 'Running Waters,' is more interesting than the destination. You wind along a cane road next to the airport runway, so close that the jets taking off and landing almost make you want to duck.

Turn off Kapule Rd just south of the Lihue airport at the marble gates (once the limo entrance to the old Westin), drive through brush and rustling grasses, then through the hotel grounds, always bearing towards the water, until you reach the lighthouse at Ninini Point. You'll have a gorgeous view of the coastline, a great spot to picnic. The beach is not safe for swimming.

Hanama'ulu Beach

A perfect crescent of soft shining sand, the beach at Hanama'ulu Bay is perfect for building sandcastles and hunting sunrise shells. In summer, the waves are gentle enough for children to enjoy. Rolling to shore in long, even swells only about a foot or two high, they break into miniature crests which turn to layers of white foam flecked with sandy gold, like the lacy borders of a lovely shawl.

Even occasional 'wipe-outs' are not serious because of the gentle, gradual slope of the sandy bottom.

Hanama'ulu Beach

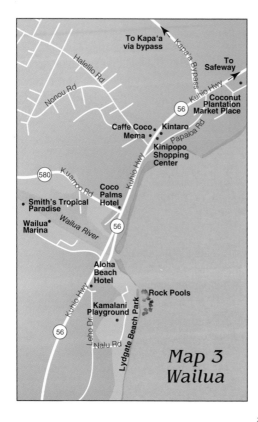

**Map 3
Wailua**

Kids can chase tiny sandcrabs, and there is plenty of shade for babies beneath the tall ironwood trees which fringe the sand. Behind the beach, the Hanama'ulu Stream forms shallow pools as it winds toward the bay, and kids can hunt for tiny crayfish and other creatures with nets. The deep gold of the river is shaded by trees so tall and dense you can hardly see the sky, and the dark green leaves trail into the water behind stalks of lavender water hyacinths with petals streaked with the colors of peacock feathers. A picnic pavilion faces the river, and tables look out over the bay. Everything is uncrowded, as this beach is frequented by few tourists. Unfortunately, it is also in the path sometimes used by helicopters returning to the airport from their scenic tours. Try to ignore the noisy choppers, and plan your visit for the morning, as the mosquitoes get hungry about 4pm.

Directions: Turn off Rt 56 Kuhio Highway towards the sea at Hanama'ulu, between the 7-Eleven and the school. Bear right at the fork. The road ends at the park. Restrooms, playground. Map 1

Wailua Area Beaches: Lydgate Beach Park

Lydgate Park just south of the Wailua River is a favorite spot for families. A rock-rimmed pool provides safe swimming for babies and toddlers, even in winter months. Adjacent is an enormous rock-rimmed pool which breaks the surf into rolling swells excellent for swimming, rafting, and floats of all kinds. The pool is one of the best year–round snorkeling

Lydgate's rock rimmed pools

spots on the island, for families of brightly colored fish feed along the rocky perimeter, so tame they almost swim into your hands. The rocky wall protects snorkelers and swimmers from surf and dangerous currents. Fly a kite, play frisbee on the wide, sandy beach, and collect shells and driftwood.

Kids will love the Kamalani Playground, 16,000 square feet of fun, with mirror mazes, a suspension bridge, lava tubes, and circular slide. South of Lydgate, the beach is ideal for long walks, very beautiful and almost deserted. Continue past the rocky point in front of Kaha Lani Condominium along the beach (or take the paved bike & walkway) towards the Hilton Hotel. The sand is firm and fine, perfect for walking, and you'll have spectacular views of the coastline, particularly beautiful at sunrise or sunset. You'll probably find only fishermen checking their lines. Swim with caution, however, for surf can be rough and currents powerful; Lydgate's pools are much safer.

Directions: If you are driving north on Rt 56, turn right onto Leho Rd just past the Wailua Golf Course. The right turnoff to the park is clearly marked. Follow this road to the Park and the rock pools. If you are driving south on Rt 56, you must turn left onto the Leho Rd just across the bridge over the Wailua River, at the Aloha Beach Resort. Lydgate has a lifeguard, picnic tables, and showers. Maps 1, 3

Wailua Bay

Wailua Bay's long, curve of golden sand is perfect for walking. Near the bridge is the mouth of the Wailua River, sometimes shallow enough to

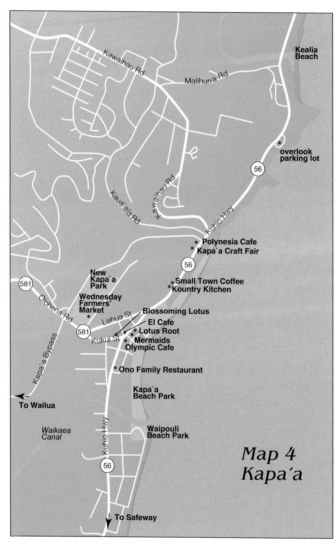

Kealia
Beach

overlook
parking lot

56

Kawaihau Rd

Malihuna Rd

Kaua'a'a Rd

Kawaihau Rd

Kuhio Hwy

Polynesia Cafe
Kapa`a Craft Fair

56

581

New
Kapa`a
Park

Small Town Coffee
Kountry Kitchen

Olohena Rd

Wednesday
Farmers'
Market

Lehua St

Blossoming Lotus

El Cafe

581

Lotus Root

Kukui St

Mermaids

Olympic Cafe

Kapa`a Bypass

Ono Family Restaurant

Kapa`a
Beach Park

To Wailua

Waikaea
Canal

Waipouli
Beach Park

Kuhio Hwy

Map 4
Kapa'a

56

To Safeway

ford, but at other times deep and treacherous. Swimming in the brackish, calm water of the river can be fun, although parents of young children should not let them stray from the edges because the water can become deep very quickly. Swimming where the river empties into the bay is not recommended because currents can be dangerous and unpredictable. Local kids often congregate here, a popular spot for surfing and body boarding, particularly in summer. A lifeguard is usually on duty. The Wailua River offers many activities: water skiing (p 142), kayaking (p 120), or (if open) touring Fern Grotto (Smith's Boat Tours 822-4111).

Directions: On Rt 56, just north of the Wailua River bridge Maps 1, 3

Kapa'a Area Beaches: Kealia Beach

North of Kapa'a on Rt 56 and just past a scenic overlook turnout, you will see spectacular Kealia Beach, a long, wide curve of golden sand ending in a rocky point. When the surf is up, lots of surfers ride the long, even rollers. During summer months, the waves can be gentle enough for children at the far end of the beach where lava rocks extending into the sea create a cove where the water is quieter. Kealia has long been one of Jeremy's and Mike's favorite beaches for surfing and body boarding. The sandy bottom slopes so gradually that you can walk out to catch some wonderful long rides, though at times the waves can be too powerful for children (even adults).

Body board fun at Kalapaki, Kealia, Anahola, Lydgate, and Hanama'ulu.

Exercise caution, particularly in winter. Stay near the body boarders, and not the hard board surfers looking for the bigger thrill. Watch out for the small, blue 'men o' war' jellyfish, which wash ashore after high surf. If you see them on the sand, they are probably also in the water. They pack a nasty sting, so head to another beach for the day.

Firm, level sand makes this a perfect walking beach, and children will enjoy playing in shallow pools behind the beach where a stream flows into the ocean. Strong rip currents near the river mouth can make ocean swimming hazardous.

Directions: Drive north of Kapa'a on Rt 56 until you see the parking lot between mile markers 10 and 11. Maps 1, 4

Donkey Beach

Donkey Beach is a lovely and peaceful spot, a long curve of sand which ends in piles of rock on both sides. Surf and currents are strong, even in summer, making swimming risky and only for experts. Waves crest with gleaming foam and break straight down with thunderous explosions of spray. We saw no one in the water, though – our first hint that Donkey

Beach was for sun-worshipers rather than swimmers. In fact, it has for years been a place where nude sunbathing was the rule. Times are changing, however, as land once devoted to sugar is developed into homesites, and security patrols help folks remember to cover up.

Directions: A scenic public bike and walking path follows the cane road from Kealia Beach to Donkey Beach. Or park in the public lot just off Rt 56 between the mile 11 and 12 markers. Map 1

Anahola Area: Anahola Bay

The beach at Anahola Bay is so long that to walk from one end to the other may take you nearly an hour. Colors are magnificent, especially at sunrise or in late afternoon as the sun moves to the west over the dark green mountains, deepening the blue of the water and the gold of the sand while brightening the tall white puff clouds until they glow with light.

Swimming can be risky, for surf near the center of the bay can be strong and currents powerful most of the year. The county park at the sheltered southern end of the bay is great for snorkeling and picnicking. On the northern end the bay, where the Anahola stream flows into the sea, children can play in shallow pools formed by the stream as it winds toward the bay, sometimes filled with tadpoles and tiny fish for kids to net. Children can also explore the stream on boogie boards where it is shallow.

Anahola Bay is a family favorite, a good choice on weekends when more well-known beaches are crowded. Watch out for small, blue 'men o' war' jellyfish which sometimes wash ashore after a storm. If you see them on the sand, they're probably in the water too, and the sting can be very painful.

A short drive (or long walk) north of the river will take you to Alio-manu Beach, popular with local families because of an offshore reef good for fishing and seaweed harvesting. Snorkeling is for experts only, who should venture out if tradewinds are light and the river current not strong. It's a great spot for a picnic, with little sandy 'nooks' along the road perfect for two. You can walk along the sand, wade among the rocks, pass homes peeking out from the vegetation, and listen to the waves.

Restrooms; showers. *Directions:* Turn off Rt 56 at the Aliomanu Rd just north of Duane's Ono Burger and the Anahola Store and follow it to the mouth of the stream. To get to the beach park at the southern end of Anahola Beach, take Anahola Rd (just south of Ono Burger which has great burgers; 822-9181), and head towards the water until you see parking area. Map 1

North Shore
Beach Adventures

*Kilauea Lighthouse
has a bird's eye view of
Secret Beach*

Map 5
North Shore

North Shore
Kauai

Ke'e Beach
Ha'ena Beach Park
Tunnels Beach
Kepuhi Beach
560
1 C
Ha'ena
Wainiha Beach
Lumahai Beach
Hanalei Bay
Pali Ke Kua ("Hideaways")
7
Pu'u Poa Beach
6 A B
5
Honoiki
Liholiho

Hanakapiai Beach
Kalalau Trail
Wet Caves
Limahuli Stream
Manoa Stream
Wainiha Powerhouse Rd
Wainiha River
Lumahai Stream
Waikoko Beach
Hanalei Pier
Hanalei
Weke
Aku

Hanakapiai Stream
Limahuli Falls
Wai'oli Beach Park
Ching Young Village
Kuhio Hwy
Wai'oli Stream
3 **4**
2 Hanalei Center
Hanalei

Hanakapiai Falls

Lumahai Beach

Hanalei Bay

Hike the Kalalau trail to Hanakapi'ai, 112

Princeville Hotel – come for sunset

Limahuli Gardens, 91
Na Aina Kai, 91

Beaches

Hotels

A Princeville Hotel
B Hanalei Bay Resort
C Hanalei Colony Resort

Kilauea Lighthouse

Most Na Pali boat tours now depart from south and westside harbors, 86

Sharing the wave at Kalihiwai

Kauai's main traveled roads: Rt 56 (Kuhio Hwy) travels north from Lihue, becomes Rt 560 at Princeville, continues west to road's end at Ke'e Beach.

Kalihiwai Bay, a jewel on the North Shore

North Shore ins & outs

Exploring the north shore takes you to spectacular beaches, magnificent cliffs, amazing vistas. As Rt 56 winds north and then west, you will pass through three main residential areas: Kilauea, Princeville/Hanalei, and Ha'ena. Each has wonderful beaches and opportunities for adventure.

Driving north from Anahola, you will first come to *Kilauea*, passing along the way the turnoff to *Moloa'a Bay* and *Larsen's Beach*, both great spots for quiet beachwalking. Just outside Kilauea town (pick up picnic supplies at Kilauea Fish Market, Kilauea Bakery, or Farmers' Market Deli). Kilauea Bay and Kalihiwai Beach are beautiful places to explore. You can visit the Kilauea Lighthouse and nature preserve; tour *Na 'Aina Kai Botanical Gardens* nearby; and shop at Kong Lung and Banana Patch.

Princeville comes next, an ocean bluff community of condos, homes, two famous Robert Trent Jones golf courses, and the spectacular Princeville Resort Hotel, well worth a stop for lunch, afternoon tea, or a sunset cocktail. Bring your camera for amazing vistas of *Hanalei Bay*.

As the road winds down the cliffside, you will see one of the loveliest beaches anywhere in the world, Hanalei Bay, and the town of *Hanalei*, with quaint shops and tiny eateries. Stop for a picnic or at least a wonderful beachwalk on firm golden sand at one of the most beautiful places you will ever see.

Continuing west around Hanalei Bay, you will pass *Lumahai Beach* (you'll see all the cars parked on the roadside). We prefer to continue on all the way to the end of the road, crossing scenic one-lane bridges, hugging cliffs, and visit *Ke'e Beach* – a great spot for summertime snorkeling and the starting point for the trail to Hanakapi'ai (and Kalalau).

The north shore – and the drive to the end of the road – are absolute musts! Take extra film/storage media for your camera.

Favorite North Shore Beaches

- Spectacular *Hanalei Bay*, an unforgettable image of Kauai for those rainy evenings back home. Great for swimming and surfing, running and walking (p 55), and sunset music at Hanalei Pavilion (p 127). Start the day at *Café Hanalei* in the Princeville Hotel for breakfast with an incredible view (p 195).

- Our favorite family beach is *Kalihiwai*, which combines spectacular beauty with wonderful summertime swimming, as well as firm golden sand, perfect for running. In winter, surf is up, to the delight of our boys, and even spectators can have fun watching the surfers catch spectacular rides. Kids will love the brackish pools behind the beach for fishing, swimming, and playing with their boogie boards (p 53).

- *Anini Beach* is gentle enough for children (p 53), and a popular spot for snorkeling and windsurfing (p 145).

- For long, solitary beachwalks, try *Larsen's Beach* (p 47); for a peaceful picnic, try *Moloa'a Bay* (p 46).

- Adventurers love hiking to *Secret Beach,* both secluded and spectacular, with magnificent views of the northern coast (p 51).

- The best snorkeling, when surf is calm, is at *Tunnels Beach* (p 58). In summer months, *Ke'e Beach* (p 60) has excellent snorkeling as well.

- From Ke'e Beach, you can hike the cliffside trail through the Na Pali wilderness to *Hanakapi'ai Beach* (p 114), magnificently beautiful, though too dangerous for swimming, and further, to *Hanakapi'ai Falls*. Try the first quarter-mile climb to a spectacular point overlooking Ke'e Beach and the Ha'ena reefs. For sunset watching, don't miss the view from the Princeville Hotel, or from *Tunnels Beach, Ke'e Beach* or, in summer months, *Anini Beach* (p 53).

Great Days on the North Shore

Day 1: Breakfast at *Café Hanalei* (p 195) or *Hanalei Wake Up Café* (p 190). Relax on *Hanalei Bay* (p 53), rent a kayak and explore the *Hanalei River* (p 120), or try windsurfing at *Anini Beach* (p 145). Lunch picnic at *Kalihiwai* (p 53) with sandwiches/wraps from *Kilauea Fish Market* (p 201). Watch the sunset from Princeville Hotel's *Living Room*; listen to Kauai's talented entertainers (p 127). Dinner at *Neidie's* (p 204).

Day 2: Breakfast at *Kalypso's* (p 199). Drive to the end of the road to *Ke'e Beach* (summer, p 60). Hike the cliff trail to the Ke'e Beach overlook (p 114) or on to Hanakapi'ai Beach. Or visit *Limahuli Gardens* (p 91).Pack a picnic and snorkel at *Ke'e Beach* or *Tunnels*. Watch the sunset: with music at *Happy Talk Lounge* (p 127), with dinner at *Bali Hai Restaurant* (p 193), or a slack key concert at Hanalei Pavilion (p 127).

Day 3. Breakfast at *Kilauea Bakery* (p 200). Hike to *Secret Beach* (summer, p 51) or trail ride (p 117). Lunch at the *Princeville Golf Course* (p 206), *Tropical Taco,* or *Hanalei Mixed Plate* (p 190). Lazy afternoon beach walk at *Larsen's Beach* (p 47) or *Moloa'a* (p 46). Or tour *Kilauea Lighthouse*. Dinner at *Postcards* (p 204).

Moloa'a area beaches: Moloa'a Bay

Just north of Anahola and before you reach Kilauea, you can visit Moloa'a Bay or Larsen's Beach, which though beautiful are more suitable for relaxed beachwalking than swimming. The road to Moloa'a winds through countryside for several miles, and you can hear wonderful sounds – the breeze rustling in the leaves, the chirping of insects, the snorting of horses grazing in tree-shaded meadows. At road's end, you will find a gate attached to an unfriendly looking fence intended to discourage parking along the shoulder. Walk through the gate and cross a shallow stream.

Moloaʻa Bay

At this point the bay, hidden by the half dozen homes which ring the beach, suddenly comes into view – an almost dazzling half-moon of shining golden sand and turquoise water. The long, sandy beach ends in grassy hills and piles of lava rocks on the left, and a sheer cliff on the right. To the left, the rocks are fun to climb and search for shells and trapped fish, although this windward side of the bay is usually too rough for swimming, and the bottom is very rocky. To the right of the stream, the bay is more sheltered, the water gentler and the bottom more sandy.

In times of heavy surf, this bay, like all windward beaches, can have dangerous currents. During these times, Moloaʻa Bay is a beautiful place for walking. The peaceful solitude is filled with the sound of waves. The crystal blue water, traced with the shadowy patterns of the rocks below, stretches out to a horizon where pale clouds fade into a limitless sky. At 5pm you might see horses wandering home after another difficult day of grazing – a spectacular sight with the light glistening on the water and the horses darkening slowly to silhouettes.

To get to Moloaʻa Bay, turn off Rt 56 about a half-mile north of the mile 16 marker onto Kuamoʻo Rd; turn right onto Moloaʻa Rd and follow it to the end. Map 5

Larsen's Beach

Getting to Larsen's Beach is half the fun. A right-of-way-to-beach road wanders through pastureland, where horses grazing peacefully seem sketched into a landscape portrait of silvery green meadows. At the end of the well-graded, sandy road is a small parking area and a gate leading to the top of the cliff, where the beach below seems a slender ribbon of white against the dark blue water. Although a second, smaller gate seems to direct you to the right, walking through it takes you to a steep path ending in rocks. Instead, walk down the hillside to the left on a well worn path with a

Larsen's Beach, a great spot for beachwalking and shell collecting, even if winter surf is too strong for safe swimming.

gentle slope. A five-minute walk brings you to a long, lovely beach curving along the coastline and disappearing around a distant bend – perfect for lazy afternoons of beachcombing and exploring. Although a rocky reef offshore seems to invite snorkeling, Larsen's Beach is extremely dangerous.

Before you begin the hike down, observe the ocean carefully and locate the channel through the reef, just to the left of the rocky point where you are standing. The churning water caused by the swift current makes the channel easiest to see from this height, and once noted, it can be recognized at sea level. Once you see this channel, you can also pick out the smaller channels which cut through the reef at several other points. Swimmers and snorkelers should avoid going near any of these channels, particularly the large one, because currents can be dangerously strong and even turn into a whirlpool when the tide is going out. Remember, Larsen's Beach has no lifeguard, and help is not close by. Currents can be exceptionally treacherous at any time, but particularly in winter months, and four years ago two experienced local fishermen drowned here. The watchword is caution: swim in pairs, never go out beyond the reef, try to stay within easy distance of the shore, and examine the surface of the water carefully to avoid swimming near a channel. If you snorkel, don't get so absorbed in looking at the fish that you lose track of where you are, and don't go out at all if surf conditions don't seem right to you. Sorry about all the 'don'ts,' but safety is a key issue here.

A trip to Larsen's Beach does not require swimming or snorkeling. If you bring reef-walking sneakers to protect your feet, you can walk around in the shallow water and watch colorful fish who don't seem afraid of people. Or walk for miles along the magnificent coastline of this picture-perfect beach. Hunt for shells, or simply lose yourself in the spectacle of nature's beauty. You will probably encounter only another person or two.

The drive back is wonderful, with spectacular views of the rolling hills, lined by fences and stands of trees, and beyond them the dark and majestic mountains reaching to touch the clouds.

The turnoff at Kuamo'o Rd that takes you to Moloa'a, (just north of the mile 16 marker on Rt 56) also takes you to Larsen's Beach. After you bear left at the Moloa'a Rd turnoff, go about 1.1 miles and look for a dirt road on the right. The right turn marked 'beach access' will be very sharp and angled up an incline. Then another beach access sign will mark the left turn onto the long, straight road to the beach. (From Hanalei, turn left off Rt 56 at the mile 20 marker, and left again onto the beach access road). Park, lock up, walk towards the cliff, where you will find a gate leading to the top of the cliff and down the trail on the left. Map 5

Kilauea area beaches: Kilauea Bay

The road to this unspoiled beach tests the mettle of both car and driver with challenges at practically every turn, and takes you past sobering reminders of the devastating and deadly flood that caused enormous destruction a year ago when the Ka Loko dam broke. Deeply rutted, even gouged by ditches and holes, the road can turn into a quagmire in rain, but in dry weather, it can be navigated without too much difficulty by a careful driver even in a rented subcompact. Pick a dry day, and the road will add the zest of adventure and heighten the excitement of discovering, just down the hill from the parking area at road's end, a bay shaped like a perfect half-moon, the deep blue water sparkling with light, and the golden sand outstretched between two rocky bluffs like a tawny cat sleeping in the sun.

At the northern end is the Kilauea stream. One year it may be shallow enough for small children at low tide; the next, too deep. The width can vary from a few yards to fifty. To the left of the stream, the beach ends abruptly in an old rock quarry, a great spot for pole fishing. To the right of the

Surfing at Kilauea on a summer day

stream, the sandy beach extends a long way before ending in piles of lava rocks which children will enjoy climbing and exploring for tidal pools. Chances are you'll encounter only another person or two and can watch in solitude as the waves roll towards to the beach in long, even swells, break into dazzling white crests, and rush to shore in layers of gold and white foam.

Surf can be dangerously strong and the currents treacherous at certain times, particularly in winter when the beach may almost disappear beneath the crashing waves. We found the swimming safe enough in summer for our seven and ten-year-olds to surf on their boogie boards in the shallow water, although even close to shore the pull of the undertow made us watch them closely.

The tiny blue Portuguese 'men o' war' are sometimes washed ashore here after a storm, so if you see any on the sand, go to another beach, for these small jellyfish pack a giant sting!

Behind the beach, the stream forms brackish pools where children can swim safely, except near the stream's entrance into the bay where the current can be swift, particularly at high tide. One August, the pools were wider than we had ever seen, like a shallow lagoon, and our family had a great time netting tadpoles. Our children loved this beach because of the variety of things they could do and the challenge of ripping the leaves off the branches that scraped the sides of the car as we maneuvered around the gullies on the way down and back. We love the beach because we have had it, sometimes, all to ourselves.

Directions: south of Kilauea town, between mile markers 21 and 22, on Rt 56, take Wailapa Rd towards the ocean. After .4 of a mile, turn left onto a dirt road and follow it (only in dry weather) for about a mile until you reach the Kahili Beach at Kilauea Bay. The road passes the area devastated March, 2006 by a tragic break in the Ka Loko dam. Traces of destruction remain. Map 5

Secret Beach

Nestled at the base of a sheer cliff just north of Kilauea, Secret Beach is well off the beaten track for good reason. You must hike down (and back up!) a rocky trail which zigzags through trees, gullies, and brush. You can drive only to the trail's beginning at the top of the cliff. From here, you can hear the waves crashing below – apparently not very far away – as you look down on a trail which seems to disappear into a tangle of jungle. The path is steep in places – sneakers are a good idea – but branches, roots, and vines offer plenty of handholds, and in a pinch, you can always resort to the seat of your pants!

The walk down will take about seven minutes, and as the path makes the last sharp plunge before leveling off to the sand, you can see, at last, through a screen of trees and hanging vines, a magnificent stretch of golden sand and a shining turquoise sea. In rainy times, this enormous triangle of sand may be partly covered by a lagoon fed in part by a stream winding down behind the beach. Towards the left, you can climb a rocky outcropping and find a small beach ending in a steep cliff. Towards the right, you can see the Kilauea lighthouse and walk a long way across the sand.

Secret Beach is not a place to come alone, for the obvious reason of its isolation. Swimming is not safe. The surf is rough, and the currents strong and unpredictable; you'd never find a lifeguard if you had trouble. During the winter, this beach, enormous as it is, can disappear almost entirely under huge, crashing waves. Instead of swimming, walk along the water, hunt for shells, and forget everything but the feel of wet sand between your toes.

The walk back up the cliff will give you time to adjust to the world you left behind – just about 10 minutes of mild exertion, with the air cool under the trees and the leaves speckled with sunlight. This would not be pleasant in the mud, though, so don't go after a soaking rain. By the time you reach your car and remember that you have to stop at the store for milk, the peaceful solitude you left behind will be as hard to recapture as a wave rippling on the sand. But for a few moments, you were lost to your working-day world. This may be the secret of Secret Beach, a secret worth keeping!

Note: One reader discovered another secret about this beach, when she and her family reached the bottom of the trail and ran into "a long-haired young man wearing nothing but a guitar!" So be prepared for strange music!

Directions: Approach Secret Beach and Kalihiwai Bay from Kalihiwai Rd, about a half mile north of Kilauea on Rt 56. Turn towards the ocean onto Kalihiwai Rd. Bear left, then turn right onto a dirt road that looks like a

Kalihiwai—our favorite family beach on the north shore. In summer, the ocean can be calm, almost like a lake (below) while in winter, thundering surf can crash onto the sand (above).

broad red gash in the landscape. Follow towards the water till it ends. Park, lock up, and walk down the trail. Map 5

Kalihiwai Bay

You'll catch your first glimpse of Kalihiwai Bay as you drive down the narrow road carved into the side of the sheer cliff which encloses it on one side. From this angle, the bay is a perfect semi-circle of blue, rimmed with shining white sand and nestled between two lava cliffs. Ironwood trees ring the beach. A freshwater stream flows into the bay near the far end, so shallow and gentle at low tide that small children can splash around safely. It becomes deep enough behind the beach for kayak adventuring up-river.

A favorite family beach, Kalihiwai Bay offers wonderful summertime fun for people of all ages. Little ones will love the shallow pools behind the beach where they can fish or float on rafts, while older kids will enjoy the ocean swimming. At times, the waves rise very slowly and break in long, even crests over a sloping sandy bottom, perfect for wave jumping and boogie boarding. One summer day we watched a dozen children celebrate a birthday with a surfing party. In winter, the surf and currents in the bay can become formidable. Even experienced surfers may have difficulty managing the currents which can be particularly strong when a swell is running. If the surf is too rough, Kalihiwai is still a lovely beach for walking or running, with firm sand and magnificent views of the cliffs. There are portapotties, but the nearest public restrooms are in Kilauea at the ball field behind Farmers Market (next to home plate!) Pick up picnic supplies at Kilauea Bakery, and browse Kong Long Center and Banana Patch next door.

A yellow siren atop a pole on the beach road is a reminder of the *tsunami* or tidal wave of 1957 which washed away the bridge originally linking the two roads leading from Rt 56 to Kalihiwai Bay. Both are still marked Kalihiwai Rd at their separate intersections with Rt 56. Either will take you to the bay. If you choose the Kalihiwai Rd just north of the long bridge on Rt 56, you'll have to wade across the stream's mouth to reach the beach. The Kalihiwai Rd just south of the bridge and north of Kilauea is preferable. Map 5

Anini Beach

This quiet, beautiful beach goes for miles along a coastline protected by an extensive offshore reef. At some places the road is so close to the water you could almost jump in. The beach park has restrooms, camping, and picnic facilities, although you can turn off the road at almost any spot, park, and find your private paradise. The reef creates a quiet lagoon, great for summertime snorkeling, and for windsurfing at any time of year. During high surf, particularly in winter, the current running parallel to the beach can become strong enough to pull an unwary swimmer out through the channel in the reef at the west end of the park. Stay inside the reef.

polo road
Across from the Beach Park, the Kauai Polo Club hosts matches on summer Sunday afternoons. Continue along Anini through a quiet residential area all the way to its western end, where a sandbar extending quite far out invites wading and fishing. Children enjoy the quiet water and the tiny shells along the waterline, and you'll love the amazing combination of sounds – the roar of the surf breaking on the reef far offshore, and near your feet, the gentle rippling of the sea upon the sand.

In summer months, you can watch the sun set into the ocean at Anini Beach, a glorious sight which can be yours in perfect solitude. The tall ironwood trees darken to feathery silhouettes against a pale gray and orange sky, filled with lines of puff clouds. The water shimmers gold as the sun's dying fire fades slowly to a pearl and smoky gray, to the songs of crickets and the lapping of gentle waves.

Just northwest of Kilauea, between mile markers 25 and 26 on Rt 56, turn towards the ocean at the Kalihiwai Rd just north of the long bridge. Bear left at the fork, and follow the road as it winds downhill past the park till it ends at the base of the cliffs at Princeville. Map 5

Hanalei area: Princeville: Pu'u Poa Beach

Tucked beneath the Princeville Resort Hotel's ocean bluff perch is a sandy beach set inside a reef. When you look down from the hotel, you can see the rocky bottom that makes swimming less than perfect. This same reef can make for good snorkeling in calm summer seas, but you must negotiate your way carefully through one of the small sandy channels into the deeper water. In winter, waves crash against the outer reef, and it becomes a challenging surfing spot.

Public access is available through a cement path leading from the left of the gatehouse entry to the Hotel. Be forewarned: on the way down the cliff, you'll have to descend nearly 200 steps (and then come back *up* those same steps later on!). You can explore the beach more easily if you visit the hotel for breakfast or lunch, both wonderful meals in a spectacular setting. After dining, take the hotel elevator down to the beach level, where lovely gardens frame the sand. Bring a camera.

Directions: Drive Rt 56 north, enter Princeville at the main entrance (pick up a free map) and stay on Ka Haku Rd until the end. Park in the hotel visitor's lot if you're going to the hotel for lunch. If not, try the small public lot just in front and to the right of the hotel entry gate. Map 5

Pali Ke Kua or 'Hideaways' Beach

At the base of the cliff near the Pali Ke Kua Condominiums in Princeville is a lovely sandy beach set inside a reef, where you can watch the sun sparkle on the waves in near solitude. It is a peaceful spot, secluded and beautiful, actually two beaches connected by a rocky point. Swimming is not the best because of the coral bottom and the offshore rocks, but snorkeling can be very good in calm summer seas. Be cautious. On all north shore beaches, snorkeling can be risky and advisable only in a calm ocean. When the surf is up, currents can become dangerous. In winter, waves can cover the beach entirely.

It's called Hideaways for good reason – hard to get to, popular primarily with surfers or with guests at Pali Ke Kua who use the condominium's improved concrete pathway down the cliff. The public right-of-way is much more difficult; initially it's steep steps with a railing, and then the trail dwindles to dirt path. It can be slippery, even treacherous, when wet. The trek down takes about ten minutes, and the way up, as you can imagine, somewhat longer.

Directions: Enter Princeville, drive to the hotel and park in the lot. The hotel staff usually doesn't mind if you take one of the back spaces nearest the cliff, where you'll see the top of the steps down to the beach. Map 5

Hanalei Bay

Hanalei Bay is simply spectacular – a long half moon of golden sand stretching for miles. Turn off Rt 560 onto almost any road in Hanalei and you will come to Weke Rd, which runs east to west along the bay. Turn right to get to Hanalei Pavilion Beach Park (showers and restrooms), where each night at 6pm, Doug & Sandy McMaster play traditional Hawaiian slack key guitar music (826-1469). At the end of Weke you will come to the Hanalei Pier, where in winter months you can pay for walk-up surf lessons and board rentals (p 137). Several Trans-Pacific Cup Races from California to Hawaii end in this beautiful bay, and during summer, gaily colored boats

Hanalei can be peaceful and calm in summer, but winter waves can reach 20 feet, and boats move to safer harbors on the south shore and westside.

rock gently at anchor. The boats are moved out of the bay, however, by mid-October, and by winter, twenty-foot waves are not uncommon. In dangerously high surf, the beach is closed to swimming.

Looking for surf? The biggest breakers are at 'Pinetrees,' near the center of the bay. During winter months, when the surf can become dangerous, Hanalei Bay is still wonderful – the wide sandy beach firm and level for hard running. Walk west to where the Wai'oli Stream, icy cold from mountain water, flows into the bay. Sometimes it's shallow, at other times the current is formidable, but at all times it's beautiful and peaceful, waves crossing from different directions in foam glistening with gold.

West of the town, you can explore almost any road turning off Route 560 towards the water. At the westernmost curve of the bay, near the mile 4 marker, you'll find a calm, protected beach where the water is relatively quiet even when most of the north shore is too rough for safe swimming.

After you pass Princeville, Rt 56 curves down the cliffside to the town of Hanalei (mile 3 marker). Aku Rd (or any other right turn) will take you to Weke Rd, which runs along the bay from east to west. Turn right on Weke to go to Hanalei Pavilion Park (showers, rest rooms, lifeguard) or past it to Hanalei pier. Turn left onto Weke, and you can choose several 'right of way to beach' streets leading to the bay. Showers, restrooms and lifeguard station are available at Ama'ama Rd, or 'Second Parking Lot.' Map 5

Ha'ena Area Beaches: Lumahai Beach

The setting for the Bali Hai scenes in *South Pacific*, Lumahai is stunningly beautiful, a curve of white sand nestled at the base of a dark lava cliff, with a giant lava rock jutting out of the turquoise sea just offshore. Keep in mind that the trek down from the road may take you through slippery mud (showers are frequent on the north shore), and the trip back up can be worse, especially if you have to carry a tired child. No restrooms.

Swimming at Lumahai Beach can be very dangerous, particularly during winter months. Without a reef to offer protection from unpredictable currents and rip tides, Lumahai Beach is one of the most treacherous spots on the island, and people drown here almost every year. Beware of climbing that spectacular offshore rock for a photograph, as a sudden powerful wave can easily knock you off!

You can also continue to the western end of Lumahai, about a mile further along Rt 560 at the mile 5 marker. Across the street from an emergency telephone is the entrance to a sandy parking area. Here the beach is wide and golden, with breakers and currents which can be big enough to make swimming dangerous. Children will love playing in the stream flowing into the sea, ice cold from mountain rainwater.

The stream meets the ocean at a huge rocky bluff, a spectacular place to sit quietly and watch the waves crash against the rocks, sending dazzling spray into the air. It is also a beautiful beach for walking although the coarse sand is hard-going near the waterline, and you must cross a vast expanse of hot sand to get from the parking area to the sea, so bring sandals! Hunt for striped scallop shells shining in the sun, or wander all the way to the other rocky bluff that separates this part of Lumahai Beach from the part pictured in all the postcards. Cross the rocks could be hazardous even at low tide, because an occasional 'killer wave' can come up suddenly out of nowhere and smash you into the rocks. A small cave etched into the base of the cliff, with powder soft, cool sand invites wave-watching.

Pass Hanalei on Rt 560, and you will soon see, at about the mile 4 marker, many cars parked on the shoulder just past a 25 mph. If you choose to hike down the cliff to Lumahai Beach, park on the right and lock up. Map 5

Tunnels

Popularly known as Tunnels Beach, Makua Beach has a large lagoon perfect for swimming because it is protected by two reefs, the outer reef favored by surfers for perfectly formed arcs, and the inner reef filled with cavities and crevices for snorkelers to explore for fish and sea life. Divers love the outer reef for its tunnels, caverns, and sudden, dramatic drop off. Tunnels is about the only beach on the north shore that is usually calm enough for those trying to snorkel for the first time although even here you may find rough surf and treacherous currents during winter.

Listen to the surf reports, and plan any winter visits for times when surf is manageable, and preferably at low tide. In calm conditions, bring the kids and let them paddle about on boogie boards while the older ones try their luck with mask and snorkel. Bring fish food, or even a green leaf, in a plastic baggy and swish it in the water and you'll be surrounded by fish (Just be sure to take the bag back out with you). Swimming through the coral formations of the reef, which is almost like a maze of tunnels, can be great fun when the water is quiet. Enter the reef through one of the small sandy channels or the large one on the right, and dozens of fish in rainbow colors will swim right up to your mask. If the showers which frequent the north shore rain on your parade, you can take shelter under the ironwood

The reefs at Makua Beach, or Tunnels, can be great for snorkeling.

trees – or under your boogie board! If you see a monk seal lying on the beach, give it a wide berth. It's probably exhausted, sleeping before heading out to sea. Seals don't trust humans and need privacy to rest.

Snorkelers at Tunnels

Warning: Even when the area between the two reefs may look calm enough for safe swimming, watch out for these danger signs: high surf on the outer reef or fast moving ripples in the channel between the reefs. These indicate powerful, swift currents that could sweep you out through the channel into open ocean. Instead of swimming, hunt for shells on the beach, or walk around the rocks to the east.

Directions: Continue west on Rt 560, and go 1.1 miles west of the Hanalei Colony Resort. You will pass the mile 8 marker and the turnoff to the YMCA camp. Parking is nearly impossible due to safety issues and also opposition by local residents. Cars parked along Rt 560, a state road, will be ticketed. You can drive ahead to Ha'ena Beach Park, park, and walk back along the beach, or try parking along the county road leading to the YMCA campground (Parking is legal on county roads). No public facilities. Map 5

Ha'ena Beach Park

Past Tunnels is Ha'ena Beach Park, where an icy stream winds across a lovely golden sand beach curving along the coastline. The water is a dazzling blue. Reefs bordering both sides of the beach, named 'Maniniholo' after the large schools of striped convict fish feeding on the coral, provide summertime snorkeling, when the waves are gentle enough for swimming and rafting. During winter months, however, large waves can break right onto the beach, making swimming, even standing, a hazardous activity. Restrooms, showers, picnic and barbecue facilities, and a lifeguard are available, as well as camping by permit. You can walk a long way in both directions, with views of the towering cliffs and shimmering sea.

Pull into the Beach Park lot at the mile 8 marker on Rt 560. Map 5

Ke'e Beach

When you can drive no further on the main road along Kauai's north shore, you will discover a beach so beautiful you won't quite believe it to be real. The Na Pali cliffs rise like dark green towers behind the golden sand, and a reef extending out from shore creates a peaceful lagoon ideal for summertime swimming. As you walk along the shining sand, new cliffs come into view until the horizon is filled with their astonishing shapes and you begin to imagine captive princesses in enchanted castles.

Like all beaches on the north shore, surf at Ke'e Beach varies with the seasons. Winter surf can reach 20 feet, when the ocean roars with crashing waves and churning foam with undercurrents far too strong for safe swimming. In summer, however, the turquoise water can be perfectly still and so clear that bubbles on the surface cast shadows on the sandy bottom.

Summertime snorkeling can be spectacular alongside the reef, where the water, though sun-warmed will feel icy along the surface from rainshowers. If the tide is not too low, you can snorkel on top of the reef itself. Be careful. The coral reef may look shallow enough to walk on, but you won't want to take a chance on coral cuts. Be careful of unpredictable currents in

Ke'e Beach's lagoon (at left in this photograph) is great for summer swimming, but thunders with surf in winter.

the channel to the left of the reef, as they can be strong enough to pull a swimmer out of this sheltered area into the open sea. A lifeguard may be on duty to warn swimmers out of the channel.

Unforgettable Hanalei sunset

Trees provide shade for babies and protection from the occasional rain-showers which cool the air and make the coastline sparkle. The dark sand can be very hot, so you'll need your sandals. Small children can play and swim safely in the shallow water or climb over the rocks at low tide. Bring nets and pails for small fishermen.

Sometimes you can walk west across the rocks and around the point. From this vantage point, the Na Pali cliffs are truly magnificent – jutting into the cobalt blue ocean in vivid green ridges, the surf crashing in thundering sprays of foam. This walk can be dangerous in any but the calmest sea, and you must watch the direction of the tide carefully so that your return trip does not involve crossing slippery rocks through crashing waves. Ke'e Beach, lovely as it looks, can have treacherous currents and unpredictable surf, and so extra caution is a must. For a spectacular, bird's eye view of Ke'e Lagoon, climb the first quarter-mile of the trail to Hanakapi'ai Beach. Public restrooms and showers. If possible come early and come midweek.

Parking is hard to come by. We drive all the way to the end of the road, passing the large lots. If we can't find a spot, we turn off by the showers and restrooms and park along the dirt road under the trees. Map 5

Beach Access

By state law, all beaches on Kauai are public. Beachfront hotels and condos along the beaches (but not private homeowners) are required to provide public beach access. That does not always mean convenient access or even parking, unfortunately. While the county has provided for many public beach access points (the sign for access is a waist high silver pole with yellow band), there may not be adequate parking spaces. On the road to Ha'ena and all its lovely beaches, for example, parking is legal only on a few designated shoulders, and not at all near popular Tunnels Beach, where parking has become next to impossible. So look for the pole – and hope for the best!

Some Useful Hawaiian Words

– (a LOW ha) hello, good-bye, love, kindness, friendship

hale – (HAH lee) house

haole – (HOW lee) foreigner white man

heiau – (HEY ow) ancient Hawaiian temple

hui– (HOO' ee) club or group

kahuna– (ka HOO and) an elder, wise person

kalua– (ka LOO a) to roast under-ground, like kalua pig

kai – the sea

kama'aina – (ka ma EYE na) a native

kane – (KA neh) man

kapu – (KA poo) forbidden, keep out

keiki – (KAY kee) child

kona– (KOH na) leeward side of the island

lani – (LAH nee) heavens, sky

lomilomi – (low me low me) massage

mahalo – (ma HA lo) thank you

makai – (ma KAI) ocean side

mauka– (MOW ka) towards the mountains

menehune– Kauai's legendary little people & builders

nani – (NA nee) beautiful

ohana – (o HA na) family

ono – (OH no) delicious

pali – (PA lee) cliff, precipice

paniolo – (pa nee O lo) cowboy

pau– (pow) finished, done

puka – (POO ka) hole

wahine – (wa HEE neh) woman, wife

wikiwiki – hurry up

South Shore
Beach Adventures

Maha'ulepu Beach

Restaurants, 208

Rt 50 (Kaumuali'i Highway) heads west from Lihue to Kalaheo, Hanapepe, Kekaha, & Waimea. Turn off Rt 50 at Rt 520 to reach Koloa and then Poipu. The Koloa Bypass Road skirts Koloa and links directly with eastern Poipu.

Map 6 South Shore

Many Na Pali Boat Tours depart from Port Allen, 86

Salt Pond Beach Park, a family favorite, 75

scuba, 130

Beaches

Hotels

The wild beauty of Maha'ulepu.

Heliconia blooms at NTBG Gardens, Lawai, 92

ATV adventure, 84

Poipu Beach Park, 67

Kahili Mountain Park

To Lihue

50

Tree Tunnel

520

Kaumuali Hwy

Omao Rd

Koloa Rd

530

Waita Reservoir

Mahuila Rd

Waikomo Rd

Koloa

9

Weliweli Rd

Koloa Sugar Mill

520

Camp Rd

8

Lawai Rd

Prince Kuhio Park

10

Kiahuna Golf Course

Koloa-Poipu Bypass

CJM Stables

Poipu Bay Resort Golf Club

Gillin's Beach

Kawailoa Bay

Ha'ula Beach

Maha'ulepu Beaches

Kipu Kai

Long Beach

Kukui'ula Small Boat Harbor

Spouting Horn

Lawai Beach

Hoonani Rd

Poipu Rd

11

Poipu Shopping Village

Poipu

Koloa Landing

Poipu Beach Park

A 12

13 B 14

Hoone

15 D

C

Keoniloa Bay

Brennecke's Beach

Shipwreck Beach

Kauai
South Shore

Great Days on the South Shore

Day 1. Breakfast *Tomkats,* Koloa (p 226). Take a boat cruise (p 86) along the south shore to Kipu Kai (winter) or Na Pali Coast (summer). At the end of the day, head to *Maha'ulepu Beach* for great walking (p 70). Sunset dinner at *Beach House* (p 207). Or watch the sky glow at sunset from Poipu Beach Park and dine at *Brennecke's* (p 210). Stroll through the beautiful *Grand Hyatt Resort* after dinner (free valet parking).

Day 2. Breakfast *Joe's on the Green* (p 216). Tour *National Tropical Botanical Gardens* (p 92), take a zipline tour to *Kipu Falls* (p 145), or trail ride (p 117). Take out lunch from *Koloa Fish Market* (p 219), then snorkel at *Poipu Beach Park*. Before dinner, enjoy Hawaiian music at Hyatt's *Seaview Lounge* (free). Dinner at *Roy's* (p 223) or *Plantation Gardens* (lite meals in the lounge, p 220). Stroll through the *Kiahuna* and *Sheraton* grounds after dinner.

South Shore ins & outs

The south shore extends along the sea from Kipu Kai (nearly inaccessible except by boat) and Maha'ulepu Beach to the Poipu Beaches, and west towards Salt Pond Beach Park, including the inland towns of Koloa and Kalaheo. Rt 50 takes you west from Lihue to the turnoff at Rt 520 (Maluhia Rd) just before the Mile 11 marker; follow it through the 'Tunnel of Trees' to Koloa, then to the fork taking you either to Poipu Beach (left) or to Lawai (right) home of National Tropical Botanical Gardens and the popular blow hole called Spouting Horn. You can also avoid Koloa and take the bypass road that goes directly to eastern Poipu; the left turn is well marked on Rt 520 after you come through the pass.

Favorite South Shore Beaches

When it's raining up north, you may want to travel south (even west) to find the sun. Usually in the island's lee, south shore beaches offer relatively calm swimming conditions all year, except during a south shore 'swell.'

- *Poipu Beach Park* is perfect for families, the rock rimmed pool a safe place for small children, and the snorkeling at the other end of the curving beach is wonderful for older ones and their parents (p 67).

- *Brennecke's Beach* is (nearly) back to pre-Iniki waves, the long rollers legendary for bodyboards and body surfing (p 68).

- Our favorite hidden beach (though increasingly popular), is *Mahaʻulepu Beach* east of Poipu. Wild and beautiful (p 66).

Poipu Beach

You could not imagine a more perfect beach for children than this lovely curve of soft golden sand sloping down to a gentle, friendly sea. The waves, with changing shades of turquoise sparkling with sunlight and dazzling white foam, break gently over a protective reef across the entrance to this small cove.

For babies and toddlers, a ring of black lava rocks creates a sheltered pool where the water is shallow and still. For older children, waves beyond the pool roll to shore in graceful swells perfect for rafts or body boards. Children can explore the long rocky point at the far end of the beach. Bring nets and pails for tiny fish in the tidepools.

Just around the rocky point, in front of the old Waiohai Hotel which is now a time-share resort operated by the Marriott, you can enjoy some of the best snorkeling on the island. Hundreds of fish in rainbow colors feed on the coral, so tame they almost swim into your hands. Carry snorkeling fish food in a plastic bag, or even a green leaf, and they'll swim right to you. Stay inside the reef to avoid being caught in a strong current.

The park has a lifeguard, restrooms, outdoor showers, barbecues, picnic tables, and shaded pavilions. Sometimes you may see a monk seal taking a sunbath on the sand. It's resting, gathering strength to face another day in paradise.

Directions: In Poipu, take Hoʻowilili Rd to Hoʻone Rd. Park in the lot. To park near the Kiahuna and Sheraton, turn off Hoʻowilili Rd at the Sheraton's sign, then turn left at Hoonani Rd and continue to the end. Enter the last driveways on the left and on the right for public parking. Maps 6,7

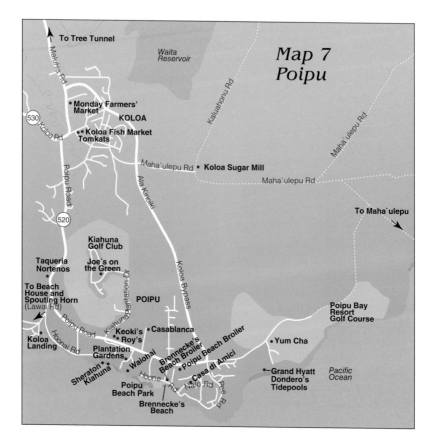

Brennecke's Beach

Adjacent to Poipu Beach Park, Brennecke's Beach was once the best beach for body surfing in Hawaii. Now, it is finally recovering from Hurricane Iniki, which smashed giant boulders into the seawall and washed away most of the sand. Today, as the sand is coming back, the waves are gradually returning to their old pattern, breaking far out for the big kids, and then again closer to shore for younger ones to catch a swift and exciting ride. After Hurricane Iwa caused a similar level of destruction in 1982, the return of the sandy bottom took ten years, and it's taken just about as long after Iniki. Wave riders must still be wary of rocks, and watch out for waves that head towards the sea wall. There is no lifeguard protection.

Directions: Adjacent to Poipu Beach Park, on the eastern side. Maps 6, 7

Shipwreck Beach

Shipwreck Beach along Keoniloa Bay was never much of a beach – until the hurricane blasted the south shore of Kauai and created a new coastline. What was once a thin curve of sand is now a long, golden crescent divided by lava rocks. It's called Shipwreck Beach with good reason; the surf is powerful, breaking in long, shining arcs which crest slowly, one at a time, with deceptive smoothness, and then crash in thunderous explosions of spray not far from shore. Local people warn that beyond the break point are dangerous currents and large rocks. A better place for family swimming would be Poipu Beach Park, and novice surfers would be better off at Wailua Beach, where rocks and wind are not a problem and a lifeguard is on duty. Be particularly careful during summer months, when a south shore swell can bring big surf.

Instead of swimming, you can climb the cliff to explore strange caves and rock formations. The colors are breathtaking – the deep blue of the water and the gold of the cliffs dazzle the eye, and the view down is a dizzying spectacle of surf crashing against the rocks. Be careful, though. Avoid going close to the cliff's edge, as the footing is slippery with loose sand. It's great for photographers but not for children.

Shipwreck Beach – walk along the rocky bluff and explore fascinating rock formations.

Directions: Take Poipu Rd past the main entrance to the Hyatt Hotel. Turn toward the water on Ainako Rd. Park in the lot. Public access restrooms and showers are by the parking lot. Shipwreck is 14 miles from Lihue; 24 miles from Kapaʻa; 44 miles from Princeville. Maps 6, 7

Mahaʻulepu

At the end of a dusty drive through winding sugar cane roads, you will find a beautiful sandy beach carved into a rocky point. This part of the south shore can be very dry and very hot – and you'll soon find a thin red film on every surface inside your car, including you. But it's worth the dust to reach a beach astonishing in its wild beauty, the surf crashing against the rocks and sand, the churning turquoise water almost glowing with sunlight. Beautiful it is, but often not safe enough for swimming. Unless surf on the whole south shore is flat, you may find the waves crashing with enough force to knock you down, and currents powerful enough to make even local people wary.

Solitude at Mahaʻulepu

Mahaʻulepu is a lovely beach for exploring. On the eastern end, a lovely half-moon of golden sand nestles at the base of a rocky cliff. A long walk to the west takes you past a rocky reef which at low tide juts out of the sand in fascinating formations. As you reach the end of the curve, the tip turns out to be a point, and on the other side, you'll find another, even longer stretch of beach. Here the water ripples in toward shore, protected by an offshore reef where the waves roll in long, even swells. You might see a fisherman casting his line or even a swimmer snorkeling among the rocks if the sea is calm. When the tradewinds are strong, windsurfers splash color on the sparkling sea. At the western most end, at Gillin's Beach, you will find a new house built on the spot where plantation manager Gillin once lived. Sun warmed tidal pools are shallow and still; kids can catch tiny fish in nets.

At the far eastern end of Mahaʻulepu is a rocky bluff. After a moderate uphill climb, you will come to a promontory with spectacular views of the coastline. Rock formations are amazing, and a tiny beach set into the cliffside shelters interesting pools of tiny sea life.

Poipu *Directions:* Take Rt 50 to Rt 520 (Maluhia Rd), and follow signs to Poipu. Take Poipu Rd past the Hyatt Regency, continue on to the unpaved road, and pass the golf course and the quarry. When you come to a stop sign, turn right and head toward the water. This is sugar company land; at road's end, park or turn left to another lot. Maps 6, 7

Kipu Kai

You can only get to Kipu Kai by boat, for the private road crossing the gap in the mountains between Rt 50 and the south shore is deeply rutted and gouged, suitable only for the sturdiest 4-wheel-drive vehicles. Some boat tour companies offer day trips to this lovely section of Kauai's coastline (p 86). Kipu Kai is actually three beaches which share a rocky peninsula shaped like an alligator. Long Beach is, as you would expect from the name, stretches out in a long line of fine sand in the shape of a half moon, nearly enclosed by outcroppings of rocks at each end. Set at the base of the rocky mountains behind Kipu Kai, Long Beach is special among south shore beaches, combining the favorable weather of the south with a rugged beauty more characteristic of the north shore. As if this weren't enough, the ocean is relatively gentle due to the rocky points which embrace the beach, breaking the surf and creating a protected lagoon.

A wonderful old rambling ranch house sits atop Turtle Beach, so named for its shape. The house was built in stages by the Waterhouse family using orders of wood and supplies floated ashore from cargo ships. From the veranda overlooking the bay, Jack Waterhouse used to communicate with the 'rest of the world' by signals. According to his will, the Waterhouse family descendents retain use of the land until the end of the next generation, when Kipu Kai Ranch is destined to become a state park.

The rocky, twisting road to Kipu Kai tracks through gullies and over steep ridges, requiring 4-wheel-drive vehicles. Instead, consider a boat tour (86).

Map 8
Westside

Miloli'i State Park

Nu'alolo Kai State Park

Kalalau Lookout

Pu'u o Kila Lookout

Koke'e Lodge & Museum

550

Pu'u Hinahina Lookout

Koke'e State Park

Waimea Canyon
(1 mile wide and
3657 feet deep)

Polihale State Park

Pokale Rd.

Waimea Canyon Lookout

Nohili Point

Barking Sands

Kao Rd.

Waimea River

Old Mana Rd.

Mana

550

Mana Point

Koke'e Rd.

50

Military Airfield

Waimea Canyon Rd.

Pacific Range Missile Center

Kokole Point

Kekaha

Waimea

Kekaha Beach Park

Kikiaola Small Boat Harbor

❻ A
Lucy
Wright ❺
Beach
Park

Russian Fort Elizabeth

50

Pakala Beach
("Infinities")

Kaumuali'i Hwy

Olokele Rd.

Hanapepe

❹❸❷

Eleele

Lolokai

❶

Port Allen

*Drive Waimea Canyon, 141
and hike at Koke'e, 116*

Lele

Salt Pond Beach Park

Port Allen Airport

Hanapepe Bay

*Na Pali Boat Tours depart
from Port Allen, 86*

Westside **Kauai**

N

0   1   2
Miles

Westside Beach Adventures

Salt Pond Beach Park – great for families, and often a sunny spot when other parts of the island are cloudy.

Restaurants & Hotels

Beaches

Salt Pond Beach tidepool — perfect for kids!

Westside ins & outs

Kauai's Westside is still small town rural, and the weather is often sunnier than the windward shores. Port Allen is headquarters of many boat tours companies and also *Kauai Chocolate Co.* In HANAPEPE, Kauai's 'biggest little town,' check out the swinging bridge, visit art galleries (like *Arius Hopman* for photographs and *Banana Patch Studio* for ceramics) and sample *Taro Ka chips* at the factory. *Hanapepe Café* is a great place for lunch or a mid-afternoon coffee on a rainy day. Stop at *Kauai Kookie Factory* on Rt 56 next to Mariko's for special flavors (like lavender shortbread); it's set back from road. Visit beautiful *Salt Pond Beach Park.*

Next is WAIMEA, with a black sand beach perhaps less appealing than the beautiful long white sand beach a few miles farther at Kekaha. For lunch and free wireless, stop at *Waimea Plantation Cottages*, or choose *Wrangler's*. Waimea is the gateway to *Waimea Canyon* and *Koke'e State Park* and its wonderful hiking. Beyond is Kekaha and then Polihale at the end of the road on the westside.

Favorite Westside Beaches

- *Salt Pond Beach Park* offers great swimming, protected by a reef, as well as usually sunny weather. Kids love the tidal pools (p 75).

- At *Kekaha*, you'll find firm sand and miles of beach perfect for beachwalking and running, as well as surf for body boards (p 77).
- Drive all the way to the end of the road to magnificent *Polihale Beach*, the western most part of the island (p 78). The beach seems limitless.
- On your trips west, enjoy a tasty lunch at *Wrangler's* in Waimea (great hamburgers and salads, p 231), or *Hanapepe Café* (vegetarian delights and espresso, p 229), or *Grinds* in Ele'ele (sandwiches on fresh home-baked bread, p 190).

Great Days on the Westside

Day 1: Drive to *Polihale Beach* (p 78) with a picnic lunch from Grinds, or drive *Waimea Canyon* Rd to *Koke'e* (p 141), and explore the forest preserve (p 116). Try shave Ice at *Jo Jo's* on the way back. Dinner at *Wrangler's* (p 231).

Day 2: Tour the *Na Pali Coast* by boat (p 86), or *Gay & Robinson Sugar Plantation* (p 84,125), or visit quaint *Hanapepe*, test its swinging bridge, browse the art galleries and have lunch at *Hanapepe Café* (p 229). Afternoon: *Salt Pond Beach* (p 75) or *Kekaha* (p 77). Dinner at *Toi's Thai Kitchen* (p 229).

Hanapepe area beaches: Salt Pond Beach Park

The beach at Salt Pond is a semicircle where the sand slopes downward with the lovely grace of a golden bowl to hold the sea. A reef near the mouth of this sheltered cove breaks the surf into slow, rolling swells that break again gently near the shore so that children can raft and swim inside this natural lagoon most of the year. At both ends of the beach, tidepools can be calm enough at low tide for babies and toddlers, and great fun for older kids when the incoming tide splashes over the rocks to make waterfalls.

Walk along the beach and explore tidal pools and the ancient salt ponds where local people still harvest sea salt. The park is spectacular, especially when brightly colored windsurfers race out across the reef, and particularly favored in terms of weather. Even when clouds and rain prevail elsewhere, this little point of land seems to escape them, and in winter, the water seems a few degrees warmer and more friendly. Showers, rest rooms, picnic tables, barbecues, and a lifeguard make Salt Pond a popular weekend spot for local families, although the beach never seems crowded. Be careful in periods of

Miles of golden sand at Kekaha

high surf, however, as unpredictable currents can create hazardous swimming, and stay inside the lagoon. For lunch, stop at the Hanapepe Café, or take out a picnic lunch from Grinds in Ele'ele, just a few miles east of Hanapepe on Rt 50.

Just west of Hanapepe on Rt 50 at the mile 21 marker, turn left at Lele St, and take the first right onto Lokokai Rd; drive until you see the parking area. Map 8

Pakala's Beach or 'Infinities'

Just west of Hanapepe on Rt 50, past the mile 21 marker, you will find cars parked along the road just next to a low concrete bridge. They belong to surfers, who head for Pakala's by way of an overgrown path crossing a pasture to the beach. Wear shoes or sturdy sandals, and stay away from the thorny kiawe which grows near the beach.

On this lovely, curving beach, the sand and sea are deep gold, as if sprinkled with cinnamon, because the A'akukui stream carries red volcanic soil to the sea. You can hear the crash of the waves as you walk across the pastureland, and by the time you pass through the trees which ring the sand, you'll feel like you're alone on a deserted island. It is a lovely spot. The waves rise gracefully in long, even lines crested with gold. Each wave breaks and rushes onto the sand in shining foam, and then rolls back out again to meet the wave coming in; they perform a fascinating ballet, sometimes meeting like dancers in perfect rhythm, sometimes colliding in bursts of spray. You could watch the waves for hours and never see two waves embrace in exactly the same way.

The bay is divided by a rocky point where local fishermen try for pompano. If you cross the stream and climb the rocky ledge, you come to a sandy beach dotted with shells, sea glass, and coral. Beyond the reef is a surfing spot famous for long, perfectly formed waves that surfers can ride on to 'infinity' (see *Surfing*, 137). Paddling out over the shallow reef takes a long time, but the ride, according to our son Jeremy, is really special. Be careful at low tide, when shallow water over the reef can expose an unwary surfer to spiny sea urchins. To the right of the rocky point, the beach stretches a long way before disappearing around a bend. The firm golden sand is perfect for walking, and the waves can be quite gentle. This western spot is a good place to try when other parts of the island are in rain.

Just west of Hanapepe on Rt 50, watch for the mile 21 marker and then the low concrete bridge. No facilities, but about 1 mile further on Rt 50 you'll find public restrooms and showers at the Russian Fort, and just across the Waimea River. Map 8

Kekaha area beaches: Kekaha Beaches

Stretching for miles along Kauai's western coast, the Kekaha beaches combine swimming, surfing, and walking with the predominantly dry weather of the island's leeward side. As Rt 50 curves toward the sea at the small town of Kekaha, the beach is narrow, but a mile or two north, it widens and becomes more golden, with long, rolling waves breaking evenly in brilliant white crests. At times, the waves can break perfectly for surfing and body boarding, although, as everywhere on Kauai, surf and currents can be dangerous and unpredictable, and you may find high surf and rip currents. Watch where local people are swimming and follow their lead – especially if they are not going into the water!

Even if swimming is not advisable, the sand is firm and flat, one of the finest beaches on Kauai – or anywhere – for walking, running, or playing frisbee or football. We recommend driving the full length of this stretch of beach so that you can select the most favorable spot and then double back to park. Despite its clear, sunny weather, the western side of the island has not yet been developed as a tourist area, and so these beaches are frequented primarily by local residents and are not very crowded. You can walk for miles along the sand, with beautiful views of Niʻihau, purple on the horizon. Or drive north towards Barking Sands and Polihale Beach, winding through sugar cane fields where silvery grasses wave in breezes against the deep red-gold of cleared fields and the vivid blues of the sea and the enormous sky.

Directions: Drive northwest of Waimea on Rt 50 until the road curves towards the water near the mile 25 marker. Map 8

Barking Sands

The beach from Kekaha to Polihale extends about 15 miles, and the section off the Pacific Missile Range Facility is open to the public during daylight hours. Post September 11, security requires an application for an annual pass. The form is available electronically but the completed application must be submitted in person with a photo ID. Processing then takes approximately 2 weeks. Contact thomas.h.clements@navy.mil for information, or to get the form by e-mail, or call the Morale Welfare and Recreation Office at 335-7936.

Like Polihale Beach, the surf here can be extremely strong, often too powerful for safe swimming. While the waves break magnificently for surfers, unpredictable currents and a sudden drop-off make swimming hazardous. You have to look carefully for channels through the coral reef fronting the beach to find sandy bottom. The wide, sandy beach is both hot and difficult to walk on, and shade is almost nonexistent. It is a spectacular place for a picnic, though, and you can see Niʻihau on the horizon, just past the golden, shining sand and glistening turquoise sea.

Directions: Main entry gate is northwest of Kekaha on Rt 50. Map 8

Polihale Beach Park

From the time you leave paved road behind to jolt north through a maze of sugar cane fields, you know you're in for something special. Gradually, beyond the tall sugar cane rustling in the breeze, a dark ridge of jagged peaks appears on the right. As you get closer, these giant cliffs reveal splendid colors – trees and bush in vivid greens against the black rock slashed with the deep red of the volcanic soil. When you can drive no further, the beach at Polihale emerges from the base of the cliffs – an enormous stretch of brilliant white sand more immense, it seems, than the cliffs which tower above and the band of deep blue sea beyond. Only the sky seems the equal of this vast expanse of glaring sand, so wide that to walk from your car to the ocean on a sunny day will burn your feet, and so long that no single vantage point allows the eye to see its full extent. 'Beautiful' is too small a word for this awesome place. Polihale – home of spirits – is more appropriate, not only because the majestic cliffs and beach dwarf anything human to insignificance, but also because here man's access to the western coast really ends. Beyond lies the Na Pali wilderness, unreachable except by boat or helicopter, or by the handful of hikers who dare to climb the narrow and dangerous trails. Polihale is the threshold between the known and the unknown, the tamed and the untamed, the familiar and the wild.

Swimming is treacherous; the rolling, pounding surf even at its most gentle is only for strong, experienced swimmers. No reefs offer protection from the powerful ocean currents. Come instead for the spectacle, to picnic and walk, to gaze at the grandeur of cliffs above the endless sea and sand, to listen to the silence broken only by the crashing surf, to appreciate in solitude the splendor of nature's power. A feeling of awe lingers even after you return to paved road and a world of smaller proportions.

You'll find the turn onto the dirt cane road to Polihale, marked by a state park sign, just before Rt 50 ends. Restrooms, showers, roofed picnic tables, barbecues. Camping by permit only. Be careful with your rental car. Don't get your wheels mired in muddy roads, or stuck in sandy dunes. Map 8

Monk Seals

You may see a monk seal lying on almost any Kauai beach. Give it a wide berth – it's probably exhausted, resting before heading back out to sea. State law requires a 'safe distance' of 50 feet from the seal. If you try to get closer, you run the risk of provoking a nasty bite, or perhaps frightening the animal into the water before it has fully rested. The Hawaiian Monk Seal is on the list of endangered species.

Beach Safety

We describe the beaches in their summer mood, when the surf and currents can be at their most gentle. From mid-October to mid-April, however, swimmers must be particularly cautious on the windward beaches to the north and northeast where the surf and currents are more unpredictable and dangerous.

On the south shore, surf is "up" in summer months, and the ocean more calm during winter.

Plan your beach adventures according to surf conditions (Call 245-6001 for a report on the size of the swell, times of high and low tides).

A few simple suggestions: Don't swim alone or too far out at a beach where currents are unfamiliar, and avoid swimming where a river flows into the sea. Never turn your back on the ocean; keep your eye on the waves. Before you swim, observe the water carefully. Look out for the fast moving water running laterally which indicates a strong current.

Should you ever find yourself caught in a strong undertow or rip current, and if your efforts to free yourself are not successful, remember this: don't panic, conserve your energy, and drift with the current until it weakens. These currents usually weaken beyond the point where the waves break, and many are shaped like horseshoes, so that at some point you will probably be able to swim back in.

Be particularly careful when you are snorkeling, when you can easily get distracted by the fish and lose your sense of direction. Stay close enough to shore that you can swim in at any time, and remember that unfamiliar beaches will have unknown currents.

You'll find the safest snorkeling in the rock-enclosed pool at Lydgate Park on the eastern shore, or at sheltered Poipu Beach to the south.

Beware of walking or even standing close to the edge of cliffs or rocks to photograph the pounding surf, as waves vary in size and strength and a huge one may come up suddenly and wash your camera away – perhaps you along with it! These sudden large waves can be treacherous because they are unexpected as well as powerful, particularly on the northern and western beaches without reefs to protect against strong ocean currents. Avoid swimming in the murky water near where a stream flows into the sea.

When surfing, watch where the local surfers ride the waves. They know where to avoid strong currents, rocks, and dangerous wave breaks. They are also experienced, however, and seek a bigger thrill. Keep an eye out for that occasional oversize wave. Rather than trying to ride it (or worse, run from it), you may want to dive through or drop down under it. These big ones often come in threes, so be ready!

Portuguese 'men o' war,' tiny blue jellyfish, pack a walloping sting in their long, trailing tentacles. They sometimes dot the waterline after heavy surf. Don't step on them or pick them up. If you are stung while swimming, pull the jellyfish off carefully, trying not to touch the stinger any more than you have to, or use some sand to scrape the stinger off. Warm water helps, and vinegar or meat tenderizer can be used as to help break down the poison. The best medicine, however, is prevention. If you see them on the sand, pack up and head out for another beach!

An even smaller critter, the bacterium causing leptospirosis has been found in Kauai's rivers and streams, so avoid freshwater swimming far from the ocean's edge if you have open cuts or sores. Instead, swim in the ocean or the brackish water where a stream flows into the sea.

Your beachbag should contain some antibiotic ointment and bandaids for coral cuts, and, if possible, some vinegar or meat tenderizer in case you meet a man o' war. Keep a spare sun tan lotion in the glove compartment of the car.

On Kauai, as anywhere, follow normal rules of self-protection: Lock your car against theft as you would at home, store valuables in the trunk, and avoid walking alone at night in unlit, deserted areas – including those romantic beaches.

Beware the Hawaiian Sun

If you lie out in the sun between 11:30am and 2:30pm you will fry like a pancake, even in a half hour, because Hawaii lies close to the equator and the sun is exceedingly strong. You'll need a good sunscreen (dermatologists recommend at least SPF 15) even on cloudy days, when ultraviolet rays can cause a burn.

The best lotions protect against both UVA and UVB rays. An Australian suncream, *Blue Lizard,* protects against UVA and UVB, and the bottle actually turns blue in UV light to alert you it's time to lotion up. Many dermatologists consider lotions containing *mexoryl* to afford the best broad-spectrum, long-lasting protection. Products containing mexoryl have a track record in Europe where they originated, and now they are FDA approved for use in the United States. One of the best is named for the town in France where it was developed, *La Roche-Posay* (renowned for the thermal spring water incorporated into its skin care products).

Read carefully: *waterproof* does not mean the same as *water-resistant,* though don't put too much faith even in that claim. So-called 'waterproof' sunscreens will wash off in salt water and should be reapplied periodically, as we do every two hours. We've had good luck with sticky gels like *Bullfrog.* Most lotions need a few minutes to dry in order to adhere to the skin before swimming.

Children need special care and effective lotions. For spots which kids rub often, like right under the eyes, you can try sticky gels or a sunscreen in chapstick form. It's a good idea to make a rule that kids get 'greased up' in the room or parking lot before heading for the beach as they hate to stand still once the sand is in sight. Bring hats and tee-shirts (the most reliable sun-protection) for after-swimming sandcastle projects. It's a good plan to schedule family beach visits for the early morning or late afternoon, and plan meals, naps, or drives for the noonday sun hours. Sunburns are often not visible until it is too late, but you can check your child's skin by pressing it with your finger. If it blanches dramatically, get the child a shirt or consider calling it a day. Keep a spare lotion in the car, for without lotion, beaches can be hazardous to your health.

Babies need a complete sunblock, a hat to protect the scalp, and protection for feet. To give babies shade, an umbrella (KMart, Wal-Mart, Longs) would be a wise purchase for the beach.

ATV

One of the newest ways to tour Kauai's wilderness areas is by ATV. *Kipu Adventures* leads tours through Kipu Ranch, a 3,000 acre cattle ranch between Lihue and Poipu. On wide wheel-base Honda 350s, you maneuver up and down grades, bounce into streams, cross valleys and forest areas, go through pastures with cattle and climb the rocky road to the Ha'upu mountain pass – a spectacular lookout to gorgeous Kipu Kai beach. You may see Nene geese, wild pigs, pheasant, turkeys, amazing trees, as well as locations of *Raiders of the Lost Arc, Jurassic Park, Mighty Joe Young*, and others. Kids must be 16 to drive; 2 seater ATVs – aka 'the bomber' – are also available. Long pants are required, and anything you wear will soon become an original red dirt shirt! ($105/3 hrs; $140/4 hrs; 246-9288; kiputours.com).

Kauai ATV's motto is 'do something dirty' – and for good reason. You'll splash through plenty of mud, climb over rocks, cruise through cane fields, and wade into a waterfall (on foot) for a photo op on tours over cane roads and through cane fields on Kauai's south side. The company provides head lights to go through an old cane tunnel (great fun!). Choose a 4-hour 'waterfall tour' with picnic ($155); a 3 hr 'Koloa tour' ($125); or the 'mudbug tour' on a 2-seater mud cruising machine which includes kayaking at the Waita Reservoir, the largest inland body of water in the state ($175). Rent mud gear (recommended), but be prepared to get filthy. Two-seaters are available for all tours, as well as a specially designed 4-seater for families. Tours include an image CD. Visit the outdoor gear store, unique on Kauai. 742-2734; 877-707-7088; kauaiatv.com.

On the westside, *Gay & Robinson* offers a 4.5 hr tour of the Robinson family's private Makaweli Ranch and uplands, with views from Polihale to Poipu: $145 for the 'mountain pool adventure' which includes a 'paniolo barbecue,' or $100 for a tour with snack (M-Sat. 335-2824).

Artists & Artisans

Kauai Products Store (Kukui Grove) is *the* place for work by island craftspeople (246-6753; kauaimade.net for links to artisan websites and contact info). *Kauai Museum's* shop has quilts, native wood boxes, Ni'ihau shell leis, and jewelry (245-6931). For pottery, visit *Kilohana Clayworks* (246-2529). In Kapa'a, don't miss *Kela's Glass Gallery* (822-4527; 888-255-3527; glass-art.com) for beautiful colors and shapes. In Hanapepe's art colony, visit *Banana Patch Studio* for pottery and beautifully illustrated books (335-5944; bananapatchstudio.com); *Kama'aina Koa Wood Gallery (335-5483);* and *Arius Hopman* (335-0227; hopmanart.com) for lovely watercolors. In Waimea, *Wrangler's Steakhouse* shop has wonderful local crafts, and nearby *Waimea Cottages* has a lovely small museum shop where you can see Gramsy's patchwork art. Stay for lunch and share free wireless.

Stop in at craft fairs for bargains in hand crafts (some local, some imported). Sᴏᴜᴛʜ sʜᴏʀᴇ: In Poipu, a craft fair goes on daily at Spouting Horn. Wᴇsᴛsɪᴅᴇ: In Waimea, it's on Rt 50 (Wed – Sun). Eᴀsᴛsɪᴅᴇ, look opposite Otsuka's in northern Kapa'a (Wed – Sun).

For info about Kauai's artists, exhibitions, and open studios contact *Kauai Society of Artists* (kauaisocietyofartists.org; PO Box 3344, Lihue HI 96766). *Garden Island Arts Council* (245.2733; gardenislandarts.org) has the latest schedule for music, art shows, dance, and poetry.

Beachwalking & Running

Our favorite running beaches, with firm sand and just the right slope, are Hanalei Bay and Kalihiwai on the north shore, Kalapaki on the east, and Kekaha to the west. For long meandering walks, we like Moloa'a and Larsen's Beach in the north, Maha'ulepu on the south, and on the eastern shore, Anahola Beach or Lydgate Park along the Wailua Golf Course, beautiful at sunrise or sunset. The Kapa'a – Kealia bike/walk trail follows the coastline. Remember the sun. Fluids, sunscreen, even a hat are a must.

Bikes & Motorcycles

On a comfortable cruising bike (wide saddle, hi-rise handlebars), you can try a 'downhill adventure' over 12 miles of winding smooth blacktop from Waimea Canyon, at an elevation of 3,500 feet, to the coast. *Outfitters Kauai* leaves daily at dawn in the beautiful early morning light or in the late afternoon for the sunset. Tours from $94 which includes a helmet. (742 - 9667; 888-742-9887; outfitterskauai.com). *Outfitters* also rents bikes.

Bike Rentals: Eᴀsᴛsɪᴅᴇ: Try the new, mostly level bike path that goes from Kapa'a north past Kealia beach, or bike south of Lydgate Park along the ocean. Call *Kauai Cycle & Tour,* Rt 56 in Kapa'a (821-2115; bikehawaii.com/kauaicycle). Nᴏʀᴛʜ Sʜᴏʀᴇ: tour Hanalei and Ha'ena. Call *Pedal & Paddle* (826-9069). Sᴏᴜᴛʜ Sʜᴏʀᴇ: *Outfitters Kauai* (742-9667). Repairs? *Bicycle John* (245-7579; bicyclejohn.com). Rent a Harley? Call *Ray's*

(822-HOGG; 1-888-527-9484); *Kauai Harley* (241-7020; 877-A-1-CYCLE; kauaiharley-davidson.com); or *Two Wheels Kauai* for Yamaha/Kawasaki/Honda (Kapaʻa: 822-2333; cyclecitykauai.com).

Boat Tours

The spectacular cliffs of the Na Pali coast are off limits to most visitors – unless they dare to hike the wilderness on narrow and slippery trails. Coastal boat tours provide a way to see these amazing cliffs up close, and enjoy a sometimes rough and ready adventure at the same time. Explore sea caves, watch sparkling waterfalls, and marvel at how tenaciously plants can cling to inhospitable rock. You'll see an enormous change in landscape, from the dark, rich green of Keʻe Beach, where rainfall measures nearly 125 inches a year, to the reds and browns of Polihale on the west side, where it's only 20 inches. During winter (November till March), if seas off Na Pali are too rough and currents too strong, tours may cruise Kauai's south shore to Kipu Kai, where humpback whales frequent Hawaii's warm waters from December to April, as well as pods of spinner dolphins.

In choosing a tour company, consider the size of the boat (only smaller boats can enter Na Pali's sea caves and snorkel at protected Nuʻalolo Kai, while larger boats can offer a smoother ride). Also consider onboard amenities (restrooms, shade, and food/beverage selection); length of the tour (how much you see and whether there is a snorkel break); activities offered (snorkeling, scuba, lunch, heavy pu pus, cocktails), and the season (rougher winter seas mean you can't get as close to the cliffs). Snorkeling

on any of these trips depends on weather and surf, but most companies try to get you get in the water even if there is nothing much to see.

Small power catamarans: In calm seas, these boats (fewer than 18 passengers) combine a comfortable ride with the agility to go into the sea caves along Na Pali (some companies close down in winter). Twice daily from Port Allen, *Makana Tours* takes 12 passengers on a 32-ft power catamaran with bathroom. Captain Mike De Silva, a Kauai native, makes sure everyone gets a bird's eye view of the amazing scenery. You may frolic with a pod of dolphins, even play in a waterfall, and see amazing fish while snorkeling at protected Nuʻalolo Kai. Flotation devices for snorkelers, excellent equipment, a buffet lunch with fresh-baked bread for sandwiches, even a fresh water rinse after snorkeling make a difference. Mike's knowledgeable and accommodating crew describes history, natural history, and local lore ($129/adult; 335-6137; 888-335-6137; makanacharters.com).

From Waimea, *Liko Kauai Cruises* owned by Liko and his Hawaiian family offers an excellent 4 hour morning or afternoon snorkeling and sightseeing tour which goes into some of the caves, as well as fishing cruises. His 49-ft power catamaran, 'Na Pali Kai III' has all forward seating, shade, plus bathroom. Liko's policy is to go as far up Na Pali as weather permits, so you can see everything, occasionally pods of whales in winter ($120/adult; 338-0333; 888-SEA-LIKO; liko-kauai.com). *Catamaran Kahanu* tours Na Pali on a 40-ft power catamaran, 18 feet wide with a 'flying bridge' for hanging over the waves to watch for spinning porpoises and humpback whales ($135/adult; 645-6176; 888-213-7711; catamarankahanu.com). Keith Silva takes *Kaulana Pali Kai*, a 27-ft power boat for 6 passengers, ideal for families or small groups (337-9309).

Zodiacs: If you crave a bigger thrill, consider zodiacs, whose 'rough and ready' ride often takes you up and over waves and head on into the surf. These rigid hull ocean rafts are not for the weak of heart – or back. The ride can be very bumpy, so ask right away for gloves to hold onto the rope, especially if you want to sit towards the front. A waterproof camera is a good idea for when the boat goes under waterfalls and through the ocean spray. On the ride home, the boat may feel as if it is driving against the waves at top speed, and so less adventurous passengers might prefer the back, in what is called the 'cadillac seat.' *Z Tours* offers scheduled tours to south shore, including Kipu Kai (742-7422; 888 9ZTOURZ; ztourz.com).

Kauai Sea Tours takes 15 passengers on a full-day tour that includes a guided hike ($139/adult), or a half-day tour that includes snorkeling but not landing ($125/adult). Seasonal sightseeing and whale watching raft tours are also available ($69-99) (826-PALI; 800-733-7997; kauaiseatours.com). *Captain Zodiac*, now operated by Captain Andy's, operates a 24-ft motorized rigid hull craft. The 6 hr Na Pali snorkeling adventure includes (weather permitting) landing at Nu'alolo Kai for lunch ($159/adult) (335-6833; 800-535-0830; capt-andys.com). *Na Pali Explorer* operates 2 boats along Na Pali, a 35 passenger rigid hull zodiac complete with restroom and shelter for higher speeds in rough ocean conditions, and a 26-ft, 16-passenger 'Hurricane' Zodiac. 3-hour south shore whale watching tours go out in winter months ($79-$125/adult) (338-9999; 887-335-9909; napali-explorer.com). *Na Pali Riders*, leaving from Kekaha, has the advantage of touring the entire Na Pali coast all the way to Ke'e Beach or, if you're lucky, Tunnels Beach. It's a long tour, but you'll see everything (742-6331; napaliriders.com).

Larger catamarans: For those who tend to get seasick, these offer a smoother ride, particularly in winter months, when seas are rougher. *Blue Dolphin Charters* tours Na Pali on the 'Blue Dolphin,' a 63-ft sailing catamaran, and the 'Blue Dolphin II,' a 65-ft catamaran, both of which have

top decks with rows of seating ($139/5 hrs). It begins, as most tours do, with a continental breakfast and safety briefing, and it is the only Na Pali tour company that offers a diving option – both for certified divers and first

Small Power Catamaran Tours
(fewer than 18 passengers)

North Shore:

Captain Sundown	826-5855

Westside:

Makana Tours	822-9187
Liko Kauai Cruises	338-0333
Catamaran Kahanu	335-3577
Kaulana Kai	337-9309

Large Catamaran Tours
(more than 18 passengers)

Westside:

Blue Dolphin	742-6731
Holo Holo Charters	335-0815
Kauai Sea Tours	826-7254
Captain Andy's	335-6833

Zodiacs

Westside:

Na Pali Explorer	338-9999
Z-tours	742-7422
Kauai Sea Tours	826-77524
Captain Zodiac	335-6833

timers ($35). After the snorkel/scuba break, a make-your-own sandwich lunch is served, and the bar opens with beer, wine, and mai tais. On our last tour, owner-operator Captain Terry took us close enough to the cliffs for a waterfall shower (not possible in rough winter seas). Sunset cruises are also offered ($109/3 hrs) (335-5553; 877-511-1311; kauaiboats.com).

Captain Andy's 55-ft sailing catamarans, 'Spirit of Kauai' and 'Akialoa' also sail from Port Allen to Na Pali ($139/adult) (335-6833; 800-535-0830; capt-andys.com). Both boats have two 'trampolines' which provide front row seats – if you don't mind getting occasionally soaked with spray. If the wind is right, the captain may hoist the sails and turn off the engine for a quiet, smooth ride. A large, partially covered area with tables and chairs offers shelter and beverages (and after snorkeling, beer and wine). Morning Na Pali cruises begin with muffins and fruit, and later a make-your-own sandwich lunch.

On its 60-ft sailing catamaran, 'Lucky Lady,' *Kauai Sea Tours* has an excellent Na Pali tour ($135/adult) with snorkeling, as well as a sunset dinner cruise ($109/adult), and, on longer summer days, a snorkel sunset dinner cruise ($135/adult). The crew is very friendly, knowledgeable, and courteous. Breakfast and lunch are served, with mai tais, wine, and beer after you get out of the water (826-PALI; 800-733-7997; kauaiseatours. com). Also from Port Allen, *Holo Holo Tours* goes along Na Pali on 'Leila,' a comfortable 50-ft sailing catamaran with little side-to-side rolling motion.

Breakfast, lunch, as well as beer and wine are included (335-0815; 800-848-6130; holoholocharters.com).

EASTSIDE: *True Blue Sailing* sails a 42-ft trimaran out of Nawiliwili Harbor near Lihue year round, with picnic & snorkel tours to Kipu Kai, snorkel tours off Nawiliwili, and charters. They specialize in small groups (20 or less) (246-6333; kauaifun.com).

NORTH SHORE: The longest operating tour boat captain on Kauai, *Captain Sundown* sails each tour personally, taking 15 passengers in his 40-ft sailing catamaran, 'Ku'uipo,' from Hanalei out along the Na Pali coast ($162/6 hrs) (826-5585; captain-sundown.com). His family-owned company has been in business since 1971– that's the record on the island – and the bearded, friendly captain knows just about all there is to know about the island, its stories, and its waters. Choose either a Na Pali snorkel sail with a stop at Nu'alolo Kai, a Na Pali sunset sail, or a whale watching trip. Na Pali tours include a lunch of deli-made sandwiches (vegetarians can bring their own for a discount).

If you have the time, consider a tour to Ni'ihau, the 'forbidden' island largely off limits to tourists, except on boats which can come close enough to snorkel and dive but not to land. For skilled divers, *Seasport Divers* offers an all-day 3-tank dive trip with a knowledgeable and friendly crew. On Tuesdays and Fridays, *Blue Dolphin Charters* takes a comfortable 65-ft sailing catamaran ($185) for snorkeling or diving ($35 extra), and *Holo Holo Charters* offers daily snorkeling-only tours ($156). See *Scuba*, 129.

Snorkeling stop at Nu'alolo Kai

When booking a tour, ask about cancellation policies for weather and surf conditions. You can check

the weather report yourself (245-6001). Companies may claim they never go out in rough seas, but a lot depends on the definition. Rocking, rolling swells are fun for some, not so much fun for others, especially if there's no shelter from wind and spray, so think twice if your tour is ready to head out in marginal weather. Compare the number of passengers with the overall boat capacity, keeping in mind that the more crowded the boat, the less comfortable you may be. Inquire about your captain's experience on Kauai; every captain must be coast guard licensed, but some have more experience than others. Keep in mind that your young tour guides appreciate a modest tip.

Bring sunscreen, especially if your craft doesn't offer shade, perhaps a hat and sunglasses for glare, a towel, a long sleeved shirt for early morning check ins, and if possible, your own snorkel mask (and anti-fog) that fits properly. Protect your camera and film in a heavy duty zip lock plastic bag, and bring a dry shirt for the long ride home when you may be soaked with spray and dreaming of a hot shower.

Botanical Tours

EASTSIDE: Above Wailua, the *Kadavul Temple* gardens are a botanic wonderland developed over 20 years, with waterfalls and plants from all over the world; call 822-3012 for tour times. From Rt 56, go up Kuamo'o Rd (Rt 580) about 4 miles; turn left onto Kaholalele Rd (see p 94). About 3 miles farther on Kuamo'o Rd is the *Keahua Arboretum*, a 30-acre preserve of grassy meadows and trees (Follow the signs, and don't get discouraged when the road gets bumpy). You'll cross a stream and come to a grassy spot for a picnic and hiking trails beneath ancient trees. From the Arboretum, *Aloha Kauai Tours* can take you by 4x4 van to the base of Mt. Wai'ale'ale, where spectacular waterfalls converge into a river (245-6400). Map 1

NORTH SHORE: In Ha'ena, a walking tour of NTBG's *Limahuli Gardens* will lead you uphill through 17 acres of lush rain forest and gardens filled with native plants to an ocean lookout. You'll love the ancient terrace constructed for growing taro nearly a thousand years ago by the earliest Hawaiians. Take a guided tour ($25; reservations: 826-1053) or self-guided stroll ($15) over the 3/4 mile loop trail. Tues-Fri and Sundays: 9:30am - 4pm. Rt 560, 1/2 mile past mile 9 marker. Map 5

Na'Aina Kai in Kilauea, a remarkable botanical garden and 'sculpture park' combines tropical gardens, an intricate Poinciana maze, a 'wild forest,' carnivorous plant habitat, desert garden, even an oceanfront gazebo overlooking the spectacular north shore coastline. A 3 hour tour proceeds on foot and by tram through gardens, waterways, and groves (T-F $35), or you can take a shorter tour on foot ($25). Families can take special tours, and kids

Allerton Gardens NTBG in Lawai

can explore a children's garden (828-0525; naainakai.com). Bring your camera. For lunch, try Kilauea Fish Market or Kilauea Bakery. Nearby, *Guava Kai Plantation* explains the propagation of this tasty fruit. Map 5

SOUTH SHORE: The guided tour of *National Tropical Botanical Gardens* in Lawai is a unique opportunity to explore a 186 acre preserve of tropical fruits, spices, trees, rare plants, and flowers of astonishing variety and beauty – 50 varieties of banana and 500 species of palm. Instead of a formal garden, the plant collections are part of the natural landscape of the Lawai Valley. Park at Spouting Horn and climb aboard a van or a vintage 1941 Dodge touring bus to Lawai Kai, the Allerton family's spectacular private gardens, a rustic paradise irrigated by an ingenious water system of fountains, streams, waterways, and rocky pools. Stroll at a leisurely pace under spreading, giant trees to pavilions where a statue reflects a graceful image in a pool speckled with fallen leaves. The 'cutting garden' has brilliantly colored heliconia.

The popular 2.5 hour tour ($35), which includes one mile of walking, takes place Mon - Sat at 9am, 10am, 1pm, and 2pm (call for Sunday tour times). Van departures for a self-guided tour (allow 1.5 hours) run every hour starting at 9:30am till 2:30pm, on a first come first served basis ($20). Bring your camera. Reservations and info: 742-2623; ntbg.org. Map 6.

Further west in Kalaheo, flower photographers will love *Kukuiolono Golf Course*'s plumeria grove – a rainbow of colors in summer. Turn south on Papalina Rd (the town's main intersection, at the traffic light); after .8 miles, turn into the entrance on the right.

Camping

Camping is permitted at Anahola, Ha'ena, Anini, Salt Pond, and Polihale Beach Parks, as well as in specified areas of the Na Pali region and other wilderness preserves. For state parks, the camping limit is 5 nights in a 30 day period per campground (less on some stopovers on the Kalalau Trail). For information, permits, and reservations contact *Department of Land and Natural Resources,* Parks Division, State of Hawaii, 3060 Eiwa St,

P.O. Box 1671, Lihue, HI 96766 (274-3444). Download permit forms at kauai.gov (click on licenses and permits). For Alakai Swamp or Waimea Canyon, contact *Division of Forestry* at the same address (274-3444). *Kauai County Parks*: camping is limited to 4 days per park, or 12 nights total. (241-6670; kauai.gov). Allow 30 days to process permits.

WESTSIDE: *Koke'e*: *YWCA Camp Sloggett* in spectacular *Koke'e State Park* has access to 45 miles of hiking trails leading to the Kalalau Lookout and its amazing views of the Waimea Canyon and Na Pali coastline. Group and hostel accommodations include tent camping and a bunkhouse with kitchenettes, shared bath facilities, and hot showers (from $20/pp/night). Reserve at least two months in advance: YWCA of Kauai, 3094 Elua St, Lihue HI 96766 (245-5959; campingkauai.com). Map 8

Those who want to be close to nature – and to a shower and refrigerator at the same time – can try *Koke'e Lodge's* cabins, which have a stove, refrigerator, hot shower, cooking and eating utensils, linens, bedding, and wood burning stove; prices start at $45/night (maximum stay of 5 nights during a 30 day period). Advance reservations: *Koke'e Lodge*, Box 819, Waimea HI 96796 (335-6061). Breakfast and light lunch 9am - 3:30pm. Bring warm clothes for cold nights, and remember, on Kauai as elsewhere, to lock valuables in car's trunk. Koke'e info: kokee.org. Map 8

NORTH SHORE: *Ha'ena*: *YMCA Camp Naue* in spectacular Ha'ena on the north shore offers beachfront camping in bunk houses (or your own tent). It's popular with local clubs and families, but individual tourists are also welcome to stay in the bunkhouse ($12/night; children half-price); if you bring your own tent, it's only $10. YMCA of Kauai, Box 1786, Lihue HI 96766 (246-9090 or 742-1200). Map 5

Rent camping equipment at *Pedal & Paddle* in Hanalei (826-9069; you can also ask about current trail conditions); *Kayak Kauai* in Hanalei (826-9844; 800-437-3507; kayakkauai.com) and Kapa'a (822-9179); or *Outfitters Kauai* (742-9667) in Poipu. Buy camping equipment in *Long's Drug Store*, *K- Mart*, *Wal-Mart*, *Costco* in Lihue, as well as small variety stores like *Waipouli Variety* (Wailua), *Discount Variety* (Koloa), *Village Variety* (Hanalei), or *Ace Hardware* (Hanalei).

Churches & Temples

The *Kapa'a Missionary Church* in (822-5594) welcomes visitors of any denomination with a shell lei and a warm greeting. *Wai'oli Huia Church* in Hanalei (826-6253) conducts services in Hawaiian and English, and the family friendly family atmosphere is evident in the announcement at the top of the Sunday Bulletin: "Our keikis are apt to wander during church. They do this because they feel at home in God's house. Please love them as we do." You'll pass many lovely old churches on Kauai, from back roads in Koloa, sides streets in Kilauea, to cane fields on the west side.

The *Kadavul Hindu Temple* in the Wailua valley draws thousands of Hindu followers each year, as well as tourists fascinated by the extensive botanical gardens, stone temple, and 300-kg crystal *Siva Lingum*. Visitors to the temple and monastery may be invited to join a *puja* (cleansing) ceremony. Kuamoʻo Rd (open to the public 9am – 11:30am; tours available; 822-3012; saivasiddhanta.com/hawaii). Map 1

Coffee & Espresso Cafés

DRINKS: *Small Town Coffee* in Kapaʻa serves great coffees. In fact, owner Anni Caporuscio won the 2006 Hawaii Barista Championship with her unique coconut coffee drink. Don't miss carrot bran muffins from the local organic bakery, the free wireless, and local friendliness in her blue storefront in north Kapaʻa on Rt 56. In Wailua, Southern California favorite *Coffee Bean and Tea Leaf* is next to Foodland; *Starbucks* is next to Safeway and in Lihue's Kukui Grove next to Jamba Juice. *Java Kai* sells drinks, beans and bakery treats in Lihue, Hanalei, Kapaʻa, and Koloa (866-JAVA-KAI; javakai.com). BEANS: *Kauai Coffee* plantation in Lawai grows beans free of insecticides on 4,000 acres where Hawaii's first coffee plantation was founded in 1836.

Wai'oli Mission Church, Hanalei

Try samples at the visitor's center (335-0813; 800-545-8605; kauaicoffee.com). *Black Mountain Premium Hawaiian Coffee* is grown near Waimea and sold in local stores. *Kalaheo Coffee Company* (kalaheo.com) sells fragrant beans along with tasty deli choices. Other home-brew favorites include *Lapperts* (510-231-2340; lapperts.com) and Hawaii brand *Lion Coffee* (800-338-8353; lioncoffee.com).

Family Beaches

Our favorite family beaches are *Kalihiwai* (p 53) and *Anini Beach* (p 53) on the north shore; *Poipu Beach Park* (p 67) and *Salt Pond Beach*

Park (p 75) on the south shore. On the eastside, we love *Kalapaki Beach* (p 33) and *Lydgate Park* (p 36). *Lydgate, Anahola, Poipu Beach, Salt Pond, Kealia, Wailua Bay, Hanalei Bay,* and *Keʻe Beach* have lifeguards.

At Lydgate you'll also find *Kamalani Playground* – a 16,000 square foot playground with mirror mazes, a suspension bridge, lava tubes, and circular slide. Walk less than a half mile along a new paved walkway/bikeway beside the beach, and you'll come to the playground's newer section just south of Kaha Lani Condominium.

With a plastic pail and an inexpensive net ($9 for an 8 inch net at Long's), children can have fun trying to catch fish trapped in tidal pools. Net fishing is fun at the rivers behind the beaches at *Anahola, Kalihiwai,* and *Moloaʻa,* and at the tidal pools at *Salt Pond Beach Park* and *Poipu Beach Park.*

Family Fun

Kids will love the free hula shows sponsored at the major shopping centers and hotels. Times may change, so call ahead to confirm. EASTSIDE: the Coconut Plantation Marketplace show is at 5pm on Wed (822-3641); the Hilton has torchlighting and hula every day at 6pm (245-1955); the Marriott in Lihue has torchlighting at 6pm in the fall and winter and 6:30pm in the spring and summer (245-5050); and the Harbor Mall in Nawiliwili has hula with 'Aunty Bev' on Wed at 12:15pm (245-6255). Kukui Grove offers free 'Aloha Friday' entertainment from 7pm - 8pm on Fridays (245-7784).

Netting tadpoles at Moloaʻa

NORTH SHORE: Princeville Hotel has hula and chanting Sunday nights at 6:30pm in the Living Room. SOUTH SHORE: Poipu Shopping Village has shows at 5pm on Tues and Thurs (742-2831). Don't miss the keiki hula show at the Hyatt. Kids can dress in their aloha finery to watch the free hula show 6pm - 8pm on Tues and Sat (*Seaview Terrace*: 742-1234; free valet parking).

At *Children's Discovery Museum* in Wailua (823-8222; kcdm.org) kids find learning adventures and hands-on activities. For a family friendly fun, try *Kauai Backcountry's* Tubing adventure (245-2506; 888-270-0555; kauaibackcountry.com). Call Gregg at *Watersports Adventures* for scuba lessons (821-1599). Would-be young surfers can call 'Uncle Ambrose' (822-7112), Charlie Smith (634-3557), or try a surf school. For first rate, kid-friendly windsurfing lessons, call *Celeste Harvel* (828-6838).

Day camps are offered at the *Children's Discovery Museum* as well as the major hotels. Hyatt, Marriott, Princeville Hotel, Kiahuna, and the Sheraton typically charge guests about $50/day.

Kids under 18 golf free (after 4pm) at *Puakea Golf Course* (245-8756; puakeagolf.com). Free lei-making workshops every Friday at W*est Kauai Technology and Visitors Center* (9:30am - 11am ; 338-1322). Young artists will enjoy *Clayworks at Kilohana*; Keith Tammarine helps them craft, glaze, and fire their creations in his studio (246-2529; clayworksatkilohana.com).

Great children's books: see Kauai artist Joanna Carolan's beautifully illustrated books (*Kauai Good Night Moon* and others) at *Banana Patch Studio* in Hanapepe.

Other great books: *Hawaii is a Rainbow, Peter Panini and the Search for the Menehune, Pua Pua Lena Lena, Keiki's First Books* board books.

For cribs and child equipment rentals, call *Ready Rentals* (823-8008; 800-599-8008; readyrentals.com). $20 delivery.

Farmers' Markets

Farmers' Markets happen almost each day of the week – some are 'official,' some informal – and all are great spots to catch the flavor of the island, talk to local people, and enjoy a kaleidoscope of tastes and colors. From truck beds, cardtables, or the trunks of cars, local farmers sell their fruits, vegetables, and flowers at prices more reasonable than supermarkets. Manoa lettuce, as little as $5 for a half-dozen small heads, will be fresh from the garden and taste of Kauai's sunny skies and salt air. You may find tomatoes and avocados; fresh basil, oregano, chives or marjoram; a shiny dark purple eggplant with just the right sound when you thump it, and bananas of all kinds – Williams, Bluefield, and apple-bananas. Don't be put off by the short, fat, drab-skinned exterior because inside, the fruit looks like golden sand at sunset and tastes like bananas laced with apples.

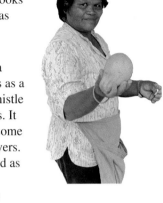

Come early for the best selection – so the starting time is important to know. At the Koloa market, a rope tied across the parking lot serves as a starting line, and the fun begins with a shrill whistle to ensure an equal chance for buyers and sellers. It drops at noon on the nose, so don't be late. At some markets, official opening time doesn't deter buyers. They simply 'reserve' their selections, permitted as long as no money changes hands. Sellers write buyers' names on bags of fruit, or on pineapple leaves, or even give out numbered tokens, like a hat check. The actual buying can be accomplished in a matter of moments – but you have to remember where everything is stashed.

Sellers quickly become friends, who may offer you a slice of their best wares. Papayas will be the local sunrise and strawberry variety, with a red-orange center even tastier with a local lime. Even if you aren't cooking,

Farmers' Markets

Monday	noon	*Koloa*, Ball Park on Rt 520 next to the ball field. Maps 6, 7
	3pm	*Lihue*, Kukui Grove by Sears. Maps 1, 2
Tuesday	2pm	*Hanalei*, west of town on Rt 560. Map 5
	3pm	*Kalaheo* Neighborhood Center, Papalina at Rt 50. Map 6
Wednesday	3pm	*Kapaʻa*, Kahau St. Maps 1, 4
Thursday	3pm	*Hanapepe*, Town Park. Map 6
	4:30pm	*Kilauea*, Kilauea Neighbor Ctr. Map 5
Friday	3:00pm	*Lihue*, Vidinha football stadium parking lot, near airport. Maps 1, 2
Saturday	9am	*Kekaha* Neighborhood Center, Elepaio off Rt 50. Map 8
	9am	*Kilauea*, Christ Memorial Church. Map 5

you'll be tempted by stringbeans as long as shoelaces, squash with squeaky skins, tomatoes still warm and fragrant, all kinds of vegetables with odd shapes, even fresh coconuts. You may even find leis of pakalana or plumeria for $5 a strand. Take home tropical flowers by the bunches – bird of paradise, parrot colored heliconia blossoms, stalks of fragrant white or yellow ginger. Be ready to bargain with sellers if you are buying in quantity, and take their advice about venturing into new tastes. Most sellers price in $2 or $5 packages, so bring plenty of bills.

The largest markets are in Kapaʻa, Koloa, and Lihue. On Fridays, the *Lihue market* is in the parking lot behind the Vidinha football stadium just south of the airport. Enter off Kapule Highway (Rt 51) at the small street leading into the stadium at its northern corner, or turn off Rice St at Holoko Rd (Map 2). The Wednesday *Kapaʻa market* is opposite the armory; take Kukui Rd off Rt 56 and turn right at the end; then make the next right onto Kahau Rd and park on your left. The bypass road from Wailua to Kapaʻa comes out just at the end of Kahau Rd. Map 4

For the *Koloa market*, turn left off Mahulia (the main road into Koloa) Rd at Anne Knudsen Park next to the baseball field. You'll see all the cars parked at the side of the road (Map 7). Monday at 3pm, the *Kukui Grove market* is in the Sears parking lot. Map 2

Just missed the market? You'll find roadside produce stands all over the island. Look for low acid, 'Sugar Loaf' pineapples from Kahili Farms, strawberry papayas, bananas of all kinds. You'll love fruit 'frosties,' a tasty confection of frozen fruit whipped smooth like soft ice cream. Try combinations of mango, banana, papaya, pine-apple – whatever is in season – at the *Moloaʻa Sunrise Fruit Stand* on Rt 56 north of Anahola and *Banana Joe's* in Kilauea. Stock up on

Bouquets of heliconia and ginger for $3.50

local fruits. Tropical fruit 'smoothies' are made at *Moloa'a Sunrise, Banana Joe's* and *Mango Mama's* (Kilauea); *Killer Juice Bar* and *Lotus Root* (Kapa'a); and *Jamba Juice (*Lihue and Kapa'a).

Shoppers wait for starting time at the farmers' market. Bananas, pineapples, papayas cost only a few dollars, flowers just a bit more.

Fitness & Athletic Clubs

EASTSIDE: *Kauai Athletic Club* next to Kukui Grove Shopping Center in Lihue offers daily, weekly, and monthly visitor rates, classes, weight machines, swimming pool, and squash courts (245-5381; kauaiathleticclub. com). *Curves*, home of the 30 minute workout for women (curvesinformation.com), is located nearby in Lihue (245-9790) as well as in Ele'ele (335-5381). NORTH SHORE: *Princeville Health Club*, in the Prince Golf Course clubhouse, has sweeping views of the fairways and ocean, and visitor rates for classes, personal training, massage, and yoga (826-1105; princeville. com). SOUTH SHORE: In Poipu, *Hyatt Resort* offers classes, first-rate gym facilities, outdoor pool, as well as massage (240-6400; anaraspa.com). Use the spa and you can enjoy the lap pool, gym, and entire health facility. You can make one treatment an all day deal.

Local Style: In Kapa'a, a 'local' style gym at modest rates: *Kauai Gym* (823-8210). Hours are limited. *At Your PACE* (822-4111) features hydraulic resistance machines ($5/visit). WESTSIDE: Try *Iron Hut* (335-3383) and *Kauai Xtreme Fitness* (335-0049) in Port Allen. NORTH SHORE: *Devaki* combines yoga with personal fitness training (826-9990). (See *Yoga,* 145).

Fresh Island Fish

You can sometimes find locally-caught fresh fish at roadside stands or farmers' markets. You can try some of the big stores, like *Costco* in Lihue and *Cost-U-Less* and *Safeway* in Wailua where high volume usually means a fresh selection. The small local markets, however, are more interesting and more fun:

EASTSIDE: Try *Fish Express* in Lihue (245-9918) for filets of shibiko (baby yellow fin tuna), ono, ulua, and snappers of all hues – pink, grey, red. Prices and selection vary with the weather, the season, the tides, even the moon; prices are generally higher in winter when fishing boats face rougher seas. The adventurous can try opihi (limpets) raw in the shell with seaweed or smoked marlin. Your fresh fish can be vacuum sealed for shipping. In Hanama'ulu, stop in at *Ara's Sakana-Ya* for homemade ahi poki (raw fish, onions, Hawaiian salt and shoyu) and sushi platters. In Kapa'a, try the inexpensive *Pono Market* (822-4581), a local favorite for poki.

NORTH SHORE: Don't miss *Kilauea Fish Market* for high quality fresh catch and prepared dishes (828-MAHI). In Hanalei, try *Hanalei Dolphin*'s fish market (822-6113).

SOUTH SHORE: *Koloa Fish Market's* seared ahi is a must try, and filets of local fish are really fresh (742-6199).

Flowers & Flower Leis

The fragrance of pikake or white ginger; the cool, silky touch of petals; the delicate yet rich colors of orchids and plumeria – no vacation is complete without a flower lei, especially on your last night. Many stores (even Safeway, Longs, Wal-Mart) offer ready-made leis in a refrigerated case, but imported carnations cannot compare with a local lei which reflects the traditions of the island and the artistry of the lei maker. Order a day in advance, and pick up your lei on the way to dinner.

The *Mauna Loa lei* ($20), a wide woven band of small purple orchids, is popular at graduation. *White ginger* is *a* spectacular creation of white, sometimes pink buds tightly threaded like feathers, fragrant enough to turn heads as you walk by. Other fragrant leis: green *pakalana* ($10/strand of 100 flowers), or small, white *stephanotis* ($10), or *pikake,* a tiny, delicate white flower for weddings ($10/strand). *Plumeria* leis are common in summer; large white, yellow, pink, or deep red large blossoms have a lovely perfume. The fragrance lingers even when petals turn brown. Dry it for a Hawaiian potpourri. You can wear your lei onto the plane, though petals quickly turn brown in air conditioning. Preserve it in a plastic bag to keep it fresh to cheer your morning coffee back home.

At farmers' markets and roadside stands, you can sometimes find leis for $7. In Anahola, Aunty Kuini sells plumeria leis ($7) from a stand opposite Ono Char Burger (822-3114). Order a lei from one of the island's artists: Winnie Cummings (821-1514) and Linda Pitman (828-1572) grow their own flowers and will create a lei just for you. In Puhi, next to Kauai Harley, *San's Flowers* is a favorite spot for lovely leis made by island women. In Lihue, try *Flowers Forever* (245-4717). Check display cases in Kapa'a at *Pono Market* (822-4581) and in Wailua at *JC's Flowers & Minimart* (822-5961). In Kapa'a, visit April at *Flowers & Joys* (flowersandjoyskauai.com; 822-1569) for leis and jewelry. April and JC will ship to the mainland.

Lei in ti leaf wrap

For those friends back home taking care of your dog, what better way to say thank you than with flowers? Order an assortment

boxed and shipped fedex, arriving fresh and gorgeous in any mainland city. *Hawaii Tropical Flower & Foliage Associations* lists contact info for island members (htffa.com).

Orchid lovers will love Kauai. In Hanapepe, visit *Mackie Orchids* (335-0240; mackieorchids.com). In Kilauea, try *Kauai Orchids* (828-0904; kauaiorchids.com). Learn about varieties; buy plants to carry home on the plane (carry your plant in a plastic bag so it can easily be inspected at agriculture to be sure the pot contains only bark and no dirt).

Geocaching

An electronic treasure hunt activity, geocaching involves searching for ingeniously hidden 'treasure' containers using a handheld GPS unit. Nearly 400,000 'geocaches' are hidden around the world, about 80 on Kauai. GPS units are available at sporting outlets or specialty GPS stores, or you can check out manufacturers sites (e.g. garmin.com and magellangps.com).

You download the longitude/latitude coordinates at *geocaching.com*, where you can register (free) for a nickname under which to log finds. Some finds involve solving puzzles, or you may locate an item in one cache which is on its 10th stop on an around-the-world journey, and you can help it along to the next cache. You can also swap your own bit of treasure for what's in the cache.

No matter where you stay on the island, there are geocaches nearby, often by points of interest you might not otherwise discover.

Golf Courses

The *Princeville Makai Course* in Hanalei, designed by Robert Trent Jones, Jr., is a 27 hole, world-class championship course with 3 challenging nines: Lake, Woods, and Ocean, famous for spectacular views and the dramatic 141-yard seventh hole, where the ocean, foaming like a cauldron, separates tee and green. Ranked 6th in the state, this course has been one of *Golf Digest's* top 25 resort courses for 20 years (Par 72; Slope 133). Fees, with cart, are $175 ($125/Princeville Hotel guests; $140/ Princeville Resort guests; $95 after 1:30pm). Enter Princeville at the main gate. (800-826-1105; princeville.com for virtual views; tee times: 826-258). Map 5

The Prince Course is Hawaii's number-one rated course, according to *Golf Digest.* The 18 hole, 6,521 yard, course, designed by Robert Trent Jones, Jr., is spectacular (Par 72; Slope 145), set in 390 acres of spectacular pastureland, with rolling hills, deep ravines, tropical jungle with streams and waterfalls. Fees, with cart, are $175 ($130/Princeville Hotel guests; $150/ Princeville resort guests; $120 after 12pm). Located just east of Princeville on Rt 56. (826-5070; 800-826-1105; princeville.com. Same day tee times: 826-5001). Map 5

Kiahuna Golf Club in Poipu, designed by Robert Trent Jones, Jr., is an 18 hole, links-style course, predominantly flat, with smooth, fast greens and tradewind challenges. At 6,353 yards from the tips, this course is geared for the recreational golfer (Par 72; Slope 128). Fees, with cart, are $110/9 holes or $75 after 2pm. Ask about a 3 round pass ($300). (742-9595; kiahunagolf. com). Maps 6, 7

Poipu Bay Resort Golf Course, Poipu, designed by Robert Trent Jones, Jr. has been the home of the Grand Slam of Golf since 1994. This Scottish links-style course, 6,845 yards from the blue tees, is set in 210 acres of sugar plantation land along the ocean. Views are spectacular (Par 72; Slope 132).

Fees, with cart, are $185 ($125/ Grand Hyatt guests; $125 after noon; $75 after 2:30pm). Inquire about discounts if you are a guest at a neighboring hotel. Adjacent to the Grand Hyatt Resort. (742-8711; 800-858-6300; poipubaygolf.com). Maps 6, 7

Wailua Municipal Golf Course, adjacent to Rt 56 in Wailua, was ranked in the top 25 US municipal courses by *Golf Digest.* This popular 18 hole, 6,658 yard course is built along the ocean on rolling terrain amid ironwood trees and coconut palms. Small greens and narrow fairways make this a real challenge (Par 72, Slope 125). Unbeatable fees: $44/weekends (and it gets crowded); $32/ weekdays; half-price after 2pm; $16/cart/18 holes. (241-6666; kauai.gov/golf). Map 1

Kukuiolono Golf Course, Kalaheo. 9 holes, par 35 with spectacular views over 178 acres and a lovely Japanese garden. Located on a bluff with challenging tradewinds. Greens fee: $7; carts available. It's a local secret most don't want to share. Turn south off Rt 50 in Kalaheo at Papalina Rd. (the stoplight) and drive .8 mile. Enter gate on right. (332-9151). Map 6

Kauai Lagoons Golf & Racquet Club, in the Kauai Lagoons Resort, Lihue, overlooks beautiful Kalapaki Bay and boasts two challenging courses designed by Jack Nicklaus. The 262 acre *Kiele Course* is geared for golfers with a 20-handicap or better, and was named one of the Top 100 courses in America by *Golf Digest.* The front nine is long and rugged with many mounds and swales. The back nine runs out to the ocean, with spectacular views of waves crashing against the rocks, and prevailing tradewinds on the southeast corner (Par 72; Slope 137). Fees in peak season, including cart, are $195 ($125 after noon; $140/Marriott guests). Map 2

An extra-long course with 4 tees, the *Mokihana Course* (previously called *Kauai Lagoons Course*) is ranked by *Golf Magazine* in the top ten of "America's most playable courses" as a shotmaker's course with many bunkers and undulating greens. 6,942 yards from the tips (Par 72; Slope 135). Fees, with cart, are $120 ($80/Marriott guests); $79 after 11am. (241-6000; 800-634-6400; kauailagoonsgolf.com). Map 2

Grove Farm 'Puakea' Course near Kukui Grove Center, Lihue, de-signed by Robin Nelson, winds through 200 acres of former sugar plantation land with sheer ravines, freshwater streams and views of Mount Hau'upu, the Hule'ia Stream, and the ocean.

Recently expanded, the Puakea 18 hole course includes a jungle and flowing stream with varying wind and weather conditions (Par 72; Slope 129). Managed by Billy Caspar Golf. 6,954 yards. $125/before 1pm and $65/after 1pm; 9 holes/$65. Kids play free after 4pm. (245-8756; puakeagolf.com). Map 2

Consider the *'Kauai Golf Challenge'* – one round at three of the following courses: Kiele, Poipu Bay, Prince, or Makai ($375 shared carts). The *'Ultimate Kauai Gold Challenge'* adds a round at either Pukea, Kiahuna, or Kauai Lagoons ($470 shared carts).

Many hotels/condos have contracts with the pro shops, so ask about a 'resort discount.'

Kauai's Golf Magic by Robert Trent Jones, Jr.

I have played golf all over the world, and I keep coming back to Kauai! The island has unique courses, offering both challenges and enjoyment. With the north shore's spectacular landscape to work with, I laid out the original Princeville Resort course in three distinct nines to take advantage of the dramatic cliffs and breathtaking ocean views. The Ocean nine have great vistas and the sounds of the sea off the cliffs; the Woods thread through the trees, with a wonderful Zen-influenced bunker, an idea from my many trips to Japan.

Ranked first in Hawaii by *Golf Digest*, The Prince Course is more bold and dramatic, and I designed it to retain some of the wilderness character of its site. Carved out of heavy vegetation, it meanders through valleys, with panoramic views. It's a tough course (I'm told the beverage cart driver sells more golf balls than drinks) but from the proper set of tees, I guarantee you'll enjoy this golf nature trek!

On the south shore, the Kiahuna Plantation Course is a fun, yet memorable test with rolling fairways, sweeping bunkers, and small, traditional greens. Our newest creation, Poipu Bay Resort adjacent to the Hyatt Regency, is the site of the PGA's Annual Grand Slam of Golf. The back nine border the ocean, where the almost constant yet variable wind is the challenge. You have to make precise shots, judging both distance and the wind, or it will blow the ball off the green. Many holes hug the cliffs, and special attention has been given to ancient Hawaiian sacred grounds.

On the east side, the Wailua Golf Course is one of the best public courses in the country. Many holes flank the ocean and are protected by palm trees. This course is a must! I am also a fan of the Kiele Course. The finishing holes really get your attention, particularly the par-three 15th, requiring skill and a brave heart to tame.

No matter which course you choose, you really can't go wrong on Kauai. The people are friendly, temperatures comfortable, the pace slow – and a nice surprise around each corner! There's something magical about Kauai that brings people back. I know. I'm one of them!

Helicoptering Kauai

Many of the most beautiful places on Kauai are inaccessible by car. For this reason, a helicopter tour is an unforgettable way to see this spectacular island. Kauai is breathtakingly beautiful from the air, almost like an America in miniature, with rolling hills and valleys on the eastside and majestic mountains on the west. The island has a flat, dry southland as well as a forested wilderness to the north, and, on the west coast, wide sandy beaches where the setting sun paints the sky with gold before slipping silently into the enormous sea. There is even a 'Grand Canyon' on a small scale, where pink and purple cliffs, etched by centuries of wind and rain into giant towers, seem like remnants of a lost civilization. So much variety is amazing on an island only 30 miles in diameter.

And what you'll see is beyond your fantasies – a mountain goat poised in a ravine, a white bird gliding against the dark green cliffs, a sudden rainbow in the mist, incredible, tower-like mountains of pink and brown in the Waimea 'Grand Canyon,' a glistening waterfall hanging like a slender silver ribbon through trees and rocks, a curve of white sand at the base of the purple and gold Na Pali cliffs, white foam bursting upon the rocky coast.

Then, like the unveiling of the island's final mystery, you fly into the very center of Mt. Wai'ale'ale's crater, where in the dimly lit mists of the rainiest place on the earth, waterfalls are born from ever falling showers. You have journeyed to the very heart of the island, the place of its own birth from the volcano's eruption centuries ago. From your hotel room, you would never have believed that all this splendor existed.

Because of the expense, we worried about picking the 'perfect day.' We began on what seemed in Lihue to be only a partly sunny day, but once in the air, we saw that the clouds would be above us rather than in our way and enhanced the island's beauty with changing patterns of light.

The helicopter touring industry was started by an extraordinary pilot, Jack Harter, who had the vision more than 30 years ago of showing visitors the island's hidden beauty by air. Jack became a legend for his extraordinary flying skill, mechanical savvy, and intimate knowledge and love of Kauai. People lucky enough to fly with Jack saw and learned more in their 90 minute flight than they could have imagined possible, and carried away memories of spectacular scenery and a flight as smooth as dandelion seed even in unexpected winds. Jack had a perfect safety record, and accomplished rescues in weather other pilots would not–or could not–dare to face. As the sign at the tour desk at the Old Kauai Surf Hotel used to say, Jack Harter was 'imitated by many, equaled by none.'

Following Jack, younger pilots like Will Squyres started companies on Kauai, piloting all the flights personally, and then, as their companies added aircraft and brought in and trained even younger pilots to fly them, the 'owner piloted' company became an economically unworkable business model. The Bell Jet Rangers, which accommodated 4 paying passengers, were gradually replaced by the larger, more economical '6 -pac' ASTARs.

Jack retired several years ago to his farm on the north shore, but you can still fly with Will Squyres, an extraordinary pilot who has earned wide respect over the years for his company's perfect safety record (no accidents in 26 years), his good judgment and intimate knowledge of Kauai, and his company's meticulous maintenance. Will has scouted locations for movies like 'Jurassic Park' and 'The Lost World,' and his company's hour-long tour coordinates pilot commentary with dramatic music on a first rate sound system as you fly over the island's most spectacular scenery.

The typical tour goes in a clockwise direction around the island starting from the Lihue airport. A unique option: Niʻihau Helicopters offers a half-day tour to Niʻihau including a 3 hour landing on a beach for snorkeling and a picnic lunch (335-3500; niihauisland.com).

Looking at our images and videos back home almost brings back the magic of that hour, when we seemed suspended in a horizon so vast as to seem limitless, and any effort to confine it within camera range was impossible. It is always the best day of the trip.

Helicopter Tours & Safety

Beautiful as Kauai is from the air, recent accidents have focused everyone's attention squarely on safety. The island's mountainous terrain, occasionally turbulent winds, and rapidly changing cloud conditions can pose real challenges for the pilot. In a review of 8 weather-related accidents statewide since 1994, the National Transportation Safety Board found that half involved pilots relatively new to air tour operations in Hawaii. The reality is that a pilot with sufficient hours to be licensed may not have extensive experience on Kauai, where judgment calls are often crucial.

In 2005, a Heli USA helicopter crashed during a 'microburst' or sudden wind and rainstorm in the waters off Ha'ena, killing 3 people. According to an NTSB report (3/5/2007), "the decision by the pilot to continue flight into adverse weather conditions" contributed to the accident. In 2004, a Bali Hai Helicopters pilot flying below the recommended SFAR minimum altitude made the decision "to continue flight into an area of turbulent, reduced visibility weather conditions" rather than deviate from his tour route, and crashed into a ridgeline; all 5 on board died (NTSB 2/13/2007). Both pilots had been flying on Kauai for only a few months.

NTSB recommends pilot training that specifically addresses local weather phenomena and in-flight decision-making, and also that the FAA increase surveillance of pilots to ensure compliance with minimum terrain clearance requirements. The Honolulu FAA recommended in August, 2006

that pilots not perform 'non-flight' duties such as operating videography, sound systems, or two-way intercoms which may distract attention from primary flight responsibilities.

Two more accidents took place in March, 2007, when four people died in a Heli USA crash at the Princeville Airport after the pilot reported hydraulic problems, according to Kauai Fire Chief Robert Westerman (as quoted in CBS/AP).

An Inter-Island Helicopter crashed near Ha'ena a few days later, with one fatality.

Then and now: The eastside seen in 1995 with fields of sugar cane and in 2006 (below).

Na Pali Coastline

Accidents may be caused by mechanical failure or by pilot error, but sometimes causes remain unknown. NTSB has still not released a final report on an 2003 accident involving Jack Harter Helicopters, which occurred in clear weather. The pilot was experienced and respected, and the NTSB preliminary report shows no mechanical problems with the aircraft. We will report the outcomes of all investigations as they are completed.

Key questions to ask when you are interviewing companies:

FAA certification: Not all companies are certified under Part 135 of Federal Aviation Regulations, which requires a company to perform a more rigorous (thus more expensive) maintenance program than other certification categories, as well as annual flight tests of its pilots. This certificate must be displayed in the company's office. Ask to see it. You also have a

2007	Inter-Island Helicopters	1 fatality
2007	Heli USA	4 fatalities
2005	Heli USA	3 fatalities
2004	Bali Hai Helicopters	5 fatalities
2003	Jack Harter Helicopters	5 fatalities
1998	Ohana Helicopters	6 fatalities
1994	Inter-Island Helicopters	1 fatality
1994	Papillon Hawaiian	3 fatalities

right to know whether the company, or *your* pilot, has been involved in accidents during the past three years. (You can check with NTSB at ntsb. gov). You should also ask if the company's FAA certificate has ever been revoked or suspended, and whether it is currently under FAA investigation for accidents or maintenance deficiencies (as opposed to record-keeping violations). Since each helicopter must display its individual 'certificate of airworthiness,' look for it or ask to see it.

Pilot experience: How long has your pilot been flying over Kauai? Will you be told who your pilot will be?

Exact length of the tour. Actual in-flight time for the around-the-island tour should be no less than 60 minutes, or Kauai will appear to whiz past your window, limiting your opportunities to explore the more remote terrain inside the island's perimeter, or to take satisfying photographs. Ask for the daily flight schedule, subtract 5 minutes for landing and changing passengers, and draw your own conclusions. In this area, in our opinion, economy is not always the best policy. Operating costs for helicopters are high; companies may try to speed up tours to squeeze as many into the day as possible. Cheaper tours will almost certainly be short, possibly too short, and the extra dollars you spend for a longer tour will be well worthwhile.

Aircraft and window configuration: Seating depends on balancing the passenger weight load. The air-conditioned, 6-passenger ASTAR seats 2 passengers next to the pilot in front and 4 passengers in the rear. For passengers in the center rear seats, the view can be obstructed by passengers

Tunnels Beach as the rain moves in

seated next to the windows as well as those in front. The new oversized windows are essential. Since windows are sealed, wearing darker colored shirts will cause less reflection in the glass and give you better photographs.

The Hughes 500-D helicopter seats two passengers in the rear and two in front next to the pilot, with a narrow middle seat. *Jack Harter Helicopters* offers a 'doors off' option on its Hughes to put passengers even closer to the scenery. The FAA has no objection, but it's not for everyone. Some will like the unique experience of being almost inside the landscape; and some, like photographers, will appreciate the absence of windshield glass for capturing the light and the vivid colors. Others may not enjoy being so close to the weather, when clouds, and the moisture they carry, can drift inside.

Cancellation policy in case of bad weather: When rain and clouds sock in the interior mountains, tours often simply go around the island's perimeter, and you miss all that gorgeous interior scenery. Even in a rainstorm, we often see choppers flying. You will want a refund if can't see very much – once you're in the air. (*Jack Harter Helicopters* and *Will Squyres Helicopters* will cancel and try to reschedule your flight if visibility is below par.)

We consider helicopter tours a unique and special way to see Kauai. We wouldn't go ourselves, or let our children fly, if we thought they were unsafe. But we make careful decisions about the pilots we fly with. We think you should do your homework carefully and have all pertinent information when making your choices as well.

Hiking

Hiking can be a spectacular way to see Kauai, for more than half of the island's 551,000 square miles is forestland, and many of its most beautiful regions are inaccessible by car. However, hiking Kauai can also be dangerous. Many trails can become treacherous from washouts and mudslides, and in the Na Pali coastal region, where trails are often etched into the sides of sheer cliffs, hikers must be wary of waves crashing over the rocks without warning, as well as vegetation which masks the edge of a sheer drop. Stick to clearly marked trails, heed posted warnings, and avoid getting too close to any cliffedge – even those overlooking beautiful waterfalls or tremendous coastlines. In December 2006, two young visitors fell to their deaths on an 'off the beaten path' trail, leading, so they thought, to a waterfall.

Careful planning is a must. Before your trip, order a recreational map of hiking trails in the forest preserves from *Na Ala Hele*, a non-profit group helping with trail improvement, by sending $6 (cashier's check or money order only) to *Division of Forestry*, Kauai District (3060 Eiwa St., Room 306, Lihue, HI 96766; 274-3433), or save $1 and pick it up at the office. The

The Kalalau trail from Keʻe Beach to Hanakapiʻai winds along the rugged Na Pali coastline, through dense vegetation, along switch-backs and over rocks, sometimes only inches away from a sheer drop. Views are incredible! Mud from the frequent rain showers can create slippery conditions, so good footgear is a must.

The Kalalau Trail into the Na Pali wilderness begins where paved road ends, at Ke'e Beach on the north shore.

Reward: The view after climbing the first quarter-mile.

Na Ala Hele trail specialist is Craig Koga, *Dept. of Land and Natural Resources*, 3060 Eiwa Street, Room 306 Lihue, HI 96766 (274-3442). For detailed maps, directions, and descriptions of individual trails, check the *Na Ala Hele* website (hawaiitrails.org) and the DLNR site (hawaii.gov/dlnr). For information on the Na Pali region, contact Wayne Souza (274-3446).

Some private companies offer excellent information. For maps of Kauai's geological, archeological, and topographical profiles, visit teok. com. The company also offers guided tours. Review Bob Smith's *Hiking Kauai,* the original guidebook to hikes on Kauai, or Kathy Morey's *Kauai Trails.* Request a catalog of books and maps for hiking and camping on Kauai from *Hawaii Geographic Society,* PO Box 1698, Honolulu, HI 96806. When you arrive, you can call the *Division of Forestry* in Lihue (274-3433) for current trail conditions.

Kauai's most famous trail, the *Kalalau trail,* is a spectacular but strenuous 11-mile hike through the Na Pali cliff region, though even recreational hikers can enjoy the first few miles. This subsection, the *Hanakapi'ai trail*, has breathtaking views of the coast along switchbacks which take you into forest and back out to the ocean. About a quarter-mile of uphill walking brings you to a magnificent view of Ke'e Beach and the Ha'ena reefs. Two more miles of rigorous up and down hiking will bring you to Hanakapi'ai Beach, nestled like a brilliant jewel in a picturesque, terraced valley. Unfortunately, this beach has currents far too dangerous for swimming, and the rip currents can be so powerful that more than one unwary hiker standing in the surf at knee level has been caught up in a sudden, large wave, pulled out to sea and drowned. On a recent hike, we helped some folks who were stranded on the sand bar by high surf; fortunately we had a rope and a tall, strong friend, otherwise they would have been in trouble. Beyond the beach, you can take the trail to Hanakapi'ai Falls. It's very strenuous; the path crosses the river in several places and at times you may have to hold onto trees to keep your balance on the rocky and wet footing. Allow 6 hours for the round trip from Ke'e Beach to Hanakapi'ai Falls, with a rest stop for a picnic. Carry plenty of water and fill up at Ke'e Beach, the last source of safe drinking water.

Important safety information: When it rains, this narrow trail gets muddy – and dangerously slippery, a fact we appreciated at first hand when we saw a woman slip over the steep edge and disappear down into the slick vegetation. Fortunately, her quick-thinking companion had managed to grab her hand so that we could pull her back up. In many places, the trail is actually a stream bed and fills with water after heavy rains. Essential items: shoes with good traction for slippery rocks and mud (instead of jogging shoes or slippers), sunscreen, water, strong insect repellent, a hat, perhaps a nylon poncho, and even a walking stick (Consider a telescoping stick that can double as a monopod for your camera; a great one by Cascade can be found at rei.com). For an update on trail conditions in Na Pali, call *Pedal & Paddle* (826-9069) in Hanalei, the *Division of State Parks* (274-3444), or *Kayak Kauai* (826-9844; kayakkauai.com), which offers guided hikes of the Kalalau Trail. *Kauai Visitor's Bureau* (245-3971; kauaidiscovery.com) can help arrange local guides.

EASTSIDE: In Wailua, we like the *Mount Nounou Trail* on Sleeping Giant Mountain. This semi-strenuous 1.75-mile hike takes you to the Ali'i Vista Hale picnic shelter on the 'chest' of the Sleeping Giant. From this vantage point, you can see the inland mountains to Mount Wai'ale'ale and the Wailua River winding to the sea. The trail head is on Halelilo Rd in Wailua. From Kuhio Highway (Route 56), take Halelilo Rd for 2 miles and park on the right near telephone pole #38. After a moderate ascent over switchbacks, about an hour or less, with some climbing over boulders, through dense guava and eucalyptus, you'll come to a junction marked by multiple-rooted hala trees. The trail to the left leads to another fork, and

Hanakapi'ai Beach

either of these paths will lead to the shelter. Avoid trails leading south towards the giant's 'head' which are hazardous.

WESTSIDE: The *Koke'e Forest* region has a different kind of beauty. Within this 4,345 acre wilderness preserve are 45 miles of trails, from pleasant walks to rugged hikes, as well as fresh water fishing streams, and the 20 square mile highland bog known as Alaka'i Swamp. From Koke'e Lodge, day hikers can choose from three trails which explore the plateau and Waimea Canyon rim, ranging from the half-mile 'Black Pipe Trail' to the 1.5 mile 'Canyon Trail' along the north rim of Waimea Canyon, past upper Wa'ipo'o Falls to the Kumuwela Overlook. From this perch you can see the canyon's 3,600-foot depth and 10 mile stretch to the sea. Contact *Koke'e Museum* 335-9975 (kokee.org) for guides, maps, brochures, and reservations for guided Sunday walks (summer). Sign up for an e-newsletter that brings Koke'e news to you all year long. Hunting and fishing licenses: *Koke'e Lodge* (335-6061).

HIKING TOURS: The *Sierra Club* sponsors hikes on Kauai each month. Popular destinations: the Kalalau Trail to Hanakapi'ai on the Na Pali; Sleeping Giant Mountain trails on the eastern shore; Shipwreck Beach to Maha'ulepu on the south shore; on the west, the first few miles along the coast beyond Polihale. Send a stamped, addressed envelope to PO Box 3412, Lihue, HI 96766 (www.hi.sierraclub.org/Kauai/kauai.html).

Princeville Ranch Adventures offers an excellent recreational hike through pastureland and along a secluded stream, with a picnic lunch at a hidden waterfall before the return trip (4 hrs/$79). Great views, peaceful quiet, and healthful lunch (826-7669; 888-955-7669; adventureskauai.com). A variation on the hiking trip includes a kayaking segment through one of Kauai's 'jungle' streams (4 hrs/$94).

You can hike to spectacular *Kipu Falls* with *Outfitters Kauai* ($155), explore a hidden but previously inaccessible gem on private land, even soar over the treetops on a zipline (742-9667; 888-742-9887; outfitterskauai. com). Guides are knowledgeable, and the group (up to 20) proceeds at a leisurely pace on foot and by kayak to the falls.

Kauai Nature Tours (742-8305; 888-233-8365; teok.com) features naturalist guides and hikes at all skill levels. *Aloha Kauai Tours* explores the back country by 4x4 to hike into the 'blue hole' at the base of Mt. Wai'ale'ale (3 hrs/$75). (245-6400; 800-452-1113; alohakauai-tours.com).

Horseback Riding

North shore scenery is breathtaking, but weather can be more uncertain than on the south, where the ride can be warmer and more dusty. A morning ride avoids the heat of the day. Take sunglasses and a hat which won't blow off. (Once you're on board, it's hard to climb down and chase it).

EASTSIDE: *Esprit de Corps* in Kapa'a gives lessons (from $35) and trail rides (you can canter on the advanced ride) in the lush Sleeping Giant Mountain area. Tour rates range from $120, including a 6 hr 'spiritual' meditation ride overlooking Mt. Wai'ale'ale ($250). Owner Dale Rosenfeld enjoys working with children (she offers ponies) and visitors with disabilities (822-4688; kauaihorses.com). Map 1

NORTH SHORE: *Princeville Ranch Stables* (formerly Po'oku Ranch) offers 4 rides across the ranch lands and towards the mountains for views – some of which include a hike to a waterfall for a picnic lunch and swim. Tours cost $80/1.5 hr; $135/3 hr; $135/4 hr (826-6777; princevilleranch. com). Groups of 6-8 are taught horsemanship, a unique feature. Closed Sundays. *Silver Falls Ranch* in Kilauea escorts groups along the beautiful Kalihiwai Ridge with lunch and swim at a waterfall. Tours cost $80/1.5 hr, $100/2 hr; $120/3 (828-6718; silverfallsranch.com). Map 5

SOUTH SHORE: Near Mahaʻulepu Beach, *CJM Stables* offers a 2 hr beach tour ($90); a 3.5 hr ride and swim tour ($115 – and you can trot); and a 3 hr breakfast beach ride ($105) (742-6096; cjmstables.com). Tour guides are very friendly and provide historical information as well as photo-opportunities. Closed Sundays. Map 6

Ice Cream & Shave Ice

Kauai has its own ice cream factory, founded by Walter Lappert who wanted to retire in paradise – and ended up in business. Demand exploded for his creamy island flavors like 'Kauai pie,' and now you can enjoy Lappert's in Silicon Valley and beyond. *Coldstone Creamery* has made its way to Kauai, in Lihue's Kukui Grove Center and next to Safeway in Wailua. Hawaiian made *Meadow Gold* ice cream, available in Foodland and Big Save Markets, makes our favorite version of Macadamia Nut. The more calorie conscious can try *Zack's* in the Coconut Marketplace or *TCBY* in Wailua behind Mema's. In Port Allen, *Kauai Chocolate Company* makes delicious homemade ice cream – a spectacular chocolate.

Shave Ice is a special island treat. EASTSIDE: *Halo Halo Shave Ice* next to *Hamura's Saimin* on Kress St is one of the originals (Lihue), or try *Ono Family Restaurant* (Kapaʻa). NORTH SHORE: The *Wishing Well* (the silver trailer by Kayak Kauai in Hanalei) has some of the best flavors and textures. The owner is a local legend for establishing the first shave ice in Hanalei, and for her sometimes less-than-sweet attitude. The shave ice alternative next to Bubba's Burgers is more conventional. WESTSIDE: On your way to Waimea Canyon or Kekaha, stop in at *Jo Jo's* on Waimea's main drag (Rt 560). You can try all 60 flavors!

Internet & Cyber Cafés

Local dial-up: AOL: 245-4284 and Earthlink: 855-0020 or 482-2916. Arrange local dial-up with Hawaiian.net for $10/2 weeks (no set-up charge). 212-0200 or accounts@hawaiian.net. Many hotels offer fee-based internet services. It's free (and wireless) at *Waimea Cottages* (Waimea) and *Small Town Coffee* (Kapa'a) where you can enjoy amazing coffee, great pastries, and old-fashioned friendliness. Look for the blue building.

Cyber Cafés: EASTERN SHORE: KAPAʻA: Free wireless at *Small Town Coffee*. Public Macs. Download images; burn CDs. 9am - 7pm (M-Sat) next to Kountry Kitchen. *Akamai Computers:* Windows. ADSL. Rentals. 823-0047. 9am - 5:30pm (M-F). 4-1286 Kuhio Hwy Suite A, next to Ono Family Restaurant. *Java Kai* in Lihue, Kapaʻa, Koloa, and Hanalei has T-Mobile.

NORTH SHORE: HANALEI: *Discount Activities Internet Portal.* Windows. 826-9117. 8am - 8pm daily. Across from Kalypso's.

Jewelry

Goldsmith's Kauai in the Kinipopo Shopping Village, Wailua is a must stop. You'll find original designs crafted of gold, silver, precious gems, or lustrous pearls. Dana Romsdal and her award-winning designers create beautiful pieces like a *humu humu nuku nuku apu a'a,* or a butterfly fish, or a plumeria on a gold chain. Check photographs of their designs, or let them create something special. Seashell designs in gold are lovely, gem settings are exquisite, yet prices are very reasonable. We worked with Dana to create a pearl birthday pendant, watching the design develop on its own page at goldsmiths-kauai.com (822-4653; 800-692-7166).

In Kapa'a, *Jim Saylor* works with fine gems. While you watch, he can sketch a special setting for a loose gemstone, or help you select from his portfolio (822-3591).

Ni'ihau shell leis can be found at *Kauai Gold* in Wailua's Coconut Marketplace, and at the *Kauai Museum Shop*, with certificates of authenticity and a guarantee of workmanship. *Hawaiian Trading Center* (Rt 50 and 560) has a large selection. Without certificates, prices are lower.

Kauai Gifts

For high quality island-made artisan gifts, including shell leis from Ni'ihau, visit the unique *Kauai Products Store* (246-6753; kauaimade.net) in Kukui Grove Center and the *Kauai Museum* (245-6931) in Lihue. *Kong Lung* and *Banana Patch* (bananapatchstudio.com) in Kilauea have wonderful island style collections. *Island Soap* (Koloa and Kilauea) is fragrant with coconut, pikake, or plumeria (handmade-soap.com).

For handmade clothes and wonderful fabrics, stop at *Kapaia Stitchery* just north of Lihue on Rt 56 (don't take the Rt 51 bypass road, or you'll miss it) where island seamstresses still make quilts, dresses, and custom aloha shirts with the same care their own grandmothers did (245-2281). *Kilohana Clothing* at Kilohana has beautiful women's and men's clothing designs in vintage cloth by Melody (246-6911). *Hilo Hattie's* in Lihue (hilohattie.com) has a huge selection of Hawaiian style clothing, and across the street, *Discount Fabric Warehouse* (246-2739; gotfabric.com) has the island's largest selection of Hawaiian fabrics. At *Vicky's* in Kapa'a (822-1746) you'll find lovely fabrics and old fashioned personal attention. Knitting supplies are scarce; try Ace Hardware in Lihue.

Bargain hunters will enjoy Kauai's flea markets. Try the daily open air market at Spouting Horn in Poipu. In Kapaʻa, it's on Rt 56 opposite Otsuka's (W - Sun) and on Rt 50 in Waimea, but wares may be imports. *Hawaiian Trading Center* (Rt 50 and 560) has an enormous selection.

Kayaking

Exploring Kauai's rivers by kayak can be fun, but increasingly controversial as rivers become more crowded. The problem is most acute at the Wailua River, Kauai's only navigable river, which offers various water sports. You may see powerboats zipping along, some towing wake boards or water-skiers, sending waves toward canoes and kayaks hugging the shore.

Tours & rentals: EASTSIDE AND SOUTH SHORE: *Rainbow Kayaks* has an excellent trip upriver to the waterfall (about a mile) in two person kayaks ($92/adult). Knowledgeable guides describe local wildlife, history, and legends. After hiking another mile, you reach the waterfall for a swim and excellent picnic lunch. Since the trail can get muddy, shoes with some sort of sole are recommended (not slippers). Tour guides will take family photos (826-9983; 866-826-9983; rainbowkayak.com). *Outfitters Kauai* (742-9667; 888-742-9887; outfitterskauai.com) also offers a Wailua River tour and waterfall hike ($98 with lunch). Both *Outfitters* and *Kauai Water Ski & Surf Company* (822-3574) will rent kayaks ($40/day/double).

For river tours of the Huleʻia River, where Indiana Jones was filmed, contact *Island Adventures*. A one-way guided paddle ($89) follows the river through the Huleʻia National Wildlife Refuge and Hawaii State Conservation District to the Alakoko or 'Menehune' Fish Pond, made, according to

legend, by the 'Menehune,' Kauai's magical 'little people.' After a short hike, where you can observe many birds, waterfowl, and beautiful exotic plants, you reach Papakolea Falls for a swim, then a picnic before a van ride to your car (246-6333; kauaifun.com).

Huleʻia River tours ($98) are also offered by *Outfitters Kauai*. They can take you to *Kipu Falls*, a beautiful spot on private land, by guided kayak tour (or a separate zipline tour, p 145) – the only safe and legal way to visit Kipu Falls. On the kayak tour, a group of up to 20 proceeds at a leisurely pace on a two-mile paddle upriver, then a hike along trails (often

After all the paddling, the waterfall!

muddy) and a 275-ft zipline ride. After a brief wagon tour of Kipu Ranch and lunch, you spend an hour at Kipu falls for swimming and trying out the 25-ft rope swing ($165). It's great for recreational hikers and kayakers who want to enjoy inaccessible places, but not those who like to push ahead (742-9667; 888-742-9887; outfitterskauai.com).

NORTH SHORE: *Princeville Ranch Hike & Kayak* offers a wonderful hike (45 min) combined with kayaking a secluded stream (1/2 hour) and a picnic lunch at a hidden waterfall before the return trip (4 hrs total). Great views, peaceful scenery, and healthful lunch (826-7669; 888-955-7669; adventures-kauai.com). *Kayak Kauai Outbound* (826-9844; 800-437-3507; kayakkauai. com) offers tours and rents 2-person and 1-person kayaks (2-hour minimum). Travel upriver, or venture downriver to Hanalei Bay. In summer, when Hanalei Bay is calm, you can paddle along the bay's edge and pull up on the Princeville Hotel's beach. Rent also from *Pedal & Paddle*. Go early for the best selection.

Sea Kayaking: For experienced kayakers, sea kayaking can be great fun in the right conditions. *Kayak Kauai Outbound* (800-437-3507; kayak-kauai.com) offers a day-long kayak excursion between Haʻena and Polihale State Beach on the westside. Views are spectacular, but be forewarned: be ready for a strenuous six hours of hard paddling, and sudden squalls and choppy water often punctuate the ride. In your kayak you can explore sea caves, play with dolphins, and visit with turtles ($195). When Na Pali waters become too rough (October through April), whale-watching tours go along the south shore to Kipu Kai ($145). Poipu-based *Outfitters Kauai*

(742-9667; 888-742-9887; outfitterskauai.com) offers guided sea kayak tours along Na Pali (summer: $195) and the south shore (winter: $140).

Tips: If you are taking a tour, review the cancellation policy carefully, or you may wind up being charged if you change your mind. We are often asked about the other kind of tips; if you are so inclined, about $5/pp would be really appreciated by your local guides.

If you are renting, check the kayak beforehand for patches and leaks. And remember the sun. A hat, sunscreen, and drinking water are a must. Bring a towel and spare shirt. Everything in the kayak can get wet, so protect your camera in a waterproof bag. A 2-hour trip may be all you need.

Great spots: In summer, rent in Hanalei and load the kayak onto your car and go to the boat pier, to Anini Beach, or Kalihiwai Bay (about 10 minutes). Eastside, rent at Kalapaki Bay or the Wailua River. When winter surf and currents are too strong, your best options will be the Hanalei, Wailua, or Kalihiwai Rivers. Remember: don't drink the river water, and be cautious if you have any open wounds. The bacterium causing *leptospirosis* found in all of Kauai's rivers can cause serious, even fatal, flu-like symptoms.

Kite Surfing

Brando Wattson (639-WAVE; surf.kauaistyle.com) offers private lessons, as does Akamai Kiteboarding School, taught by Jeremy Fry (821-1000; trykauai.com). Best spots are off Tunnels Beach and Anini Beach.

Luaus

For centuries, Hawaiians have celebrated birthdays, weddings, anniversaries, and festive occasions, with a luau feast, featuring a whole pig roasted in an imu (underground oven), fresh island fish, chicken cooked in coconut and taro, tropical fruits, and salads. The major hotels offer luau extravaganzas. EASTSIDE: *ResortQuest* Kauai Beach at Makaiwa (823-0311) features a Tihati production (tihati.com) every night except Mondays ($55/one child free with adult). In Wailua, *Smith's Tropical Paradise* (821-6895; smiths-kauai.com) offers Asian/Polynesian dances ($65/adult), and you can buy a ticket to the show ($15), presented in a natural amphitheater, without also paying for the buffet (gates open at 7:30pm). Go early to see the gardens, though the bar does not open until 6:15pm, even for soft drinks. *Kilohana Plantation* tells the story of Kauai as well as Tahitian, Maori, and Polynesian dances. The buffet includes vegetarian items ($50/adult; $20/child; 245-9593; gaylordskauai.com).

NORTH SHORE: At the *Princeville Hotel* on the north shore, dancers perform by the oceanside pool; kids will love the view from the bridge (826-9644). SOUTH SHORE: At *Grand Hyatt Luau*, Tihati Entertainment (tihati.com) features an all Polynesian extravaganza on Sundays/Thursdays at $75/$65/$40 (742-1234). Some entertainment is free, or nearly free. See *Music on Kauai* (p 128) and *Family Fun* (p 95).

Massage, Kauai Style

For something truly special, try an unforgettable, Hawaiian lomi lomi massage at *Mu'olaulani* in Anahola. This unique massage experience, developed by Auntie Angeline, begins in a wood steam room, with a 'sea salt scrub' to cleanse your skin in preparation for the amazingly soothing lomi lomi performed by a team of two with fragrant oils. Angeline, her family and staff consider lomi lomi sacred to the Hawaiian tradition of healing. This extraordinary, incredibly relaxing two-hour experience costs a reasonable $150. Since the steamer is shared, specify if you prefer being with your own gender (though steam makes a nice curtain). Mornings only. Closed weekends (822-3235; info@auntyangelines.com).

A tranquil retreat facility, *Kahuna Valley* in the hills above Kapa'a offers massage, hot stone work, Watsu water-based therapy, and instruction in the Chinese healing experience of Qigong. Contact Daisy or Francesco (822-4268; kahunavalley.org). At *Tri Health Ayurveda Spa* in Kilauea, try Samvahana, a healing oil massage. Following centuries old Kerela Ayurveda tradition, two therapists massage warm oils fragrant with herbs into your skin. Treatments from $130, also massage oils (828-2104; 800-455-0770; trihealthspa.com).

Day Spas: *Spa Makaiwa* in the Kauai Coast Resort, Wailua (821-2626) offers wraps, facials, manicures, and massage, including a 'Hot Stone Raindrop Therapy': warm essential oils drip gently onto your back and are then massaged into the skin with smooth, hot rocks.

Private practitioners: They offer a reasonable price, flexible hours/ locations. EASTSIDE: the exceptional *Bonnie Morris* in Anahola (639-3459) and *Carol Launch* in Lihue (245-7005). Local companies: *Waipouli Massage* (821-0878) and *A Touch in Paradise* (639-0389). *Aloha Day Spa* in Lihue is close to the Marriott (246-2414; touchofalohaspa.com).

Resorts: At *Hyatt's Anara Spa,* a massage ($145) or pedicure ($90) allows you to use spa facilities, including lap pool, steam room, sauna, weight room (240-6440; anaraspa.com). *Aveda Spa* at Waipouli Resort in Wailua, offers signature massages, soaks, and wraps (823-1488).

Museums & History Tours

The story of Kauai is in many ways the story of the sugar plantations which shaped the island's multi-ethnic culture as much as its agriculture and economy. For this reason, *Grove Farm Homestead* in Lihue offers a fascinating glimpse into the island's past. One of the earliest Hawaiian sugar plantations, Grove Farm was founded in 1864 by George Wilcox, the son of Protestant missionary teachers at Wai'oli Mission in Hanalei. Planting and harvesting Grove Farm's sugar crop, which grew from 80 acres to more than 1,000, ultimately involved several hundred Hawaiians, Chinese, Koreans, Germans, Portuguese, and Filipino laborers, who brought to Kauai a rich heritage of ethnic cultures. A two-hour tour takes you through Grove Farm's cluster of buildings nestled amid tropical gardens, orchards, and rolling lawns. You'll see the gracious old Wilcox home, where large rooms are cooled by breezes from shaded verandas and elegantly furnished with oriental carpets, magnificent koa wood floors and hand crafted furniture of native woods. You'll see the 'board and batten' cottage of the plantation housekeeper, who came to Kauai, as a Japanese 'picture bride.' All buildings are covered by traditional 'beach sand paint' (sand thrown against wet paint) to protect them against both heat and damp (as long as 20 years).

Like other Hawaiian sugar plantations, Grove Farm was established at a significant point in the island's economic history. In the 1850's, when the monarchy began to sell land, Hawaii entered the age of private property. Before this time, land was not sold but given in trust to subjects in pie-shaped slices, from the interior mountains to the sea, so that each landhold would include precious fresh water as well as coastline.

The leisurely, friendly tour includes a stop in the kitchen for cookies and mint ice tea. For students and scholars, the library's extensive collection of Hawaiiana and plantation records is available by appointment. Tours: Mon, Wed, Thurs at 10am and 1pm. Reservations (well in advance): 245-3202 (PO Box 1631, Lihue HI 96766). Map 1

Grove Farm Homestead was planned by Mabel Wilcox in 1971 at age 89. A public health nurse, she was decorated by both France and Belgium for outstanding service in World War I. Elsie Wilcox, a Kauai School Commissioner, was the first woman in the territory elected to the State Senate. Elsie and Mabel restored *Wai'oli Mission House* in Hanalei (T, Th, Sat 9am – 3pm; 245-3202).

If the Grove Farm tour doesn't fit into your schedule, visit the *Kauai Museum* on Rice St in Lihue. The Rice Building exhibits the *Story of Kauai* – the volcanic eruptions which shaped the land; the Polynesians who voyaged to the island in canoes and left behind marvelous petroglyphs; the missionaries who altered its culture; and the sugar planters who, like George Wilcox, defined much of its agricultural destiny. The adjacent Wilcox building features local artists and rotating exhibits (an exhibit of Japanese, Chinese, Hawaiian, and Filipino wedding dress and traditions). The museum shop sells books, maps, crafts (free admission to shop). If you don't finish touring by the end of the day, you can ask for a free pass for the next. Mon – Fri: 9:30am – 4:30pm; Sat 10am – 4pm. Families free the first Saturday of the month. 245-6931; kauaimuseum.org.

Man in gourd mask by John Weber, artist with Captain Cook

The last family-owned sugar plantation in Hawaii (one of only 3 left statewide), the *Gay and Robinson Sugar Plantation* in Makaweli offers a unique 2-hour tour of sugar production. Visit the fields to see how cane is grown and harvested, then it's into the plant, with hard hats & safety glasses, to see every phase from unloading the cane to spinning it into raw sugar. Sample sugar from syrup in its molasses-like stage, then raw sugar form. Tours ($30) twice daily M-F (335-2824; gandrtours-kauai.com).

History buffs will enjoy online history of Kapa'a (kauaihistoricalsociety.org). For a catalog of books on Hawaii as well as hard-to-find Hawaiian authors, check Basically Books (808-961-0144; basicallybooks.com).

Movie Tours

A 5 hour guided narrated tour of Kauai's movie locations takes you in an air-conditioned van to locations of *South Pacific, Raiders of the Lost Ark, Honeymoon in Vegas*, and others, while at the same time showing the actual scenes on a TV monitor in surround sound ($111/adult). Some love the tinsel and the comic commentary, others are not so enthusiastic. The real advantage may be seeing a good chunk of the island in a comfortable touring van (822-1192; 800-628-8432; hawaiimovietour.com). The 'off road' tour (by 4x4 van) takes you to south shore Kipu Ranch, where you can scout forest and river locations of *Raiders of the Lost Arc, Outbreak, Six Days & Seven Nights, Mighty Joe Young, Hook, Jurassic Park,* and other box office hits ($123/adult). The more adventurous can tour them by ATV with *Kipu Adventures* (246-9288; kiputours.com). You roll through the streams, into the forest, over the rocks, following the Hule'ia River where Indiana Jones took off in his seaplane.

Music

Hawaiian music has a wonderful contemporary sound, thanks to Keali'i Reichel's wonderful original compositions in the Hawaiian language. Keali'i's first album, *Kawaipunahele*, exploded onto the music scene in 1994 and has become the bestselling album of Hawaiian music, earning a gold record in 2007 (the first gold for a Hawaiian language album). *Lei Hali'a, E O Mai,* and *Melelana* should be in your rental car's CD changer, at home too. *Ke'alaokamaile* ('The Scent of Maile') is a beautiful tribute to family, especially his grandmother. The Keali'i Reichel Collection, *Kamahiwa* (a CD of music and one of chants) is a must have, and his new Christmas album, *Kamahiwa,* is a delight (p 240).

The classics include the Brothers Cazimero (*Hawaiian Paradise* and *The Best*), The Makaha Sons of Ni'ihau, whose album *Na Pua o Hawai'i* features some of Hawaii's singing greats like Robert Cazimero, Cyril Pahinui, and Dennis Pavao. Also listen to Israel Kamakawiwo'ole's albums *E Ale E,* and *Facing Forward,* and Hapa's *Namahana* and *Collection.* Slack key guitar music brings you haunting melodies. Listen to Keola Beamer's album, *Island Born,* featuring his original music and lyrics. *Great Grandmother-Great Grandson* is Kapono Beamer's instrumental tribute to the songs of Helen Desha Beamer. Don't miss *Makana,* an up and coming star, and *Hahani Mai* by female vocalist and songwriter, Kekuhi

Keali'i Reichel
Ke'alaokamaile

Kanehele. On the re-release of Gaby Pahinui's 1972 album, *Gaby*, this legendary performer sings with his 4 talented sons; the first track is his original 1947 recording of 'Aloha 'Oe.'

Find the newest releases, sample tracks, links to musicians' home pages, on mele.com and hawaii-music.com. Listen to Hawaiian music radio while you surf: alohajoe.com.

Musicians of Kauai

Kauai's own Norman Ka'awa Solomon has recorded what is becoming the island's 'signature' album, *Na Mele O Kauai*, a unique collection of favorite Kauai songs, including guest spots by some of the great names in Hawaiian music – a real must for your rental car! Norman devotes the profits to help children on Kauai (songsoftheislands.com). In his earlier album, *Aloha Ke Kahi*, his wonderful original compositions include one of our favorite Kauai songs, his unforgettable 'Kalapaki.' Norman plays at *Happy Talk Lounge* and also helps plan weddings (for info and to order CDs: 823-6281; geocities.com/kaawakauai). Other performers at Happy Talk Lounge (call for times) include slack key guitarist Ken Emerson (kenemerson.com).

For more than twenty years, Doug & Sandy McMaster have delighted audiences with traditional slack key guitar music. Each evening they can be found serenading the sunset at the Hanalei Pavilion Beach Park. They also perform weekly benefit concerts ($10) at Hanalei Community Center (Fridays at 4pm; Sundays at 3pm; 826-1469 for ticket details). On cold winter evenings, their hauntingly beautiful music will call you right back to Hanalei. Don't miss their CDs *Hanalei Sunset, Kauai Homecoming,* and their newest *In A Land Called Hanalei* with a slack key 'Puff the Magic Dragon.' A resource for Hawaiian music and slack key, Doug and Sandy's web site (alohaplentyhawaii.com) features slide shows of Hanalei sunsets. *Hal Kinnaman* plays Hawaiian, contemporary or classical guitar on his CD of wedding music (for info, 335-0322).

Pacific Tunings by the Kauai group Na Pali collects the group's vocal numbers, accompanied by steel guitar, acoustic bass, and ukulele.

Find CDs at Borders (You can listen before you buy), Paradise Music (hawaiianparadisemusic.com) at Coconut Marketplace, Koloa Big Save, and

Princeville Center. On Kauai, KKCR (91.9), north shore public radio, plays Hawaiian music (listen at home on hawaii-music.com). KSRF (95.9) features local musician DJs.

Natural History Tours

Halfway between Kapa'a and Princeville, the *Kilauea Lighthouse*, built in 1913, once warned mariners away from Kauai's rugged north coast until technology replaced light flashes with radio transmissions. Come for spectacular views of the coastline and Mukuae'ae island, and if you're lucky, a glimpse of Spinner Dolphins or Humpback Whales on winter vacation in the waves. This is the northernmost point of Kauai, indeed of all the Hawaiian islands, and changes in weather are often first detected by the weather station here. Best of all, you will see a tiny part of the *Hawaiian Island National Wildlife Refuge*, which shelters more than 10 million seabirds in a chain of islands scattered over 1200 miles of ocean – like the Red-footed Booby. You will hear the amazing story of how 4 tons of French prisms were carried up a sheer cliff for the giant clam shaped light (10am - 4pm daily except federal holidays; 828-1413; kilauealighthouse.org).

More of Kauai's rare birds and plants can be seen at the *Koke'e Natural History Museum* in Koke'e State Park (10am - 4pm daily; 335-9975; kokee. org). Donations welcome. Interested in birds? Go to kauaibirds.com for photos and facts. Arrange tours in areas adjacent to Koke'e with *Kauai Nature Tours* (742-8305; 888-233-8365; teok.com).

Night Life

Call for local musicians' performance schedules:

* EASTSIDE : *Rob's Good Times Grill* (246-0311), *Caffe Cocco* (822-7990. *Duke's Barefoot Bar* (246-9599)

* NORTH SHORE: *Princeville Hotel* (826-9644), *Happy Talk Lounge* (826-6522), *Hanalei Gourmet* (826-2524), *Sushi and Blues* (826-9701)

* SOUTHSHORE: *Keoki's* (742-7534), *The Point* (Sheraton, 742-1661), *Seaview Terrace & Stevenson's Library* (Hyatt, 742-1234), *Joe's on the Green* (742-9696)

Photographing Kauai

* Shoot in early morning or late afternoon, which creates a warm, golden light. Strong sunlight can wash out colors and shadow your subjects' faces. Light is best coming from the side rather than over the photographer's shoulder.

* Vary your composition. For a 3-D effect, combine something in the foreground, like a palm tree, with the middle-ground and background. Try vertical shots, great for people and flowers; a vertical composition of sky, ocean, surf and sand can look like a "slice of Kauai."

* Watch out for horizons. They should be level, not tilting. The sea might look like it is 'dumping water' to the right or left if it's not straight. Placing the horizon across the middle of the picture cuts it in half. A higher horizon emphasizes the foreground; a lower one is a better 'sky shot' for great sunsets or cloud scenes.

* Use ISO 200 film or set your digital ISO to 200 to give you faster shutter speeds and sharper images. For action shots, use ISO 400.

* A polarizing filter can enhance color and improve the appearance of clouds, the ocean, and the surf break, but it slows your shutter speed.

* A cap or lens filter, a zipper case, are a big help in protecting against sand and salt.

* Download images/burn CDs: *Small Town Coffee* (Kapaʻa). (See *Internet & Cyber Cafés,* p 118).

* Move in close for people pictures. Fill the frame with your subject. If you are trying to show the location as well as your companion, try placing the person to one side, the location to the other. Watch out for the palm tree that may appear to be growing out of the subject's head.

* The Pentax Optio, small and waterproof to 5 feet, takes great snorkeling pictures.

* Great spots for great shots: Sunsets & rainbows from Princeville Hotel's terrace; Na Pali cliffs from Keʻe Beach (or first mile of Kalalau trail); windsurfers at Anini, Mahaʻulepu, or Ha'ena; the Allerton Gardens, Kukuiolono Park plumeria grove, Limahuli Gardens, Na Aina Kai; farmers' markets; sunrise at Lydgate Park, sunset overlooking Menehune Fish Pond from the road.

Scuba

You can dive Kauai's reefs and play with sea turtles on the south shore near Poipu or, weather permitting, on the north shore near the Haʻena reefs. More than a dozen companies offer introductory and refresher lessons, 3-5 day PADI certification, shore and boat dives, full or half-day charters, as well as free introductory pool lessons.

Contact Gregg Winston at *Watersports Adventures* for professional, careful, yet friendly scuba instruction, PADI certification, even refresher classes for 'rusty' divers. He has a perfect safety record, and reserved parking at Tunnels Beach. The company specializes in educa-tional 'naturalist' dives, and night dives (even night snorkel-ing) when the sea lights up in vivid colors, the coral comes alive, and you can see glowing fish and eels, turtles hunting for a place to rest (821-1599; watersportsadventures.ws).

If you have never tried diving, Gregg will make it special. In a free introductory lesson, you learn about diving equipment and safety and have a chance to practice with the gear in a swimming pool. Your first real dive ($105) will probably be at sheltered Koloa Landing (winter) or Tunnels (summer). Gregg is terrific with beginners. If you feel nervous, he may ask

you to swim next to him and hold onto his arm. Gregg is a very strong swimmer, so when you swim next to him, holding on to his arm, you actually cover a lot of territory. You are soon absorbed in the amazing sights – magnificent arrays of red and green coral, schools of silver or brilliant yellow fish swimming in geometric precision. You may see a ray gliding along in the shimmering water, possibly an eel hiding in the rocks, maybe even an octopus. Before you know it, you are swimming along quietly and comfortably, relaxed on your adventure! Gregg makes sure you have a good time and develop confidence. It's so great you want to head out again! Certified divers will appreciate Gregg's extensive knowledge, careful planning, and well-maintained equipment. Certified divers pay $85/one tank and $135/two.

Seasport Divers (Poipu: 742-9303; 800-685-5889; seasportdivers.com) offers boat dives along Kauai's south shore as well as in the waters off Ni'ihau. Their two-story dive boat is extremely spacious, the largest on the island, with 2 hot water showers, perfect after the chill of a 90 foot dive. Dive masters are friendly, extremely knowledgeable about Kauai's reefs, and very resourceful (2 wetsuits may help with cold ocean temperatures). In the winter months, the captain may take passengers whale watching during the surface interval. Excellent equipment includes computers to gauge depth and bottom time.

Among the other companies, the longest established on Kauai, *Ocean Odyssey* (Lihue: 245-8681) offers a full range of lessons, shore and boat dives, certification classes.

Others include: EASTSIDE: *Dive Kauai* (Kapa'a: 822-0452; 800-828-3483; divekauai.com), *Nitrox Tropical Dives* (800-NX5-DIVE), *SeaFun Kauai* (Lihue: 245-6400; 800-452-1113). NORTH SHORE: *North Shore Divers* (828-1223).

SOUTH SHORE: *Fathom Five Divers* (Poipu: 742-6991; 800-972-3078; fathomfive.com) offers classes in a new fully loaded multi-media classroom, certification, boat dives, night dives and trips to Ni'ihau. If you want to see fish but avoid carrying scuba gear, *Snuba of Kauai* offers tours with your air source attached on a flotation raft (823-8912; snubakauai.com).

The best diving in all of the Hawaiian islands can be found off Niʻihau, the privately owned, largely undeveloped island which has been preserved by the Robinson family as a place for Hawaiian people and culture. It's a unique opportunity to explore untouched reefs, though surf is too rough in winter months. *Seasport Divers* does an all-day boat dive to Niʻihau for experienced divers ($265/3 tanks).

Snorkeling

On the south shore, *Poipu Beach Park* offers excellent and relatively safe snorkeling most of the year. Just west of the rocky point dividing the park from the new Marriott (old Waiohai), you can find yellow tang, striped manini fish, butterflyfish, parrot fish, and silvery needle fish feeding on the coral. More than once, we have met a spotted box fish (Lauren has nick-named him 'Fred') who seems curious enough to swim right up to our masks. When surf is strong, watch out for the current at the edge of the reef.

Our family also enjoys *Tunnels* on the north shore, so named (in part) for the intricate 'tunnels' along the edge of the reef where the water seems to plunge to unfathomable depths. In summer, we like *Keʻe Beach*, where we find *humu humu nuku nuku apu aʻa*, Hawaii's state fish. At all seasons, *Lydgate Park* has friendly schools of fish in its huge, sandy bottomed, rock-rimmed pool.

Plan snorkeling with an eye to the tides, the weather, and the season. North shore is best in summer, when the ocean is relatively calm – even pancake flat. In winter, when surf is up on the north, Poipu Beach Park and Lydgate Park will probably have calmer water. Snorkel where

Fred

others are snorkeling so you can get help if you need it – avoid deserted beaches. Try not to lose track of where you are in the water, and stay dry if the surf looks rough or a rippling wave pattern indicates strong current.

Feeding the fish can be lots of fun. Packaged snorkel fish food can cause a problem when the plastic film casing begins to disintegrate in the

Renting Gear

$3-$5/day or $15/week for a good quality mask, fins, snorkel
$5-$8/day for a body board. $15-$25/day surfboard

Lihue

Kalapaki Beach Boys at the Kauai Marriott	246-9661

Wailua

Kauai Water Ski & Surf	822-3574
Kayak Kauai, Coconut Plantation Marketplace	822-9179

Hanalei

Pedal & Paddle	826-9096
Snorkel Depot	826-9983

Poipu

Nukomoi Surf Co.	742-7019
Snorkel Bob's	742-8322

Snorkel Tours

SeaFun Kauai	245-1113 or 800-452-1113	alohakauaitours.com
Kauai Snorkel Tours	742-7576	kauaisnorkeltours.com
Watersports Adventures	821-1599	watersportsadventures.ws

water, bringing lots of fish, perhaps too many fish, for your taste! This plastic is biodegradable, not like the tougher plastics which are dangerous to sea life. Carry fish food in a plastic zip-lock bag for more control (and be sure to take the empty bag back out with you). It

really doesn't matter what you put inside the bag as long as it stimulates the fish's curiosity. (Just don't use frozen peas, which are hard for the fish to digest.) Try a green leaf or piece of seaweed – it attracts the curious, rather than the ravenous, fish. Tuck your bag, or simply the leaf, securely into your suit, then once you are in the ocean, let the leaf float around as a 'visual display.' You'll be amazed at how much interest it creates.

Watersports Adventures (821-1599) and *SeaFun Kauai* (245-6400) offer land-based snorkeling tours, where shallower water shows you a different kind of sea life than the deep waters you may find on a boat tour off Na Pali. Some boat tour companies can take you to Ni'ihau, whose age and remoteness create unique opportunities for exploring (See *Boat Tours,* p 84).

A well-fitting mask is important. To test the fit, place the mask on your face (without using the straps) and breathe in; a well-fitting mask will stay on by itself. Pack your own if you can. A dilute solution of detergent and water – even spit – coats the lens to avoid fogging. Gregg Winston's tip: find a Naupaka leaf, crush it and rub it into the mask, then rinse. Or try rubbing some toothpaste, or even baby shampoo, then rinse. The Pentax Optio is waterproof to 5 feet and takes underwater digital images (see above).

Coral cuts can be dreadful. Keep bandaids and antibiotic cream in your bag and avoid touching the coral with any body part. Don't walk on it or try to pick it up. Even fins won't completely protect your feet.

Sport Fishing

Kauai's warm tropical waters offer great fishing for big and medium to light tackle game fish. No fishing license is required, and you can depart from ports all over the island, depending on surf and season. The north shore is beautiful, though too rough during winter months. From Port Allen on the west side, you have the advantage of being close to the spectacular Na Pali coastline and its amazing cliffs – fishing with a view!

Most companies equip their boats with sonar, and help to pair you up with other anglers to share the cost. Expect to pay upwards of $100 for a half-day shared rate, or as much as $875 for an all-day exclusive.

EASTSIDE: Kapa'a: *Hawaiian Style Fishing*, owned by a seasoned commercial fisherman, takes only 4 passengers on a 25-ft Kauai-built Radon, emphasizing reasonable prices and personal attention. People have a great time, and the catch is shared generously ($182/8 hrs or $125/4 hrs as well as charters; 635-7335).

Hana Pa'a Sport Fishing Charters offers a larger craft, a 38-ft Bertram with fly bridge, full tuna tower, main cabin, 2 bunk rooms, and full head. Fish are filleted and shared on 4, 6, and 8 hr private and split charters (823-6031; 866-PRO-FISH; fishkauai.com).

True Blue Charters operates the 42-ft trimaran, 'Rainbow Runner,' for fishing and snorkeling charters, or touring Kipu Kai, specializing in smaller groups and shorter tours (246-6333; kauaifun.com). *Captain Don's Charters* offers charters and/or Na Pali cruises (639-3012; captaindonsfishing.com).

NORTH SHORE: *Anini Charters* (828-1285; kauaifishing.com) departs from Anini Beach; Captain 'Honeybear' Bob shares the catch. Also try *Kai Bear Sportfishing* (652-4556). WESTSIDE: *Kauai Fun Tours* represents 5 small companies (335-5555; kauaifuntours.com). Also try *Open Sea Charter* (332-8213; 877-332-8213).

Sunset Watching & Sunset Drive to Hanalei

Watch spectacular sunsets from the 'Living Room' at the Princeville Hotel (best in summer when the sun sets into the water) and enjoy cocktails and music, or try the Beach House Restaurant on the south shore (better in winter). Or go to the beach with a blanket, possibly beach chairs, CD player with headphones, a Keali'i Reichel CD, an ice chest with drinks and snacks.

The most fun, however, is the *Sunset Drive to Hanalei*, if your accommodations are on the eastside. Check the paper for the exact time of sunset, which may be earlier than you expect because Hawaii never changes to daylight savings time. As you begin the drive, hundreds of clouds, already tinged with peach and gold, float in an azure sky above a shimmering sea. Rt 56 winds through the countryside and along the coast, with fields of sugar cane turning silver, and the colors of land and sky changing almost mile by

Sunset in the rain near Bali Hai Restaurant

mile as the declining sun deepens the greens and blues and touches everything with shades of pink and gold. At Kilauea, where the road curves to the west, a line of tall, graceful Norfolk pines stands starkly silhouetted against the blazing sky, and feathery grasses waving gently in evening breezes are touched with pink. Near Princeville, clouds luminous with reflected golds and pinks seem enormous, dwarfing cliffs whose great jagged peaks have turned an astonishing purple.

We never tire of this drive, as each sunset is different. The gleaming expanse of ocean, the sharply angled mountains, the masses of clouds are blended each night by the sun's magic into a composition of colors that will never occur again in exactly the same way. One night the sun's descent may be screened by great masses of clouds rimmed with gold and glowing tangerine against the deep purple mountains and the shimmering blue grey sea. Another time, the sun may almost blind you with its blazing, fiery gold, suffusing nearby clouds with orange and pink, and brushing distant clouds with peach. As seasons change, so does the angle of the sun, gilding the landscape with new patterns of light and color.

A sunset in the rain is the most amazing of all. Mountains are shrouded with grey, yet above the sea, the sky is brilliant with color, with sunny clouds stretching along the horizon, rimmed with pink light. Dark showers move across the horizon like 'legs of the rain,' blurring the line between ocean and sky, reaching for the sun as it slowly descends, then disappears. As the last light fades, dark clouds hovering above the cliffs slowly creep across the mountains, and the world turns slowly still and dark.

If the clouds are not too thick, you can enjoy the sunset from several places in Hanalei. Less than a mile past the entrance to Princeville, you can park at a scenic overlook on Rt 56 and see most of Hanalei's western side. But you have to contend with the distractions of traffic and car radios as well as conversations of other sunset seekers ("Ralph! I *told* you we were going to miss it!"). For a more panoramic view with greater privacy, enter Princeville and follow the signs to Pali Ke Kua, park in the lot, and enjoy the view discreetly from the lawn between the buildings.

The drive home after dinner is another sensuous experience of cool evening breezes you can almost taste as well as feel. As you drive south, you can hear wonderful sounds – the chirping of crickets, the leaves rustling in the breeze – and see the different shades of darkness in the landscape, lit by the moon against an enormous star-filled sky and the shimmering waves of the wide ocean beyond.

Surfing & Body Boarding

Surfing, like everything on Kauai, depends on the tides, the winds, and the season. In summer, the surf is 'up' on the south shore. In winter, the ground swell is mostly on the north and west shores, and experienced surfers will look for surf along the North shore from Kilauea to Ha'ena and on the westside from Kekaha to Polihale. In the summer, experienced surfers look to the south from Kalapaki Bay to Poipu. The eastside picks up tradewind swell year round. At any season, and no matter your skill level, be careful: the wave pattern varies at each beach and some spots are safer than others. Hawaiian swells rise more quickly than Mainland swells, and Hawaiian waves are more powerful than Mainland waves. Avoid going out alone, respect the local surfers, and as always, if in doubt, do not go out.

Channel 15 on local cable TV recycles National Weather Service buoy readings on water, surf and wind conditions. Check hanaleisurf.com or kauaistyle.com for current surf information and links.

Sharing the wave at Kalihiwai

Surf Lessons: Want to learn to surf? On the south shore, several surf schools operate next to the Sheraton Resort in Poipu, where surf conditions are usually relatively safe – waves less than four feet and winds moderate. With *Aloha Surf Lessons,* run by Kauai-born surfing pro Chava Greenle and his father Danny, his first teacher, you can have a first-rate lesson combining one hour of personalized instruction followed by one hour of surfing on your own. One instructor works with up to six students. Skilled and supportive, Chava and Danny make sure everyone gets 'up,' and they really love making that happen ($75/pp; also private lessons; 639-8614). Also in Poipu, *Margo Oberg*, winner of 7 world title crowns, has a surf school for all skill levels, with 6 students per instructor ($60/1.5 hrs). Private lessons are also available (652-9085; surfonkauai.com).

Surfing pro Charlie Smith offers lessons island-wide. He will drive you to wherever he thinks he'll find the island's best surf, and his unique personalized 2-hour lessons ($75) can extend to include family picnics and snorkeling. For experienced surfers, it's a great way to learn the island; he knows the best breaks, has high performance boards (634-6979; blueseas-surfingschool.com).

NORTH SHORE: The Hanalei pier is the best spot for beginners, and several companies base there for lessons and rentals. At *Learn to Surf* (826-7612; learntosurfkauai.com), Nephi Kalani Quereto has a friendly, supportive manner, with a limit of 3 students per instructor. He has the best island rate ($40/90 min) and goes where surf conditions are best for safety and weather. His guarantee: stand up or lesson is free. He gives private lessons also. *Titus Kinimaka* also offers walk-up lessons at Hanalei Pier and by appointment (652-1116). *Celeste Harvel* teaches surfing and windsurfing (828-6838), and *Brando Wattson* teaches surfing and kitesurfing (639-WAVE; surf.kauaistyle.com). EASTSIDE: *Ambrose*, one of Kauai's most experienced teachers (822-7112); *Kayak Kauai* (826-9844).

Rentals: (about $25/day): EASTSIDE: Wailua: *Tamba Surf Shop* (823-6942) is first rate, the choice of local folks. Also try *Kauai Beach Boys* in Lihue (246-6333) and Poipu (742-4442). NORTH SHORE: *Hanalei Surf Co.* (826-9000), *Kayak Kauai* (826-9844), and *Kai Kane* (826-5594), and you can usually find rental boards at the Hanalei pier.

SOUTH SHORE: *Nukomoi* (Poipu and Waimea; 742-8019), *SeaSport Divers* (742-9303), and *Progressive Expressions* (Koloa; 742-6041), which also arranges surfing lessons with *Garden Island Surf School* (652-4841). Repairs: Bruce Pleas: same-day if possible, with a loaner board if necessary (Kekaha; 337-9509; 639-2850; hisurf3@hawaii.rr.com).

Body Boards: When they were small, our kids loved to take their boogie boards to Poipu Beach Park. Then they grew up and craved the bigger waves. Family favorites for body boards are Kalihiwai on the north shore and Kealia on the east, also Hanalei and Kalapaki, according to surf conditions.

At Brennecke's Beach, the famous wave pattern is forming once again (after Hurricane Iniki washed the sand away in 1992), and you can see dozens of kids riding the first break, and younger ones catching the wave as it re-forms closer to shore. Be careful of the rocks by the seawall

When surf is too flat (or too rough) for body boards, kids can use skimboards to catch long, exciting rides across the shallows at Kalihiwai and Hanalei (where the rivers flow into the ocean) and Kalapaki.

Sweets & Treats

You'll love fruit 'frosties,' a tasty confection of frozen fruit whipped smooth like soft ice cream. Try combinations of mango, banana, papaya, pineapple – whatever is in season – at the *Moloa'a Sunrise Fruit Stand* on Rt 56 north of Anahola and *Banana Joe's* in Kilauea. Stock up on local fruits. Tropical fruit 'smoothies' are made at fruit stands like *Moloa'a Sunrise, Banana Joe's* and *Mango Mama's* (Kilauea), *Killer Juice Bar* and *Lotus Root* (Kapa'a), and *Jamba Juice (*Lihue and Kapa'a).

Lilikoi chiffon pie is a Kauai tradition – a light confection of passion fruit. A local legend, *Omoide Bakery* (Rt 50 in Hanapepe), has baked the island's best pies by secret family recipe since 1956. Pies are sold frozen (order in advance 335-5291) and will keep for several hours in the car (best in a cooler). Sample pies at *Hamura's Saimin* in Lihue, *Camp House Grill* in Kalaheo. On your way to the airport, pick up a frozen pie at Hamura's to bring onboard in a carry-on plastic insulator pack ($10 at Wal-Mart).

EASTSIDE: Don't miss *Anahola Granola*, wonderful with apple bananas for breakfast. Sample local sweets at *Pono Market* in Kapa'a, like coconut manju or Shagnasty's natural rawhide honey. Try the light, sweet pretzel cookies at *Hamura's Saimin*. Macadamia nut cookies taste like Kauai even if you're back home. In Waipouli Complex, *Po Po's* mixes macadamia nuts with chocolate chips or coconut. *Kauai Tropical Fudge* has wonderful island flavors, including banana, macadamia nut, Kona coffee, and even pina colada. Look for it in the *Kauai Products Store* in Kukui Grove, Lihue.

Huli Huli Sauce is a family favorite marinade for fish or chicken. *Kauai Bread-sticks Company* makes incredible 'killer guacamole' and mango bean salsa. Look for these treats in grocery stores, even Wal-Mart.

WESTSIDE: In the Port Allen Marina, try *Kauai Chocolate Company*'s homemade ice cream – macadamia nut, dark chocolate, coconut, and island fruit flavors – or chocolates created while you watch by Don and Marlene Greer and their family. Open 12pm - 5pm daily. A great treat after a long boat ride (335-0048).

In Hanapepe, taro chips are still made in the *Taro Ka* factory. When taro is scarce, they make potato chips flavored with special Chinese spices, as well as sweet potato chips. The traditional island favorite *Kauai Kookie Kompany* is found in most supermarkets or at the factory store in Hanapepe which gives free samples.

Papaya seed dressing, created in Kalaheo, gives salad a whole new dimension. Also look for *Aunty Lilikoi*'s mustard, with perfect bite and sweetness at the outlet in Waimea. NORTHSHORE: try the Hawaiian favorite: *Hanalei Poi* (826-4764; hanaleipoi.com). Local folks like it for dipping fresh ahi poki – or even raw vegetables.

At the end of the Waimea Canyon Road, a spectacular lookout.

Tubing

As the island's economy shifts from sugar cultivation to tourism, the vast sugar lands are finding new uses. Tubing along Kauai's sugar plantation irrigation system doesn't require washboard abs and can include the whole family. You meet in Hanamaʻulu, drive upcountry to a launch dock where, encircled by your big innertube, you wade into the canal, then float with the gentle current towards the sea along the route carved out of dirt and rock by Chinese immigrant workers in the 1870's to bring water to the cane fields.

Make it a bumper car ride if you like, kicking off rocks or the sides of the canal, or even off each other, spin the tubes, or just relax and float through hidden Kauai. You'll pass through amazing tunnels, wearing your headlamp through the first four, trying the last one in the dark. The ride goes over a mini waterfall, supervised by a staff member, which is lots of fun. At the end, there's a picnic lunch ($99; 245-2506; 888-270-0555; kauaiback-country.com). Map 1

Waimea Canyon Drive to Koke'e State Park

The drive to the top of Waimea Canyon, the 'Grand Canyon of the Pacific,' makes a great day trip. The drive along the Koke'e Rd (Rt 550) from Rt 50 to the end of the winding road will take about 45 minutes. As you travel along the canyon's rim, ten miles long and 3,600 feet deep, pull over to enjoy spectacular scenic overlooks.

At *Koke'e Lodge*, stop for lunch – excellent soups and sandwiches – and visit the *Koke'e Museum* (donation) for exhibits and trail maps. Plan your hikes in advance and sign up for an e-newsletter at kokee.org.

If possible, plan some time for exploring this wilderness preserve (see *Hiking,* 112). Even a short hike shows you great views. Bring a jacket; at nearly 4,000 feet, temperatures can be very cool.

Some hikes are suitable for families and take only a couple of hours, like the trail to Waipo'o Falls which descends through wild ginger and orchids to a beautiful two-tiered waterfall. Mosquito spray, sun screen, canteen, camera (wildflowers are beautiful), and a hat are musts.

Even if you don't hike, the drive takes you to a spectacular lookout, the *Kalalau Lookout*, with a vista of the island's west side. (Parents be careful: the railing won't keep small children safe.) Rental car companies will advise you to go easy on the brakes and transmission, and use low gear as you negotiate the curving road, even more important on the way down.

The road is hard on cars, as we learned when our 1984 red Suburban made it to the top, then coughed and sputtered to a halt in front of Koke'e Lodge. Your rental car will probably do just fine, but we'll never forget the trip back down, with 'Red Rover' – the family suburban – riding in style atop the gleaming flatbed, whimsically named 'A Tow in Paradise.' Only on Kauai would the driver park his enormous rig a half dozen times to share his favorite photo-stops!

Although commercial tours of Koke'e are no longer allowed, you can see some of the ecosystem, as well as Waimea Canyon, with *Aloha Kauai Tours* in 4x4 vans (245-1113; 800-452-1113; alohakauaitours.com).

Kauai Nature Tours offers unique naturalist guided tours with an emphasis on Kauai's natural and cultural history (742-8305; 888-233-8365; teok.com).

Water Skiing

The Wailua River on the eastern shore is a great spot for water skiing, wake boarding, kneeboarding, slalom, and other water sports. At *Kauai Water Ski & Surf Co*, you can get a driver, equipment, lessons, and the boat for an hour for $120. Put up to five people onboard (822-3574; 800-344-7915).

Weddings on Kauai

There are no residency, citizenship, blood test, or waiting period requirements. Bride and groom must both be at least 18 years old to marry without parental consent, and both must apply in person for a license, valid for 30 days (pay in cash: $60). For a free "Getting Married" pamphlet, contact the *State Department of Health,* Marriage License Office, 1250 Punchbowl St, Honolulu HI 96813 (Honolulu: 586-4544; Kauai: 241-3498; hawaii.gov/doh/records). For a Kauai company list, check bestplaceshawaii. com for links to company sites like *Kauai Aloha Weddings,* operated by Huanani Rossi, a native Hawaiian who emphasizes Hawaiian traditions (822-1477; kauaialohawed.com). Marcia Sacco has a wonderfully supportive manner and excellent connections (800-776-4813; kauai-wedding.com); she arranged a beach wedding for cruise travelers (below). Musician/composer/vocalist *Norman Ka'awa Solomon* (127) plays his unforgettable Hawaiian music and also does wedding planning (823-6281; geocities.com/kaawakauai). Gregg Winston of *Watersports Adventures* has even arranged weddings underwater (gregg@watersportsadventures.ws).

You can make some important arrangements yourself. Contact the *Division of State Parks* for a list of scenic wedding sites (274-3444). *Na 'Aina Kai Gardens* in Kilauea has a great beachfront site, unique garden areas, including a maze (828-0525; naainakai.com). Kauai has many talented musicians who can make your wedding sound really special. *Hal Kinnaman* plays Hawaiian, contemporary or classical guitar (335-0322). For a reception, reserve a private tea room at *Hanama'ulu Tea House* (call Sally or Arlene at 245-2511), or the small private room at *Kintaro* (822-3341). Restaurants with elegant private dining rooms include *Plantation Gardens* (742-2216), *Gaylord's* (245-9593; gaylords-kauai.com), and *Hukilau Lanai* which also has a dance floor (822-0600; gaylords-kauai.com). Order traditional leis from *Irmalee Pomroy* (822-3231) or contact April at *Flowers and Joys* in Kapa'a (877-822-0027; flowersandjoyskauai. com).

Kahili onboard at Anini Beach

Windsurfing

Sheltered Anini Beach's offshore reef creates a peaceful lagoon in most winds, and on most days, you can see brightly colored sails and students from two windsurf companies. At *Windsurf Kauai,* Celeste Harvel can teach the basics as well as a complete certification course ($85/3 hr session, 9am or 1pm M-F; 828-6838). A gifted teacher, she has special sized boards for kids, and a special dog, Kahili who actually may hop aboard and go for a ride. *Anini Beach Windsurfing* (826-9463) also uses the latest in equipment and teaches surfers at all levels. Both companies offer small group lessons. Drop-ins are welcome; you can rent equipment. Stop in at *Hanalei Surf Company* for advice. EASTSIDE: *Kauai Beach Boys* (246-6333) for rentals and lessons.

Yoga

EASTSIDE: Studio programs: *Kauai Athletic Club* (Lihue: 245-5381; kauaiathleticclub.com) and *Bikram Yoga Studio* (Kapaʻa: 822-5053) or *Creative Yoga Kauai* (Kapaʻa: 822-1881; creativeyogacenter.com) including Tai Chi. Or schedule private sessions with internationally recognized healing practitioner *Elandra* (635-8687).

SOUTH SHORE: *Anara Spa* at the Hyatt (742-1234; anaraspa.com). *Joy's Oceanfront Yoga* (639-9294; aloha-yoga.com) offers hatha yoga classes and private lessons, guided hikes, and yoga/wellness vacation planning.

NORTH SHORE: With *Michaelle Edwards*, practice reasonably-priced, personalized yoga in classes, private sessions, or even retreats with accommodations in a serene rural setting. Her 'yogalign' method emphasizes breathing, natural alignment, and painless yoga from the core. She can help you recover from an injury or back pain and has an excellent DVD (826-9230; manayoga.com). *Prince Clubhouse* ($55/hr) offers classes and private sessions (826-4093). *Yoga Hanalei* has classes and private sessions (826-YOGA; yogakauai.com).

Zipline

Adventurers can have a bird's eye view of Kauai's beautiful terrain on a zipline tour. Ziplining is empowering – even the most timid will come to love leaping off a platform (sometimes you are told to get a running start), sailing over trees, and surveying beautiful streams and waterfalls below before touching down hundreds of feet later. With up to 11 people on the tour, however, you can wait around a bit to be hooked up. Three tour operators take you to Kipu on the south shore and Hanama'ulu on the eastside to explore rainforest and rolling ranch land you would not otherwise see. Most specify age (12 and over), weight (100-280 pounds), and require long pants and closed-toe shoes.

Kauai Backcountry offers a 3 1/2 hour tour through 7 ziplines, ranging to 950 feet. After guides describe the tour and the safety measures, each adventurer zips off down the cable while a second guide waits at the other end, either to reel in those who don't quite make it all the way, or to act as a brake. The tour starts with a slow, easy 'bunny slope,' then advances to increasingly exciting rides. $120 includes sandwiches and Kauai cookies (245-2506; 888-270-0555; kauaibackcountry.com).

Princeville Ranch offers a 4.5 hour tour with 8 ziplines and a suspension bridge ($125). Adventurers zip across the first 7 ziplines and cross a wooden plank suspension bridge before stopping for lunch (make your own pita sandwiches, fruit, and Kauai cookies) and a swim at a small waterfall. Each adventurer receives a souvenir water bottle filled with water at the beginning of the trip and can borrow a backpack. Guides make sure that every adventurer is comfortable and safe, describing the locale, its trees and flowers (826-7669; 888-955-7669; adventureskauai.com).

Outfitters Kauai's unique tour ($120) ends at beautiful – and otherwise off limits as private property – *Kipu Falls*. In addition to regular ziplines, the tour features a 'zippell' (a fairly vertical line in which you use the braking concepts of repelling to slow your progress) and a tandem zip (2 people zoom across a stream on side-by-side ziplines). With Outfitters you also get a shoulder harness so that you can turn upside down – easier said than done! At beautiful Kipu Falls, you can try a 10 foot cliff jump and a 10 foot rope swing. It's great fun! The tour includes snacks (cheese and crackers, salami, grapes), juice, and water (742-9667; 888-742-9887; outfitterskauai.com).

Café Hanalei, Princeville Hotel

Eastside: Lihue, Hanama'ulu, Wailua, Kapa'a, 152

Lihue

Barbecue Inn	245-2921	Oriental	153	$$	BLD
Café Portofino	245-2121	Italian	157	$$$$	LD
Dani's	245-4991	Island-style	159	$	BL
Duke's Canoe Club	246-9599	Seafood/steak	159	$$$	D
Duke's Barefoot Bar	246-9599	Burgers/sand	161	$$	LD
Garden Island BBQ	245-8868	Chinese/BBQ	161	$$	LD
Gaylord's	245-9593	Continental	162	$$$$	LD
Hamura's Saimin	245-3271	Saimin	163	$	D
JJ's Broiler	246-4422	Steak/seafood	168	$$$	D
Kalapaki Beach Hut	246-6330	Burgers/sand	168	$	BLD
Kauai Pasta	245-2227	Italian	170	$$	D
La Bamba	245-5972	Mexican	173	$	LD
Ma's Family Inc.	245-3142	Island-style	175	$	BL
Naupaka Terrace	245-1995	American	178	$$$$	BD
Okazu Hale	245-6554	Island-style	179	$	LD
Oki Diner	245-5899	Island-style	179	$	21 hrs
Sushi Bushido	632-0664	Japanese	184	$$$	LD
Tip Top Café	245-2333	Amer/Oriental	184	$	BL
Tokyo Lobby	245-8989	Japanese	185	$$	LD

Hanama'ulu

Hanama'ulu Tea House	245-2511	Chin/Japanese	164	$$	D

Wailua

Bull Shed	822-3791	Steak/PRib	156	$$$	D
Caffé Coco	822-7990	Vegetarian	156	$$	BLD
Coconuts	823-8777	Pacific Rim	158	$$$$	D
Eggbert's	822-3787	American	161	$$	BL
Hong Kong Café	822-3288	Chinese	166	$	LD
Hukilau Lanai	822-3441	Pacific Rim	166	$$$	D
Hula Girl	822-4422	Steak/seafood	167	$$$	D
Kauai Pasta	822-7447	Italian	170	$$	D
King & I	822-1642	Thai	171	$$	D
Kintaro	822-3341	Japanese	172	$$$	D
La Playita Azul	821-2323	Mexican	174	$	LD
Lemongrass	821-2888	Pacific Rim	175	$$$	D

Mema Thai Cuisine	823-0899	Thai/Chinese	176	$$	LD
Monico's	822-4300	Mexican	177	$	LD
Pacific Island Bistro	822-0092	Chinese	182	$$	D
Papaya's	823-0190	Vegetarian	182	$	BLD
Wahoo's	822-7833	Seafood	186	$$$	LD
Wailua Marina	822-4311	Everything	186	$$	LD
Waipouli Deli	822-9311	Island-style	187	$	BLD
Kapa'a					
Blossoming Lotus	822-7678	Veg/vegan	154	$$$	LD
Kountry Kitchen	822-3511	American	173	$$	BL
Lotus Root	823-6658	Veg/vegan	155	$	BLD
Mermaids Café	821-2026	Veg/vegan	176	$	LD
Norberto's El Café	822-3362	Mexican	178	$$	BD
Olympic Café	822-2825	American	179	$$	BLD
Ono Family	822-1710	American	180	$$	BL
Pizzetta	823-8882	Italian	190	$$	LD
Polynesia Café	822-1945	American	183	$$$	BLD
Sukothai	821-1224	Thai/etc.	183	$$	D
Wasabi's	822-2700	Japanese	187	$$	D

North Shore: Kilauea, Princeville & Hanalei, 192

Kilauea

Farmers Market Deli	828-1512	Sandwiches	187	$	L
Kilauea Fish Market	828-6244	Seafood	201	$	LD
Lighthouse Bistro	828-0480	Italian	203	$$$	LD
Pau Hana Pizza	828-2020	Pizza	200	$	LD
Princeville					
Bali Hai	826-6522	Steak/seafood	193	$$$$	LD
Café Hanalei	826-9644	Pacific Rim	195	$$$$$	BLD
C J's Steakhouse	826-6211	Steak/seafood	197	$$$	LD
La Cascata	826-9644	Italian	202	$$$$$	D
Princeville Restaurant	826-5050	American	206	$$	BL
Hanalei					
Bar Acuda	826-1177	Pacific Rim	194	$$$	LD
Dolphin	826-6113	Seafood/steak	197	$$$	LD

$ under $15/pp $$ under $25/pp $$$ under $35/pp $$$$ under $45/pp $$$$$ over $45/pp

Hanalei Gourmet	826-2524	Sandwiches	194	$$	BLD
Neidie's	826-1851	Brazilian	204	$$	LD
Kalypso's	826-9700	American	199	$$	LD
Postcards Café	826-1191	Seafood/veget	205	$$$	BD
Sushi & Blues	826-9701	Japanese	207	$$	D

South Shore: *Poipu, Koloa & Kalaheo, 208*

Koloa

Koloa Fish Market	742-6199	Fish/local eats	219	$	L
Pizetta	742-8881	Pizza/pasta	187	$$	LD
Tomkats Grill	742-8887	American	226	$$	LD

Poipu

Beach House	742-1424	Pacific Rim	207	$$$$	D
Brennecke's	742-7588	Seafood/steak	210	$$$	LD
Casablanca	742-2929.	Italian	213	$$$	LD
Casa di Amici	742-1555	Italian	214	$$$	D
Dondero's	742-6260	Italian	215	$$$$$	D
Joe's on the Green	742-9696	American	216	$$	BLD
Keoki's Paradise	742-7534	Steak/seafood	218	$$$	D
Naniwa	742-1661	Japanese	219	$$$	D
Plantation Gardens	742-2216	Steak/seafood	220	$$$	D
Poipu Bay Clubhouse	742-1515	American	220	$$$	L
Poipu Beach Broiler	742-6433	American	221	$$$	LD
Roy's Poipu Grill	742-5000	Pacific Rim	223	$$$$	D
Shells	742-1661	American	224	$$$$	BLD
Taqueria Nortenos	742-7222	Mexican	225	$	LD
Tidepools	742-6260	Seafood/steak	225	$$$$$	D
Yum Cha	742-1515	Chinese	227	$$$	D

Kalaheo

Brick Oven Pizza	332-8561	Pizza	211	$$	LD
Camp House Grill	332-9755	Burgers/sand	212	$$	LD
Kalaheo Coffee Deli	332-5858	Deli/coffee	217	$	BL
Kalaheo Steakhouse	332-9780	Steak/PRibs	217	$$$	D
Pomodoro	332-5945	Italian	222	$$$	D

Westside: *Hanapepe, Ele'ele & Waimea, 228*

Hanapepe Café	335-5011	Vegetarian	229	$$	LD
Toi's Thai Kitchen	335-3111	Thai	229	$$	LD
Waimea Brew Pub	338-9773	American	231	$$	LD
Wrangler's Steakhouse	338-1218	Steaks/sandw	231	$$	LD

Readers' Choice...

For ocean view

Eastern Shore

Bull Shed	155
Duke's Canoe Club	159
Café Portofino	157

North Shore

Bali Hai	193
Café Hanalei	195
La Cascata	202

South Shore

Beach House	207

For pasta

Eastern Shore

Café Portofino	157
Kauai Pasta	170

North Shore

La Cascata	202

South Shore

Casablanca	213
Plantation Gardens	220
Pomodoro	222

For family friendly dining

Eastern Shore

Barbecue Inn	153
Bull Shed	155
Duke's Canoe Club	159
Hanama'ulu Tea House	164
Hong Kong Café	165
Kountry Kitchen	173
Norberto's El Café	178
Ono Family Restaurant	179

North Shore

Café Hanalei	195
Postcards Café	205

South & Westside

Brennecke's Beach Broiler	210
Brick Oven Pizza	211

Camp House Grill	212
Joe's on the Green	216
Pomodoro	222
Wranglers's	231

For steaks & prime rib

Eastern Shore

Duke's Canoe Club	159
Bull Shed	149

South Shore

Keoki's	215

For Oriental food

Eastern Shore

Hanama'ulu Tea House	159
King & I	171
Kintaro	172
Lemongrass	175
Mema Thai Cuisine	176

South & Westside

Toi's Thai Kitchen	229
Yum Cha	227

For fresh island fish

Eastern Shore

Duke's Canoe Club	159
Bull Shed	155
Hukilau Lanai	166

North Shore

Café Hanalei	195
Hanalei Dolphin	197
Kilauea Fish Market	201
Postcards Café	205

South Shore

Beach House	207
Brennecke's Beach Broiler	210
Plantation Gardens	220
Roy's Poipu Grill	223
Tidepools	225

Eastside Restaurants

'favor...eats'

The eastern shore's potpourri of dining reflects Kauai's rich multicultural heritage. *Hanama'ulu Restaurant and Tea House* combines reasonable prices and friendly service with excellent Japanese and Chinese cuisine. In LIHUE, *Barbecue Inn's* bargain-priced lunches and dinners include soup, a beverage, fresh-baked bread, entrée, even dessert. In this family-friendly restaurant, you'll find some of the tastiest food and best values on the island. Looking for local saimin? Try *Hamura's Saimin* or *Okazu Hale* for great noodles.

Gaylord's at Kilohana provides a romantic garden setting for lunch and dinner in an elegantly restored sugar plantation estate house. At the Kauai Marriott, *Duke's Canoe Club* offers a beautiful beachfront setting, as well as excellent food, reasonable prices, and the most sumptuous salad bar on the island. *Duke's Barefoot Bar* downstairs has well-priced burgers and sandwiches, and next door, *Café Portofino* serves excellent Italian cuisine. Nearby, at *Kalapaki Beach Hut*, try a first-rate hamburger or fish sandwich.

Ten minutes north of Lihue, WAILUA has a range of cuisines and prices. Try *Blossoming Lotus*; you'll be amazed at how tasty vegan food can be. *Mema Thai Cuisine* and *King & I* offer excellent Thai cuisine at a great price. *Kintaro* prepares about the best Japanese dinners, sushi, and sashimi on Kauai, though you'll probably have to wait for a table along with the local folks who like it too. *Hukilau Lanai* serves wonderful fresh fish and local vegetables. Don't miss the *Bull Shed* for the biggest, tastiest prime rib on the island as well as steaks, chicken, and excellent fresh fish – with an ocean view – at excellent prices. Go early to avoid the rush.

Vegetarian, or even vegan cravings? Try lunch or dinner at *Caffé Coco* or *Blossoming Lotus* (*Papaya's*, *Mermaid's* or *Lotus Root* for take out). On a budget? One of the island's best values is tasty Mexican food at *Monico's* in Wailua's Kinipopo Shopping Center. At the Coconut Marketplace, try *Aloha Kauai Pizza*. For hearty breakfast it's *Ono Family Restaurant* or *Kountry Kitchen* in Kapa'a, and for outstanding coffee and muffins (and free wireless) *Small Town Coffee* next door. For fresh fish wraps, curries and salads, *Mermaids* in Kapa'a is an absolute must stop.

Barbecue Inn 245-2921

Where do local folks go for a lunch which includes soup, a beverage, fresh bread, an entrée like a teriyaki chicken sandwich, and dessert for only $8? In this family-owned restaurant, you'll find some of the tastiest food and one of the best food values on the island. A local favorite since 1940, Barbecue Inn is the rare kind of place with something special for everyone in the family. At dinner, more than 30 choices – fresh fish, seafood, steak, prime rib – include soup or fresh fruit, a salad, bread, vegetable, dessert, even a beverage ($12-$18). At lunch, entrées cost even less, averaging $9 (but you don't get salad).

Kids will love the cheeseburger ($4.50), still sizzling on a toasted sesame bun, smothered with melted cheese and garnished with lettuce. Kids can order fried chicken, hamburger, spaghetti, or chow mein dinners, ten choices in all, including a beverage, or a grilled cheese sandwich made on home-baked bread toasted crisp and golden. Grown-ups will love teriyaki steak ($19), a tender rib-eye with homemade sauce, or teriyaki beef kabob and light, crispy shrimp tempura ($15).

You will be surprised at the high quality of the extras which many restaurants pay scant attention to. Miso soup is superb. Bread is homemade – light, fragrant, and exceptionally tasty. The fruit cup appetizer is so fresh – pineapple, papaya, watermelon, honeydew, and mango – that you'll almost hope your kids will refuse to eat theirs because there are no canned peaches. The green salad would win no awards for imagination, but you'd be surprised at how much fun the kids have picking out the shredded cabbage and homemade croutons. And everyone will devour the homemade pies – coconut, chocolate, or chocolate cream – pies so light they are almost as amazing as the price: $2 a slice. Buy a bag of home-made cookies or crispy 'cinnamon toast' to keep in the car.

You will see a lot of working people coming off the job, and the portions are so enormous you can understand why. Waitresses are unfailingly cheerful, even when small children decorate the floor with crumbs and ice cubes. All this makes Barbecue Inn a great choice for hearty eaters and hungry families, and for anyone who appreciates ordinary food cooked extremely well.

Lihue, 2982 Kress St off Rice St. 245-2921. Closed Sundays. Breakfast 7:30am - 10:30am; Lunch 10:30am - 1:30pm; Dinner 5pm - 8:30pm (4:30 - 8:45pm F, S). Air-conditioned. Credit cards. Maps 1, 2

Blossoming Lotus *822-7678*

In this remarkable restaurant in downtown Kapaʻa, you'll find some of the most interesting and inventive dining on Kauai. Even meat eaters should not be put off by the advertisement of 'vegan world fusion cuisine' and instead give it a try. You may be surprised at just how tasty this cuisine can be. Once a tiny take-out storefront, the now spacious, elegant dining room is nearly always full, hosting local entertainers and serving some of the most delicious food on the island. Even non-vegan diners can navigate the menu to find a new taste adventure, like spanikopita with marinated tofu and fresh organic island greens ($16), a spicy enchilada casserole with baked tempeh, beans, rice, chili sauce, and cashew cheese layered between sprouted wheat tortillas ($17), or the 'Live Lasagne' (nothing cooked above 116 degrees) 'with macadamia riccotta, so fresh tasting that the zucchini, tomatoes, and red bell peppers seem right from the garden ($16). You can actually distinguish individual flavors despite the masterful blend, and the presentation is fresh and attractive. No wonder it's won several dining awards, including the 2006 Ilima Award for best restaurant on Kauai.

For lunch, try light and carefully seasoned soups, like squash vegetable ($7). 'Gaia's Greenwich,' an open faced sandwich of beautiful fanned avocado on one side and marinated, grilled tempeh with caramelized onion, sprouts and lettuce on the other side, layered on homemade lotus spelt bread (don't panic – it's like a marvellous whole grain wheat) ($10). Or try tempting wraps, sandwiches, and salads like 'Mighty Aphrodite's Greek salad' of greens with soy 'feta' or 'Garden of Eden Salad' ($15).

Blossoming Lotus is both a philosophy and a kitchen, or an infusion of one inside the other. Owner Mark Renfeld works hard to promote healthful living on Kauai with pro bono activities, in the cyber community with his informative website (sign up online for an e-newsletter), and a cookbook that has won 8 national awards. Give it a try. You will like the attractive dining room, spacious with high ceilings and fans, and built almost entirely with environmen-

Tastes so good! Is it really vegan?

tally friendly materials. And you will enjoy the adventurous menu, with its exciting flavors and color. Don't miss the wonderful fruit drinks, flavored waters, and teas.

Kapa'a, town center. 822-7678. Lunch 11 - 3pm M-Sat; Dinner 5:30 - 9pm daily. Kosher and green certified. Credit cards. Personal chef services. blossominglotus.com. Maps 1, 4

...& the Lotus Root 823-6658

Lotus Root occupies the original Blossoming Lotus location and offers a more informal menu with terrific smoothies, cakes, cookies, deli sand- wiches, and salads to take out or eat in at the picnic tables in front. 'Miss American Chai' is the best tea drink we found, a chilled smoothie version made with banana, soy milk, and a spice blend that gives it an interesting. Wraps are tasty and inventive, and tempeh 'tuna salad' is first rate. Corn bread with apple butter packs a chili inside, so be cautious. Lotus Root is a great place to stop on the way to the beach when you want a really good smoothie or a fresh and tasty picnic lunch.

Kapa'a, Kuhio Hwy. 823-6658. 7am - 6pm daily. Credit cards. Maps 1, 4

The Bull Shed 822-3791

Since 1973, The Bull Shed has been famous on Kauai for high quality meals at unbeatable prices. Bull Shed's prime rib is truly special – a thick slice of tender beef, perfectly cooked with a tasty bone (if you ask for it), delicious au jus, and fresh horseradish sauce – at $27 the best deal for the best portion on Kauai. Fresh island fish is another winner, a huge portion filleted by manager Tom Liu himself and then perfectly grilled. At Bull Shed, 'surf and turf' sets the island standard.

A glance at the menu will tell you why the Bull Shed is so popular. Prices are amazingly reasonable; entrées come with rice and the salad bar; and several cost less than $16. Combination dinners are served with a 7.5 oz tenderloin filet instead of the usual

the best prime rib & fresh fish

small sirloin. The wine list is also reasonable, with half the primarily California selections around $20-$25.

The Bull Shed has become a favorite with each member of our family, in itself a small miracle. Our 6:45pm arrival time is early enough to beat the crowds, and all four of our children eat everything served to them – a rare achievement. Teriyaki chicken breast ($15 or $7/child) is perfectly soft and juicy. Mike loves the teriyaki sirloin ($15), and Jeremy orders fresh island ahi, a huge portion, or rack of lamb, tender and tasty with a delicious teriyaki marinade. Even better, all four put away huge and healthful salads, picking their pickiest best from the salad bar ($7 by itself).

The Bull Shed offers one of the best food values on Kauai in a pleasant dining room with friendly, efficient service. It's popular, so try to arrive before 7pm to avoid the traffic jam. Or invite some friends because 6 or more can have a reservation. If it's warm, request a table by a window that opens (not all do). Bull Shed has not only great food and prices, but an ocean view. In fact, it's built as close to the ocean as technology allows, and our favorite table, in a tiny room by itself just a few feet from the edge of a seawall, offers a spectacular view of the waves rolling towards the wall and crashing in torrents of spray. During a storm, the waves splash right against the glass, an awesome sight. Come on a night when the moon is full, and watch the waves send gleaming ripples through the darkness.

Wailpouli, in Mokihana Resort, Kuhio Hwy (Rt 56). 822-3791. Dinner 5:30pm - 10pm nightly. Credit Cards. Children's menu (under 13). Look for the sign (it's small) opposite McDonald's, north of Coconut Plantation Marketplace, south of Waipouli Resort. Turn towards the water. Maps 1, 3

Caffé Coco *822-7990*

In almost any season, something is blooming or bearing fruit at Caffé Coco. The dining room is actually a tropical grove of mango, avocado, pomolo (a grapefruit cousin), and papaya, with 'walls' of thick, tall sugar cane. The decor is a bower of bougainvillea, ferns, and orchids. Garden chairs surround a collection of tables, none quite matching, and plastic garden chairs, beneath a honeysuckle-covered arbor. The cuisine emphasizes the natural – local vegetables, fruits, and herbs – and everything is fresh and organic. Some dishes are outstanding, like local mahi mahi crusted with black sesame seeds and accompanied with rice and a tasty wasabi cream sauce. Or try fresh ono with cilantro pesto, served with 'silver noodle salad' of bean threads with a delicious homemade peanut ginger dressing. Green salads arrive with unusual dressings – creamy feta, for example – and vegetables are imaginative, like fresh corn and green beans with eggplant, or a tasty sweet potato dumpling. Lighter choices include an ahi nori wrap, with soup and salad as well as omelets and vegetable salads. At lunch we enjoyed homemade soup and an ahi sandwich on foccacia bread. A spicy fish burrito contains a generous portion of ono, as well as rice and black beans.

Dinner is even more pleasant with local entertainers, a different performer each night. You'll have to bring your own wine or try non-alcoholic beverages served in blue or yellow goblets, like ginger lemonade or pomolo fizz, made when the enormous pomolo tree bears its fruit. Desserts feature local fruits, like mango tart from their mango tree.

You place your order at the counter where a refrigerated case displays the day's fresh ingredients. The staff will describe their favorites, even identify what's on a plate headed for the dining room, and everything is reasonably priced. Dine in the garden, or inside, in what is called with a grin, the 'Black Light Art Gallery.' The paintings glow – you will too, if you are wearing anything white. If mosquitoes pick on you while ignoring your friends, bring some 'Off' and request a mosquito coil. Browse the adjacent antique shop, Bambuli. Just turn left under the mango tree.

Wailua, 4-369 Kuhio Hwy (across from Kintaro). 822-7990. 11am - 9pm (T-F). FAX 822-0066. Credit cards. Call for entertainment schedule. Maps 1, 3

Café Portofino. 245-2121

Café Portofino's oceanside location at the Marriott, and its well-earned reputation for great food during more than 20 years, make it a favorite for Italian cuisine. From tables on the deck, you can watch the waves roll across Kalapaki Bay and enjoy the evening breezes. Giuseppe Avocadi, a one-man band of talent and energy, is committed to high food quality and professional service. After twenty years on Kauai, now the torch, or rather the fork, is passing to the next generation, as son Alex is learning the business from his talented father.

The dining room is spacious, with tables separated for privacy, covered in linen and set with shining crystal. The menu offers fresh fish, homemade pastas, chicken, veal, and fish. Portofino's Italian cuisine is light and healthful, with sauces based on vegetable flavors rather than heavy with cream. Flavorful minestrone is served in a generous portion for a modest price ($7), and kids will love mozzarella marinara ($9). Vegetable lasagne

($20) is as festive looking as a wrapped birthday present with wonderful marinara sauce and tasty chunks of tomatoes. Our fresh ono was tender and moist, if on the small side, served with a delicious mushroom sauce. Other good choices are 'scampi alla limone' ($28), zesty and attractive, served with perfectly cooked broccoli. A dinner salad ($9) is nicely presented; goat cheese salad with fresh mixed greens is excellent. Tiramisu is a great finish to the meal.

Everyone seems to care about your dinner, willing to fetch extra bread or answer questions, or help you choose from a well selected wine list. If prices are on the high side, there are also some bargains, like a respectable vintage of Pinot Grigio. At Café Portofino, you'll find an attractive setting, nightly music, and friendly service.

Lihue, across from Kauai Marriott. 245-2121. Dinner 5pm - 10pm nightly. Live music. Credit cards. cafeportofino.com. Credit cards. Maps 1, 2

Coconuts. 823-8777

Described as an 'Island Style Grill and Wine Bar,' Coconuts has a kind of Maui style chic, the signature of owners who hail from island life in a faster lane than Rt 56, Wailua. Inside an exterior decorated with rowboats and tiki torches, the hum of happy diners blends with lite rock music, and all the surfaces shine, down to wood tables lit with candles. There's a feeling of energy in the relatively small dining room, due in part to other diners waiting for their tables (waits can be more than a half hour).

Coconuts offers an extensive menu, ranging from a hamburger to fresh island fish, so you can find something for every degree of hunger and expense. Salmon is flavored with teriyaki, while onaga tasted disappointingly bitter from the grill. Ahi wasabi was the best. Menu prices ($11-$27) are reasonable except for expensive nightly specials, which can add to the dinner price, so clarify when you order. Most entrées are imaginatively prepared, like a very tasty fresh island mahi with macadamia nut rice, with portions occasionally on the small side. A salad or an appetizer will add $6 to $10 more. Lobster ravioli is tasty if somewhat dense, and coconut crusted shrimp is delicious though surprisingly expensive for the portion of only two shrimps. Dinner starts with fresh baked buns and homemade hummus, and ends with tasty desserts including a first rate crème brulée. The wine list includes many good choices in the $25-$40 range, including excellent wines by the glass, as well as wonderful tropical drinks. Service is usually polite if sometimes slow.

Coconuts has a following for its island-style cuisine. Waiting is almost inevitable, so consider making friends with some folks on the beach and going in as a six – then you can have a reservation.

Wailua, 4-919 Kuhio Hwy (Rt 56). 823-8777. Full bar. Dinner 4pm - 10pm. Closed Sundays. No reservations. Credit cards. Maps 1, 3

Dani's *245-4991*

At Dani's, you won't find an orchid on your plate, but you will find hot, tasty, and filling meals, emphasizing local-style Hawaiian foods. Kona coffee comes free with breakfast, and you can choose from eggs, omelettes, pancakes, and tasty Hawaiian dishes from $3.50. The ham and cheese omelette is very cheesy and stuffed with ham, though the hotcakes are on the heavy side. The lunch menu offers a wide variety of Hawaiian, American, and Japanese dishes, as well as sandwiches and hamburgers. Prices start at $5.40 and include soup or salad, roll, rice, and coffee or tea.

With prices this low, expect to sacrifice atmosphere. The color scheme is woodgrain formica accented by fluorescent lights, but on the other hand, the large dining room is bright, clean, and comfortably air-conditioned, and service swift and efficient.

Lihue, 4201 Rice St. 245-4991. 5am - 1:30pm (1pm on Sat). Closed Sundays. Credit cards. Maps 1, 2

Duke's Canoe Club *246-9599*

One of the most popular restaurants on Kauai, Duke's offers a sumptuous salad bar, which can truly be a meal in itself, as well as high quality, reasonably-priced steak and seafood dinners. Duke's also offers the Polynesian glitz which has made its sister restaurants, Keoki's on Kauai, as well as Kimo's on Maui, so successful, plus it has a bonus: since Duke's is perched right on the edge of Kalapaki Bay, you can be in the real Hawaii as well as the Hollywood version.

From the downstairs bar, a stone stairway carved into an indoor waterfall draped with trailing flowers takes you up to the dining room, a perfect spot to look out over Kalapaki bay while listening to wonderful Hawaiian music. Friendly performers stroll from table to table, offering to play your favorite Kauai songs, like 'Beautiful Kauai' or 'Hanalei Moon.'

A banana flower bearing fruit

Duke's reasonable dinner prices (from $18 for chicken) include the wonderful salad bar, with freshly made Caesar salad as well as an array of fresh vegetables and lettuces, fruits, pasta salads, tofu, fresh-baked banana macadamia nut muffins, and even rice – great for vegetarians ($13 alone).

Fresh fish entrées ($25-$28) can be prepared 6 ways, including baked, sautéed, steamed in ti leaf, clean grilled with pineapple salsa, roasted 'firecracker' and 'seven-spice.'

Since some sauces may seem too strongly flavored, you might ask for sauce served on the side. Most fish filets (8 to 10 oz) are pre-glazed, but you can request clean grilled.

The prime rib ($35 or $26/smaller cut), however, stopped the flow of conversation. Nearly 22 ounces, it was so thick that you didn't know where to begin to tackle it. More like a family-size roast, it was a significant dining event, tender as well as juicy, served underspiced rather than over-salted. Described on the menu as "while it lasts," you might reserve a portion as soon as you arrive. The wine list offers several good choices in the mid-$20 range. Try the famous 'Hula pie.'

Everyone in the family will enjoy Duke's. Children's dinners include fries and the salad bar (about $6), and adults can order 'Lighter Fare' (pasta, pizza, or a cheeseburger) for under $10.

beachfront with salad bar

What comes to your table will be well-prepared and efficiently served in a setting where you can watch the ocean and enjoy wonderful Hawaiian music. An unbeatable combination (that's why you see so many local families crowding the tables).

Reservations help somewhat, though there's usually still a wait; one section is set aside for walk-ins. Think twice about going in the rain, however, for you won't see the view when they close the shutters.

Duke's Barefoot Bar *246-9599*

Downstairs, right next to Kalapaki Beach, Duke's Barefoot Bar serves lunch, informal dinner, and munchies all day. Try excellent hamburgers and sandwiches ($7-$11), as well as salads and crisp, hot french fries. You'll love the fresh island fish daily dinner special – one fin each night, perhaps teriyaki ahi, or grilled moonfish. The vegetable plate is fresh and colorful, and, if you are lucky, you can visit the salad bar upstairs.

Tropical Friday means tropical drinks are priced under $6 (4pm - 6pm). Many evenings, you can listen to live music in one of the few island nite spots, a favorite with the island's help staff on their time off.

Lihue, Kalapaki Beach, access through the Kauai Marriott. 246-9599. Free valet parking. Reservations at least a day in advance but be prepared to wait anyway. Dinner 5pm - 10pm nightly. *Duke's Barefoot Bar* downstairs: 11am - 11pm. dukeskauai.com. Call for entertainment schedule. Credit Cards. Maps 1, 2

Eggbert's *822-3787*

Once upon a time, when eggs were king, many an enormous omelette was whipped up at Eggbert's in Lihue. Hurricane Iniki changed all that in 1992. Eggbert's closed, and the world synched with a different diet. Now Eggbert's has re-opened in Wailua at a time of low cholesterol chic. When you've got 'egg' all over your name these days, you take a hearty risk!

For 23 years, Eggbert's has been known for breakfast, particularly omelettes (even eggbeater options), and eggs benedict in 5 styles and 2 sizes (from $8). You can also try tasty banana pancakes with coconut syrup or french toast ($6). Kids have special breakfasts. The location in the Coconut Plantation Marketplace is great for families. Plastic chairs provide adequate comfort, and blue formica tables have rounded corners, safe at eye level for short persons who like to explore underneath. Service can be a bit on the slow side, but there's cappuccino and espresso while you wait.

Wailua. Coconut Plantation Marketplace Kuhio Hwy (Rt 56). 822-3787. Opens daily at 7am. Credit cards. Maps 1, 3

Garden Island Barbecue & Chinese *245-8868*

Garden Island Barbecue in downtown Lihue serves large portions for small prices. At lunch or dinner, the rather spartan dining room will probably be full of local folks, and a glance around will show you why. Platters are mounded with colorful heaps of noodles and vegetables, and the four page menu has prices around $8. Food quality won't win any awards for inventiveness, but what the chef cooks is tasty and hot. Saimin steams in the bowl; wontons feature shrimp as well as ground meat, and vegetables are still crunchy. Lunch or dinner entrées include scoops of rice and macaroni salad. Barbecue plate ($7) with rice includes a generous teriyaki chicken breast and beef thinly sliced and delicious. Shrimp with locally grown choi sum, a green vegetable similar to broccoli leaves and flowers, is very tasty.

The dining room is clean, cooled by fans, and seems friendly from the moment you walk in. Garden Island may not be fancy, but if you're on a budget, you'll appreciate the generous portions of inexpensive, tasty food.

Lihue, 4252A Rice St. 245-8868. 10am - 9pm. Closed Sundays. Cash only. Maps 1, 2

Gaylord's. 245-9593

Once the heart of a 1,700 acre sugar plantation, Kilohana is a special place. Rooms have the spacious beauty of large proportions and wide verandas, and you can easily imagine the gracious pace of life before airplanes and traffic lights. Named for Gaylord Wilcox who built Kilohana, the restaurant's dining room and veranda look out over the mountains, a manicured lawn, and garden lush with leafy ferns and brilliant tropical flowers. In the evening, the flagstone terrace is lit with lanterns, and rattan chairs surround comfortable tables decked with white linen. Gaylord's is one of the most romantic restaurants on Kauai, with the kind of setting you'd want to star in if your life were a black and white movie.

At Gaylord's you'll do best if you order simply, with sauces served on the side. Sautéed fresh island onaga and grilled ahi were both perfectly cooked, moist and flavorful, much better without the strongly flavored sauces. The special steamed vegetable entrée made to order for our vegetarian was fresh, attractive, and flavorful. Prime rib is a good bet ($27/10oz or $29/13 oz), served with lots of *au jus*. Entrées arrive with rice, potato, or pasta, as well as a vegetable, like still crunchy sugar peas in the pod and sliced red peppers. Most cost more than $24 (fettucine with chicken) unless you come for 'light supper' (5pm - 6:30pm). Soup or salad pushes up the cost of dining quickly. While expensive, Gaylord's wine list has some good choices at a reasonable price.

The dining experience at Gaylord's can be wonderful. Waitpersons are polite, attentive, and professional, and in the quiet courtyard, you escape the usual noisy distractions of clattering trays and dishes. Small details get lots

of attention: water is served in elegant iced glasses with tangy lemon slices, and coffee cups are watched carefully. If you like to linger after dinner, bring a sweater, for winter temperatures can be chilly.

With such an elegant setting, Gaylord's is one of the island's special dining experiences, an image to haunt you when temperatures plunge back home. The food never quite seems to match the setting – possibly because of the setting.

We have had better luck at lunch, with excellent sandwiches, salads, vegetable platters, burgers, and fresh seafood ($11-$13), like fresh mahi mahi salad ($13) with 3 large pieces (we were glad we ordered the rather spicy sauce on the side). You can enjoy the garden in the full splendor of sunshine.

Lihue, on Rt 50 just west of Kukui Grove Center. 245-9593. Lunch 11am - 3pm; Dinner 5:30 - 9pm daily. Sunday brunch: 9:30am - 3pm. Weekly luaus. Credit cards. Children's menu. Weddings. gaylordskauai.com. Maps 1, 2

Hamura's Saimin *245-3271*

According to legend, Oahu businessmen have flown to Kauai just to have lunch at Hamura's Saimin. The newly painted (bright blue) small building encloses – just barely – three horse-shoe shaped counters with stools. Although a recent face-lift has made the room look cleaner and more like a luncheonette, you can still watch the cook stir and chop and make

hidden saimin

things sizzle. The inevitability of change, yes, though some traditions die hard. A sign still warns: "No Gum Under the Counter."

On this counter is served some of the finest saimin around, and you come to want to believe the legend about the Oahu businessmen and their expense account lunches. Airfare could certainly be offset with bargain food prices: $7 buys the saimin special – tasty and fragrant soup with noodles, chock full of vegetables and meats. Perfectly flavored won ton soup or won ton min is only $4. To take the saimin out costs 25 cents for the container, but you can escape the cramped little room and head for the beach. Perfectly spiced barbecued beef or chicken sticks ($1.25) are another find.

Kids love homemade *manapu*, a sweet cousin of the pretzel ($2/bag). Don't miss lilikoi chiffon pie ($2) or one of the best buys on Kauai, $12 for the whole pie. (We order one in advance to take home on the plane, frozen, in a soft plastic picnic cooler from Wal-Mart.)

When the waitress takes your order, she passes a bowl of the appropriate size and color over the counter to the cook, who inserts the proper mix of ingredients, then covers all with ladles of steaming broth. If you visit often enough, you begin to appreciate technique, the consumer's as well as the cook's. Experienced diners mix hot mustard and soy sauce in their spoons, dipping the mixture into the soup as necessary, and using chopsticks to pull the noodles through.

There's not much variety, but what the cook cooks is very good indeed, and the visit is like a trip into the island's past – about seventy years – a time before tourism brought butcherblock tables and bentwood chairs, air-conditioning and gourmet teas – a time when sticking gum under the counter, though frowned upon, was still possible. So throw away your Bubble Yum before going inside, and try this taste of authentic Kauai!

Lihue, 2956 Kress St. 245-3271. M-Sat 10am - 9pm. Open (and less crowded) Sundays for lunch. Cash only. Maps 1, 2

Hanama'ulu Café & Tea House . 245-2511

You could not select a better place to share a really special evening with friends than the Tea House. This restaurant combines delicious food with the friendliest service on the island, and, as if that weren't enough, a Japanese garden setting to make everything seem just a bit magical. Here you can dine on soft mats at low tables next to the goldfish and water lilies.

Children can wander around and count the carp (tell them to be careful; one of our two-year-olds tumbled in). Local families have been coming here for more than seventy years. Today they still appreciate excellent cooking at reasonable prices, and it's a rare wedding, anniversary, welcome, or farewell party that does not take place in one of the tea rooms by the garden.

> *Island style & family friendly*

The Miyake family cooks with subtlety and flair, and creates a genuinely special cuisine, with 35 Chinese and Japanese entrées at reasonable prices from $4.75-$14.75. We recommend the won ton soup ($6) garnished with scallions, pork, and slices of egg foo young. Outstanding! Children will love crispy fried chicken with its delicate touch of ginger ($6); the boneless pieces are just the right size for little hands.

When our party is large enough, we ask the owner to order a several course dinner, and we are always delighted with the new dishes we discover. Tempura with fresh island fish or shrimp is spectacular, served on an enormous platter, and the taste is just as wonderful ($9.75). Vegetarians will love the vegetable tempura ($6.50) or crispy tofu tempura ($4) served with teriyaki sauce and green onions. Sashimi of ahi and ono is fresh, elegantly arranged, and of the best quality. A specialty, mushrooms stuffed with crab ($5.75) is lighter than many versions of the dish, and very tasty. Chinese chicken salad has lots of chicken, lettuce, crispy noodles, and wonderful dressing. The sushi bar features excellent salmon skin handrolls with crispy grilled salmon.

Reserve at least three days in advance to choose where you dine. Avoid the rather non-descript front dining room, and try the teppan yaki room and sushi bar. Our favorite, however, is the tea house by the gardens, where we can listen to crickets sing the songs of evening while stars light up the velvet sky. If mosquitoes like to pick on you while ignoring your friends, don't be bashful about asking for a mosquito coil. The incense smell is pleasant and keeps the bugs away.

In more than twenty years of dining, this special restaurant has never let us down. The cooking is consistently excellent, the prices remarkably reasonable, the service exceptionally friendly, and children are treated with more than usual tolerance by waitresses like Sally and Arlene who genuinely love them. This is a restaurant where you should sample as many dishes as possible, and because it is such a special place, we save the Tea House for our last night, asking any *kapunas* who might be listening to speed our return. You shouldn't miss the Tea House either.

Hanama'ulu, Kuhio Hwy (Rt 56). Reserve a tea room in advance. 245-2511. Lunch 10am - 1pm; Dinner 5pm - 8:30pm. Take-out from 3:30pm. Sunday night buffet ($22/adult). Closed Mondays. Full bar. Banquet facilities. Ask Sally and Arlene about special wedding menus. Credit cards. Map 1

Hong Kong Café 822-3288

Wailua's Hong Kong Café offers an excellent alternative to generic fast food. It looks like a luncheonette, with about nine green and black formica tables in an air-conditioned dining room. It's often full because the menu offers many choices – roast duck, crispy chicken, lo mein and chow mein, sweet and sour dishes, or vegetarian creations – and almost everything is inexpensive ($7 - $14). Choose plate lunches ($7 - $9), bentos ($7 - $8) or many vegetarian dishes, including a delicious eggplant with tofu. We like saimin, of which there are nine varieties, served in huge, steaming bowls of noodles, vegetables, and flavorful broth ($4 - $8). Bring your wine or beer. Hong Kong Café is not pretentious, and you can enjoy reasonable food at reasonable prices. They will deliver nearby. Fax your order.

Wailua Shopping Plaza, 4-361 Kuhio Hwy (Rt 56). 822-3288. 11am-9pm weekdays; 1pm - 9pm weekends. Credit cards. Maps 1, 3

Hukilau Lanai 822-3441

The restaurant in the Kauai Coast 'Beachboy' Resort combines excellent dinners with a wonderful location looking out over the landscape to the sea. As darkness falls and evening breezes cool the open air patio and dining room, you can enjoy the night sky, spectacular when moonlight silvers the gardens and sparkles on the waves.

In the comfortable two-tiered dining room and dining lanai, every table has a view, enhanced by soft lighting, soft music, and performances by local musicians several nights a week. Dinner begins with homemade foccacia, which you can enjoy with a first-rate pineapple martini.

The menu features flavors of the Pacific Rim – fresh island fish, as well as poultry and meat. Entrées come with rice, potatoes, even risotto, and the kitchen will even prepare pasta you bring in yourself. Start with ahi nachos or sweet potato ravioli. If you are a seafood lover, try Hukilau mixed seafood grill ($24), a family favorite, with two good-sized pieces of fresh fish, like ahi and ono, and a shrimp skewer; be sure to ask for delicious homemade teriyaki sauce. Other fish choices include grilled ono, shiitake mushroom and panko crusted opah ($19), and opakapaka dusted with herbs baked in a ti leaf with lop cheong, cilantro, and green onion ($24). Or try a

generous seafood linguini.
Meat lovers can try the grilled
rib-eye steak with garlic
mashed potatoes ($22). When
asked, the chef created a fresh
steamed vegetable plate for our
vegetarian, a spectacular array
of grilled eggplant, tomato,
mushrooms, vegetable ragout
($13). Beach Boy Burger is at
the low end ($11). Don't miss
desserts – tropical shortcake
with lemon curd is a stand-out,
and chocolate lovers will love
the chocolate macadamia nut
cheesecake.

Hukilau will satisfy the
most exacting palates and diets.
Switch what comes with the
entreés? No problem. Bring
your own pasta? A snap. Steam
fish or vegetables in their own juices? Easy. And what's best, no extra charge
for this personalized service. Children are welcomed with a special menu.
An interesting idea, the wine list announces 20 wines costing around $20. A
banquet room is a great spot for a party.

Wailua, behind Coconut Plantation Marketplace in Kauai Coast Resort, Rt
56. 822-3441 for reservations and entertainment schedule. Dinner from
5pm. Closed Mondays. Credit cards. Banquet room. Weddings. For menus
and info, visit the sister restaurant website at gaylordskauai.com. Map 1

Hula Girl *822-4422*

Hula Girl serves Hawaiian family style lunch and dinner. As you might
expect, the décor is island style, with postcard type pictures of Polynesian
hula girls on the wall as well as a giant mural of the island. Dinner is served
to the tunes of live entertainment, sometimes with staff joining in with an
impromptu hula. Mai tais ($5) are excellent. Pork tacos ($10) are generously
stuffed, served with sour cream and delicious papaya salsa. If you are in the
mood for sashimi, though, you might prefer a specialty restaurant like
Kintaro or Wasabi. Entreés include chicken, steak, and seafood, and come
with soup or salad, as well as rice, baked potato, or linguini. Onion soup is

excellent, with chunks of onion and romano cheese, a better choice than the rather sparse dinner salad. Pork medallions ($24) and macadamia nut crusted ono ($23) were tasty, though the sauce (too salty on the former, too sweet on the latter) might best be ordered on the side. Macadamia nut rice is an interesting, crunchy accompaniment. For a pleasant combination of dinner and entertainment, Hula Girl is a good choice.

Wailua, Coconut Plantation Marketplace, Kuhio Hwy (Rt 56). 822-4422. Dinner 4pm - 9pm daily. Credit cards. Full bar. Map 1

JJ's Broiler 246-4422

More than thirty years ago, Kauai's first steak house opened in an old plantation house on the main street of Lihue, then a sleepy town with a single traffic light. JJ's achieved local fame for its specialty, 'Slavonic steak,' a sliced London broil marinated in garlic sauce. When anyone in JJ's was served this dish, everyone else knew it! When JJ's opened right on Kalapaki Bay, its garish, hot pink sign issuing a neon challenge to the hotel restaurants just down the beach. Just as the contest was getting interesting, Iniki struck and blew all the dining spots out of business.

Today, JJ's offers a reasonable meal at a reasonable price (dinners $20 - $30) when you consider the salad bar which arrives at your table in a huge bowl of greens surrounded by vegetables and condiments in a lazy susan (by itself, one of the best inexpensive meals on Kauai). On one visit, the New York steak was tasteless and tough, while fresh opakapaka was well prepared, though served with a sauce so heavy that we were glad to have ordered it served on the side. Macadamia nut rack of lamb was both tender and moist, if a bit heavy on the mustard sauce. Bread is undistinguished, served without a plate to hold the crumbs.

JJ's multi–level design affords each table privacy as well as an ocean view. Above the polished wood tables, in the enormous space of the open beam ceiling, hang actual sailboats. JJ's costs the same or even more than other steak houses like The Bull Shed in Wailua, or Duke's Canoe Club right down the beach, where, in our opinion, portions are larger and the food tastier.

Lihue, Anchor Cove Center. 246-4422. Lunch 11am - 5pm. Dinner 5pm - 10pm daily. Full bar. Credit cards. Maps 1, 2

Kalapaki Beach Hut 246-6330

In the green building right behind Kalapaki Beach, you will find one of our favorite sandwiches on Kauai – a fish sandwich with ono (usually) flash

Wailua sunrise

frozen, (always) cleanly grilled, (always) moist and tender, and wrapped in a soft roll with lettuce and juicy tomatoes. You will also find some of the best hamburgers on Kauai – no surprise since the owner, Steve Gerald, originated 'Ono Burger' in Anahola more than twenty years ago. Since then, the term 'Ono Burger' has achieved near legendary status, a name spoken with reverence whenever fine hamburgers are discussed on Kauai.

Steve Gerald has flame-broiled many a burger, either beef or turkey, or even buffalo. Beef burgers are extra juicy, extra tasty, and delicious. The entry level burger comes with lettuce, tomato, and mayonnaise on a sesame bun. Buffalo burgers are about $2 more (though just think of the savings for your arteries). Teriyaki or barbecue style, or bacon and cheddar or mushroom melt can be had for $1-$2 more. Kids' burgers include fries and soft drink. French fries are hot and tasty, with vinegar as well as catsup available. Vegetarians can try a veggie sandwich or a salad. Everything is cooked to order, so be patient, or phone the order in ahead.

It's open every day from 7am (8am Sundays) until 7pm. Start your day with a 'breakfast sandwich' or omelette, and all the coffee you can hold.

You can hardly spend your food money more wisely. Take it out, or dine in the upstairs porch with a view of the bay.

Lihue, on Kalapaki Bay, 3464 Rice St. 246-6330. BLD: 7am - 8pm daily. Cash only. Maps 1, 2

Kauai Pasta. *822-7447*

Popular with local folks who appreciate good food in generous portions, Kauai Pasta delivers on both price and value. Lasagna ($10) fills the plate, and pesto grilled chicken breast ($11) is tasty and ample. Kids have a great menu ($5).

The dining room in Kapa'a, built on two tiers, is comfortable, clean and bright, with colorful paintings, wood chairs and formica tables.

Your plastic glass will be filled immediately with ice water, and garlic bread arrives soon after. Salad of Wailua Farms baby greens comes with a delicious balsamic reduction dressing ($6). Try panini sandwiches (from $8)

The ne ne, Hawaii's state bird and an endangered species, is slowly increasing in numbers on Kauai

or pasta entrées (from $7 – add $2.50 for chicken).

Service is friendly and efficient at tables roomy enough even for large parties, For dessert, try coffee with lady fingers ($2.50). Local folks love it so much that a second branch is now open in Lihue. Catering also available.

Wailua, 4-9398 Kuhio Hwy (Rt 56). 822-7447. Dinner 5pm - 9pm. Closed Mondays. Also in Lihue, 245 2227. Credit cards. Map 1

King & I 822-1642

The King and I is one of those wonderful restaurants you always dream of discovering tucked away in a shopping center, like your child's favorite toy under the socks in the corner of his closet. The owners are a family who fled Cambodia by boat, trained at the famous Keo's restaurant in Honolulu, then settled on Kauai to follow their dream of opening their own place. Their air-conditioned dining room is attractive and clean-looking, with colorful orchids on the tables, lots of Thai hangings on the walls, and comfortable tables with white linen tablecloths topped with glass.

The real attraction at the King and I is the delicious food. Spring rolls ($7.50/6) are crisp, light and wonderfully tasty, attractively arranged on manoa lettuce, served with delicious peanut vinegar dipping sauce. Don't eat too many because it would be a mistake to miss lemon grass soup ($7.50), piping hot, with fragrant clouds of steam. Shrimps with peanut sauce are extremely tender, or try fried rice ($8) flavored with tomato, cucumber, and cilantro and garnished with sliced water chestnuts. Siam Mee Kaob ($7.50) is a small mountain of crispy rice noodles, bean sprouts, and scallions, served with a delicately sweet peanut sauce. Sa-teh with beef or chicken ($8.50), or the truly amazing mahi mahi ($11.50), is crisp and light, served with spicy peanut sauce and cucumber dipping sauce.

You'll love ginger fish ($11), mahi mahi fried crisp and served with a mild sauce flavored with ginger and scallions, or try one of the outstanding curries ($7.95-$9.95). Yellow curry is served with potatoes and onions; colored with saffron, it would be the easiest to identify as a 'curry.' Green curry takes its color–and flavor–from fresh basil, as well as coconut, lime leaves, and lemongrass. Red curry is the sweetest, flavored with coconut. Best of all, in our opinion, is a mild, sweet curry flavored with peanut and coconut and chock full of tender chicken; it's not on the menu but ask for it as 'Evil Jungle Prince' ($10). Siam eggplant ($8.50) is pungent and wonderful. Vegetarian specials (from $7.50) are tasty with basil and spices grown fresh in Kilauea. For dessert, try Thai tapioca pudding is flavored with delicious apple-bananas and coconut. Most wines cost around $20.

King and I is great choice for those times when you find it hard to look at another ahi or ono. The distinctive cuisine and friendly family atmosphere are great, and when you get your bill, your royal pocketbook will hardly notice.

Wailua, Waipouli Plaza, 4-901 Kuhio Hwy (Rt 56). 822-1642. Dinner 4:30pm - 9:30pm daily. Reservations suggested. Credit cards. Map 1

Excellent Japanese cuisine & sushi

Restaurant Kintaro 822-3341

There's almost always a line out the door of Kintaro, and with good reason. For nearly 20 years, Kintaro has remained Kauai's most popular Japanese restaurant, a must if you are looking for delicious food in an attractive setting. A fountain set in blue tiles and a sushi bar take up one long white wall. Nut-colored wood tables are set with chopsticks, blue napkins, and blue and tan tea bowls. Ceiling fans and air conditioning make Kintaro comfortably cool.

Even with a reservation, you'll probably have to wait, a bit more pleasant in the new waiting area than in the old days, when there wasn't much room between the door and Rt 56. Cocktails and pu pus are served in a comfortable, attractive lounge.

In the main dining room, you can sit at the teppan yaki tables and watch talented chefs chop and flip and make things sizzle. As they will be happy to show you, the raw ingredients are fresh and of the best quality. Teriyaki New York steak ($20) or island chicken teriyaki ($15) are tender, tasty and juicy.

If you prefer the reasonably-priced dinners on the regular menu, you might be seated in the smaller dining room next to the sushi bar. Dinner begins with delicious miso soup, followed by entrées presented on traditional sectioned wooden platforms with rice, zaru soba (chilled buckwheat noodles with a seasoned soy-based sauce) and pickled vegetables, along with tea served in a blue and tan pottery teapot. Crispy shrimp tempura with vegetables ($14) is light and delicious, particularly the green beans. Teriyaki beef with slices of NY steak is exceptionally tender ($17). Beef sukiyaki in a cast iron pot ($16) is dark and dusky with translucent noodles, meat, and vegetables. Teriyaki chicken is a family favorite with great sauce.

Take a seat at the sushi bar and watch the chef prepare rolls at lightening speed. Local people consider the sashimi (high volume means everything should be very fresh) the island's best: thin slices of ahi, translucent slivers of ono, dark strips of pungent smoked salmon, shrimps cooked so perfectly that they seemed to melt as you taste them. Spicy tuna rolls are great, as are California rolls which Kintaro makes with fresh crab meat, scallop rolls, hamachi rolls, soft shell crab hand rolls, salmon skin hand rolls, and a specialty seafood mix grilled in foil. Don't miss the Kilauea Roll or 'Bali Hai Bomb.'

Children are welcome, as is appropriate for a restaurant named in honor of a legendary Japanese boy hero, and service is polite and usually unrushed. As our children have grown up, Kintaro has become not just their favorite Japanese restaurant, but a favorite, period.

Wailua, Kuhio Hwy (Rt 56). 822-3341. Dinner 5:30pm - 9:30pm. Closed Sundays. Reservations necessary, but be prepared to wait anyway. Say 'Hi' to Evelyn when you check in at her desk. Credit Cards. Maps 1, 3

Kountry Kitchen *822-3511*

For years, and despite changes in ownership, a great spot for breakfast on the island's eastside has been the Kountry Kitchen, with terrific food at equally terrific prices. The large menu offers delicious eggs, expertly cooked bacon and sausage, as well as omelette creations, including sour cream, or bacon and tomato, or 'vegetable garden.' You can also design an omelette by ordering a combination of separately priced fillings. Kountry Kitchen's om-

Family breakfast favorite

elettes are unique – thin pancakes of egg rolled around fillings almost like a crepe – tender, moist, and delicious.

Or try Eggs Margo, a version of Eggs Benedict with turkey instead of ham. Our children loved Cheesy Eggs – a toasted English muffin with bacon and poached eggs, covered with golden cheese sauce, and our babies have all loved the honey and wheat pancake. All come with perfectly golden and crisp pancakes of shredded potatoes. For homestyle breakfasts, you can't do much better.

Kapa'a, 1485 Kuhio Hwy (Rt 56). 822-3511. Breakfast 6am - 9am; Lunch 11am - 2:30pm. Credit cards. Maps 1, 4

La Bamba *245-5972*

In Kukui Grove Shopping Center, La Bamba serves generous portions at reasonable prices. The hardworking owners try to combine the best ingredients at the best price into their family's favorite dishes. The dining room is roomy and cheerful, with red and green chiles painted around windows, Southwest scenes painted on walls, Mexican hats tacked up above booths. Green vinyl tablecloths combine with genuine friendliness to make for a pleasant dining experience.

The teen-age daughter may take your order, while her father, the chef who hails from El Salvador, works in the kitchen, and her mother looks on, managing and encouraging. You will be delighted with the fresh ingredients in generous portions. If you order a Mexican salad ($8), it fills the plate, stuffed with beans and chunks of chicken ($8). Entrées range from $7.50 - $12, including rice and beans, as well as and à la carte choices, like a delicious chicken enchilada ($3) with lots of tasty sauce.

La Bamba is a good choice for generous portions, reasonable prices, and the somewhat slow service that goes hand in hand with an informal, friendly family atmosphere. Try Mexican beer, wine, and margaritas.

Lihue, Kukui Grove Ctr. 245-5972. 11am - 10pm daily. Credit cards. Map 1

La Playita Azul *821-2323*

Tucked under Safeway's wing in the Kauai Village Shopping Center, La Playita Azul is a tiny, clean eatery with a half-dozen tables. Generous portions of chicken, pork, beef, vegetables, or seafood are tasty and reasonably priced (between $8 and $12, with à la carte items at about $3).

The fish burrito ($14) is filled with fresh ahi. Seafood burrito ($25) adds scallops, shrimp and vegetables to the mix. All plates are served with rice

Island sunsets are especially lovely when reflected on eastern shores.

and homemade beans. The house specialty '3 Tier Burrito' with fish, chicken, and steak is enough for two and delicious ($22). Each dish is cooked individually, so service may be leisurely.

Enjoy some beer or wine while you wait, or read the many testimonials scrawled by happy patrons on the walls, an interesting idea for decor.

Wailua, Kauai Village on Rt 56, next to Safeway. 821-2323. Take out. Dinner 5:30pm - 9:30pm daily. Call about lunch. Credit cards. Map 1

Lemongrass Grill 821-2888

An offshoot of the popular Mema's, the two-storey Lemongrass has an upstairs pine-paneled dining room open to the rafters and cool with breezes. (An outdoor dining terrace lit with tiki torches and rimmed with wagon wheels is more visible from the street). Dinner begins with wonderful fresh baked dark bread, and Pacific Rim entrées are colorful with vegetables and some deft Thai seasoning. Salads are attractive with fresh local greens and tasty dressings like guava pineapple or lemongrass vinaigrette. Pork with tangy Thai barbecue sauce is a generous, tasty appetizer for only $7. Grilled fresh island fish ($23) is perfectly cooked, flaky and very tasty, and, since we ordered sauce served on the side, we could experiment with combinations. We found the fish tasted even better with the light Thai salad dressing, and our server cheerfully brought us seconds. At Lemongrass, service is polite and efficient, and everyone works hard to make the dining experience enjoyable.

Wailua, 4-885 Kuhio Hwy (Rt 56). 821-2888. 5pm– 10pm daily. Full bar. Credit cards. Maps 1, 3

Ma's Family, Inc. 245-3142

Ma's tiny luncheonette is so far off the beaten path in Lihue that you'd probably never find it if you didn't stumble onto it by chance. For more than 40 years, Ma and daughter Amy have earned a reputation for generous, well-priced, and well-cooked breakfasts (about $5) and lunches. You'll probably find the dozen tables filled with local people on their way to work in the morning or stopping off at lunch.

Visitors who happen onto it will love Ma's expertly cooked eggs, delicious pancakes ($4), french toast ($3), and waffles ($3) that our children describe as "about the best." The menu also lists Hawaiian dishes like roast kalua pig ($3) that shreds perfectly for little fingers. Even toast is excellent, and fried min noodles with eggs and sausage may open your eyes to new possibilities for breakfast. Service is fast and extremely friendly in the sunny, spartan dining room. If you don't like canned milk in your coffee, ask Amy for a small glass of the fresh stuff. When you leave, you'll be astonished to find how little your meal has cost you. When a hungry family can dine so inexpensively, you feel like popping into the kitchen to give Ma a big hug! And some of our readers do just that.

Lihue, 4277 Halenani St. 245-3142. 5am - 1pm daily. Closed for New Years Day. Coffee/tea free with breakfast. Cash only. Maps 1, 2

Mema Thai & Chinese. 823-0899

Mema features Chinese and Thai dishes, and its Thai food is a tad spicier than nearby King & I. What comes to the table is both tasty and attractive. Spring rolls ($7) are crisp, attractively served with fresh leafy lettuce and peanut sauce, and can be ordered vegetarian style. On the Chinese menu, cashew chicken ($10) is chock full of nuts, and lemon chicken ($10) is excellent, very crispy and golden with a lightly flavored lemon sauce.

Thai dishes can be very spicy, so ask your server for advice. Each dish can be prepared with vegetables or tofu ($9), with chicken, beef, or pork ($10) or with shrimp, fish, or calamari ($12). Green curry with coconut milk, lemon grass, kaffir lime leaves, eggplant, and fresh basil is not overly spicy. On the other hand, red curry looks deceptively placid, garnished with fresh basil and chopped cabbage, but it's a scorcher ($10). Mahi mahi sa-teh ($11) is delicious. Vegetarians have many choices on the menu, and the chef will also tailor dishes to specific tastes.

While experts may grumble that no authentic Thai peppers blister the dishes at Mema, the temperature is up a few degrees from the King & I, with reasonable prices, lots of variety on the menu, and (mostly) friendly service.

Wailua, 4-369 Kuhio Hwy (Rt 56). 823-0899. Lunch 11am – 2pm M-F; Dinner nightly 5pm - 9:30pm. Credit cards. Maps 1, 3

Mermaids Café 821-2026

At the tiny, walk-up window, you can order some of the tastiest, most inventive dishes on Kauai – with a healthy (vegan) emphasis for good measure. Portions are generous bordering on enormous, seasoning judicious, and prices amazingly reasonable. Choose wraps and burritos made with tofu, chicken, or fresh fish ($8-$10), tempeh burgers, bakery treats, tea and espresso. Don't miss the ahi wrap ($9), one of the best taste treats on Kauai: fresh grilled ahi and nori are stuffed into a giant, delicious spinach tortilla. Or try an excellent coconut chicken curry heaped with vegetables and rice

($10), or local organic salad ($9). Foccacia is crisp and fluffy, a treat all by itself, or as a sandwich with chicken, tofu or fish ($9). Have some hibiscus iced tea ($2). It's not fancy, and the only seating is outside: a couple of chairs in the sun or some stools. So pack up and head for the beach – as lots of local folks do.

Kapaʻa, Kuhio Hwy. 821-2026. 11am - 9pm daily. Credit cards. Maps 1, 4

Monico's Taqueria *822-4300*

Monico's in Kinipopo Shopping Center has attracted loyal followers for excellent food at unbeatable prices. Fresh ahi burrito is packed with tender fish, cleanly grilled perfectly medium rare, and delicious rice ($11). Vegetarian burrito has sautéed fresh vegetables (or grilled upon request) with beans and rice ($9). Or try a tasty garden salad ($6). Kids have a great menu (quesadilla, bean and cheese burrito, or nachos for $4).

Dine in the small, quiet courtyard or carry your meal out to nearby Wailua Bay for a picnic. Take-out orders are packaged with chips and salsa. While you wait for your food to be prepared, visit Goldsmiths Kauai next door for beautiful jewelry designs at reasonably prices.

At Monico's, prices are reasonable, portions generous, and the service swift and polite. A great combination, and first-rate value.

Sandy beaches rim the Eastside near Lydgate Park in Wailua

Wailua. Kinipopo Shopping Center, Kuhio Hwy (next to Kintaro). 822-4300. Lunch 11am - 3pm; Dinner 5pm - 9pm. Closed Tues. Credit cards. Maps 1, 4

Naupaka Terrace, Kauai Hilton. 245-1955

In the newly renovated Kauai Beach Hotel, Naupaka Terrace has a clean new look, with a bright new menu and a seasoned favorite in the chef department, Mark Sasson. His new menu is designed to please a variety of diners, those who like beef and chicken favorites as well as those intrigued by the unusual, say a diminutive lobster omelette as a dinner appetizer.

Execution is proficient and generous. Fresh mahi mahi ($26) was perfectly prepared, lightly sautéed and served with a delicate mango sauce and a garnish of radish sprouts. Macadamic nut rack of lamb ($27) is moist and tender, with a dark, resonant sauce. Dinners include a house salad and either white or a delicious mixed grain rice. Don't pass up macadamia tart or ice cream pie.

Service is polite and attentive, and the dining room attractive. A pleasant dining lanai winds around a lagoon where the occasional carp leaps into the air. If mosquitoes like to pick on you, request a coil. The incense smell is great, and it keeps the bugs away.

Kauai Hilton, Kuhio Hwy (Rt 56) near Hanama'ulu. 245-1955. Breakfast 6:30am - 11am; Dinner 6pm - 9:30pm daily. Credit cards. Map 1

Norberto's El Café. 822-3362

In the heart of Kapa'a, Norberto's has served Mexican food on Kauai since 1977. White stucco walls, hanging plants and sombreros, and wood-grain tables create a setting like a cantina. Over the years, prices have not changed much (dinners from $13-$17), and almost everything is reasonable, including margaritas by the pitcher and à la carte entrées, as well as complete Mexican dinners with soup, vegetable, beans, chips and salsa for $18 or less. Ask for chips made with flour tortillas. Nachos are generously covered with cheese. When we finished our bean soup, we were offered seconds!

The Burrito El Café deserves to be called a house specialty – a tortilla generously stuffed with flavorful beef, beans and cheese, baked enchilada style and topped with guacamole and fresh red tomatoes and lettuce. The tostada is a huge colorful salad mounded over a crisp tortilla, and the chili relleno is dipped (not drowned) in egg and gently cooked. An El Café specialty, taro enchiladas are first rate, the taro leaves tasting a bit like spinach. Almost all dishes can be ordered vegetarian style.

Service is friendly, prices are reasonable, and children are treated with tolerance, even when cranky. When the salsa proved too hot for the short people, our fast-thinking waitress brought over a bowl of bean soup. Once kids started dipping chips, all you could hear was happy crunching.

Kapa'a, 4-1373 Kuhio Hwy (Rt 56). 822-3362. Dinner 5:30pm - 9pm. Closed Sundays. Credit cards. Maps 1, 4

Okazu Hale 245-6554

Okazu Hale's saimin has great noodles with steaming broth and vegetables. Or sample the Japanese style noodle soup, Miso Ramen, which has a richer flavor and more spice. In this tiny eatery inside the strip mall next to Ace Hardware in Lihue, you'll find saimin, sushi, Japanese style 'local food,' as well as teriyaki and barbecue dishes, even old-fashioned pot roast. Prices are inexpensive ($7-$10). The decor is spartan, to put it mildly. It's jammed when the plate lunch crowd arrives, but the saimin is worth the crush. Saimin special ($6) comes with shrimp tempura, chicken katsu and vegetables. This is local style Kauai – don't miss it.

Lihue, 4100 Rice Street. 245-6554. Lunch 11am - 2pm. Dinner 5pm - 9pm. Closed Sundays. Cash only. Map 1

Oki Diner 245-5899

Your body's still on east coast time and you're hungry in the middle of the night! Well, Oki Diner is open 21 hours a day, 7 days a week, with local style food. For breakfast, a full range of eggs and pancakes (from $7) including banana with strawberry syrup; for other times, there are sandwiches, burgers, noodle dishes of all kinds, and 25 'local favorites' like stir fry or beef stew, Hawaiian style ribs and pork, complete with rice and salad, and hot, tasty saimin. Choose the 'Mongolian Bar' to pick out your vegetables, meat, seafood, select a sauce, and the chef will cook your meal to order ($12). Don't forget the pies. 'Pumpkin crunch' is a local legend, available by the slice for $3.40 (it's square).

Oki Diner has a new, more comfortable dining room opposite the County Round Building in downtown Lihue. For large portions of straightforward meals at honest prices, and at any hour, it may just be what you need on Hawaiian time.

Lihue, Rice St. 245-5899. 6am - 3am daily. Credit cards. Map 1

Olympic Café 822-2825

On the upper floor of the Hee Fat building, Olympic has a view of the mountains above main street Kapaʻa, a great spot for people-watching while you eat one of your 3 squares, or down a beer or cocktail. Lunch and dinner choices include burgers, salads (including a tasty tofu salad), sandwiches, wraps, burritos, and fresh fish tacos (from $10). Coffees and cappuccino, as well teas and herbal blends, fill out the full bar menu.

The main attraction here is portion, as in huge. Presentation lags behind, as your food may be heaped on the plate rather than arranged. At dinner, stir fry chicken, for example, arrived more or less inverted over a pile of rice ($16). Ahi burrito was smothered with so much guacamole you could hardly find the fish ($13). Calamari ($10) closely reassembled onion rings. Fresh island fish (grilled or blackened $20) was adequate, though best was the quesadilla ($10).

The lunch menu, available all day, offers sandwiches (from $8), salads (from $6), wraps (from $8), and burritos. Tofu may be substituted for chicken, or ordered on a giant bed of lettuce and tomatoes. Chicken salad, a moist chicken breast, arrived with mixed greens and delicious dressing ($9.50). Sandwiches come with either chips or a half papaya – a healthful option. Olympic is a good choice for lean pocketbooks and hefty appetites.

Kapaʻa, 4-1345 Kuhio Hwy. BLD: 7am-9pm daily. Credit cards. Maps 1, 4

Ono Family Restaurant 822-1710

Ono Family Restaurant is a long-time local favorite for delicious, wholesome, and inexpensive family meals. Breakfasts and lunches (inquire about dinners) are served in a cozy dining room, with polished wooden booths, some with a removable partition to accommodate large families. Breakfasts are a favorite among local and tourist families; more than 30 egg creations are priced from $6, including 17 omelettes. Banana and macadamia nut pancakes with coconut syrup are a local legend, as are eggs benedict. Lunches are filling and tasty, with sandwiches, salads as well as steaks and fresh fish choices, including buffalo burgers ($6-$10). You may find 'Ono Ono' shave ice served in a stand out front.

Service can be slow, as each dish is cooked to order, but everyone is friendly and cooperative. Wait persons are helpful with things like crackers, straws, extra napkins, and extra cups for tastes of grown-up coffee – those etceteras of family dining that don't seem essential until they're missing. On one occasion, when we could not find our waitress to get a glass of water that had suddenly become a necessity, an adjacent Daddy passed over an

Wailua sunrise

extra. Just outside the door, two old timers shared their donuts with a wandering seven-year-old, patted his head as he chewed, and listened politely to his latest fish story.

4-1292 Kuhio Hwy (Rt 56), Kapaʻa. 822-1710. 7am - 2pm daily. Credit cards. Maps 1, 4

Ono Char Burger *822-9181*

For years, the shack at Anahola was famous among local people for delicious hamburgers and fresh fruit smoothies. As tourists heard about the hamburgers, the shack, along with its reputation, expanded. Picnic tables grew up under the tree, and the menu lengthened. Despite new owners, the burgers are still delicious, if somewhat smaller than before (from $4.15). Quarter-pounders can be made with various cheeses (even blue cheese) or teriyaki style.

Our favorites remain the 'local girl' with teriyaki, swiss cheese, and fresh pineapple, and the vegetarian sandwich. Children can order 2.5 oz hamburgers or deep fried chicken strips and fries that will make the rest of the party want to order the adult portion. Add sizzling crisp french fries, and wash it down with smoothies and ice cream shakes, floats, and freezes. Service can be slow, particularly at peak lunchtime. Be patient, pack up your sandwiches (each half will be separately wrapped) and head for beautiful Anahola Beach just a mile down Aliomanu Road.

Fishing net floats wash ashore from as far away as Japan

Anahola, Rt 56, next to Whalers Store. 822-9181. 10am – 6pm daily;
Sunday from 11am. Save time; phone in your order. Credit cards. Map 1

Pacific Island Bistro *822-0092*

Pacific Island Bistro has replaced Panda Garden, though the menu
features many of its favorite dishes, like hot, tasty duck won ton soup
($6.50), crisp spring rolls ($5), and as an entrée, piquantly flavored chicken
fried noodles ($12). Of the new 'fusion' style cuisine, pan fried opakapaka
($20) is light and flaky. The menu also includes lamb ($24) and NY steak
($19), as well as chicken ($16), Peking duck ($20), and Oriental chicken
salad ($11). White tablecloths covered with shiny glass tops are set with
blue and white china, and the white room is both cheerful and bright.
Portions are generous, the menu varied, the food tasty, and service, though
occasionally slow, politely pleasant.

Wailua, Kauai Village Center, Rt 56. 822-0092. Lunch 10:30am - 2pm
except Wed; Dinner 4 - 9:30pm daily. Credit cards. kauaibistro.com. Map 1

Papaya's *823-0190*

Papaya's is actually a full-service natural foods store. The deli offers a
wide range of organic vegetarian and vegan foods, including sandwiches and
casseroles flavored in Mexican, Cuban, Indian, Szechwan, Thai, Greek and

Italian styles, as well as tempeh, fish, or chicken burgers, 'garden lasagne,' or spanakopita ($4 to $10). Grilled tofu is excellent, as is the fresh ahi sandwich. We also love the tofu 'egg-less' salad and tempeh 'tuna' salad. You'll also find espresso, cappuccino, lattes, mochas and teas. Dine outside at tables on the patio (more accurately the walkway of the mall)

The second branch in Hanalei village has a wonderful fresh soup and salad bar, great smoothies, and sandwiches.

Wailua, Kauai Village Shopping Center (near Safeway), Kuhio Hwy (Rt 56). 823-0190. 9am - 8pm. Closed Sundays. Credit cards. Map 1

Polynesia Café 822-1945

At the northern end of Kapa'a, the new branch of Hanalei's Polynesia Café has big ambitions: 3 meals a day, including a full range of vegetarian options, and an art-venue take on décor. In the spacious dining room, tabletops are painted with colorful scenes, each a unique work by a local artist. In addition to surfboards and even a boat, paintings of Polynesian scenes hang on the walls, all available for purchase. But it's the portions you may remember; they're huge. The kitchen, staffed by a sous chef from the popular Pacific Café (now closed), prepares every meal from scratch, down to the bread baked in a bakery located in the rear. Appetizers include delicious vegetarian spring rolls, coconut shrimp, and sashimi. For an entrée, try ahi, a generous cut, and specify sauce on the side so you can enjoy a clean-grilled, delicious fish ($19). Entrées arrive with rice and vegetables. Breakfast options ($5-$10) go well beyond bacon and eggs to include items like cheese blintzes.

Northern Kapa'a, 4-1639 Kuhio Hwy. 822-1945. Breakfast 7am - 10:45am; Lunch 11am - 2:30pm; Dinner 5pm - 9:30 daily. Credit cards. Maps 1, 4

Sukothai 821-1224

Sukothai offers a larger menu than King & I or Mema – Thai-Chinese-Vietnamese, and, as if that weren't enough of a challenge for the kitchen, barbecue. The small dining room welcomes you with flowered tablecloths and flowers, and air conditioning makes dining comfortable. Most dishes cost about $8. 'Tom Kar,' or coconut and lemon grass soup, is presented in a lovely earthenware serving bowl ($8). Deep fried rice pancakes filled with minced chicken are also delicious ($8). Vegetable fried rice is colorful with vegetables ($7), and pad Thai, made with rice noodles, is excellent ($8). Don't ask to alter a dish or to modify the spicyness, as sauces are prepared in advance. Lunch specials are a bargain.

Kapaʻa Shopping Center (by Big Save), Kuhio Hwy (Rt 56). 821-1224.
10:30am - 9:30pm daily. Air-conditioned. Credit cards. Map 1

Sushi Bushido. 632-0664

At Sushi Bushido you'll find specialty rolls that are really special, like the 'Lava Roll' in which scallops, crab, and shrimp are rolled with yellowtail, cucumber, gobo, and avocado, then wrapped with fresh salmon, topped with saki aoli, and baked – truly a unique taste combination ($13). Or consider 'Sunrise roll' filled with yellow fin, tuna, yellowtail, flying fish eggs, cucumber and papaya ($11). Miso soup is richer, more intense than the usual ($2.50), and seaweed salad ($3.50) spikes the palate. Sashimi is first rate, the yellowtail like butter and the salmon fresh. Edamame is served cold with no salt, and cold tofu is spicy ($5). The only sour (sharp?) note was raw onions in the vegetable roll.

Local folks who appreciate excellent quality for a reasonable price frequent Sushi Bushido's dozen red tables with plastic garden chairs, sitting on the lanai with a distant lanai view of Kalapaki Beach. Or choose to sit at the small sushi bar inside for a closer view of the chef. Japanese beer and sake round out the meal.

Lihue, Anchor Cove Center rear. 632-0664. 11am - 10pm daily. Credit cards. Maps 1, 2

Tip Top & Sushi Katsu 245-2333

With a name that conjures up 1950's expectations (a clean room, a square meal), Tip Top still delivers after nearly 80 years. If you manage to find it on a side street in Lihue, you'll find more local people than tourists in the spartan dining room, and you'll enjoy roomy booths, comfortable air-

conditioning, and the breakfasts – delicious macadamia nut pancakes (also banana, pineapple or raisin), french toast, omelettes, or bacon and eggs, accompanied by a scoop of hash browns (most cost less than $5). Meals are well-prepared if unexcit-

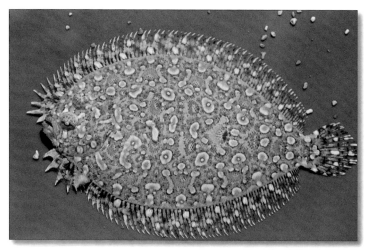

Political fish – blends in with current conditions!

ing, but homemade pineapple and guava jam is special. Have it on toast, but that's à la carte. The specialty is oxtail soup, available even at breakfast. Check out the bakery as you pay your bill for take-out treats. At lunch, try burgers, plate lunches ($6), or visit Sushi Katsu, a small sushi bar (there are only 8 seats) inside Tip Top, and sample California roll, or a spicy ahi roll, or an enormous bowl of saimin. In the evenings, you can enjoy Sushi Katsu's complete Japanese dinners at modest prices. In the motel on the second story (plain is beautiful) rooms go for about $50/night.

Tip Top is a Kauai family tradition. Breakfasts are hot, fast, and filling – perfect for those mornings when you're on the way to the airport and need every ounce of strength to get those bags through agriculture inspection and security without misplacing anything – or anybody!

Lihue, 3173 Akahi St. Tip Top: 245-2333. 6:30am - 2pm. Sushi Katsu: 246-0176. 11am - 2pm; 5:30pm - 9:30pm. Closed Mondays. Credit cards. Map 1

Tokyo Lobby *245-8989*

Tokyo Lobby is informal and comfortable, offering a wide variety of Japanese lunch choices from $5 and dinners from $12. Hibachi lemon chicken is tender, if a bit peppery, served with a rather bland miso soup, rice and a salad with coconut dressing — a reasonably priced ($13) and filling meal. Tempura is crisp though not particularly light; order it as an entrée ($13) or appetizer portion ($8). Try tasty shu mai (fried shrimp dumplings $4) or agadeshi tofu ($5) instead of overcooked edamame ($3). Vegetable roll and kappa maki were disappointingly small. On the whole, though, Tokyo Lobby is a good choice for large appetites on small budgets.

Lihue, Harbor Mall, 3501 Rice St. 245-8989. Lunch 11am – 2pm (M-F) Dinner 4:30pm – 9:30pm daily. Beer, wine, sake. Credit cards. Map 1

Wahoo's Seafood Grill & Bar . . . 822-7833

Don't be put off by the location next to a fast food joint. Wahoo's Seafood Bar and Grill offers imaginative seafood created with flavors of the Pacific Rim, some at an attractively reasonable price. Wahoo's pleasant dining room has a breezy feel, with colorful silk draped on the ceiling, shimmering like golden waves. You are actually seated on an open air porch, next to a coconut grove, or you can choose the more sheltered inside section.

The menu features seafood entrées, many elaborate (plain grilling is hard to find unless you choose the ahi sandwich, a bargain at $11). Pair the ahi sandwich with a bay shrimp salad, a small, colorful mountain of really fresh greens, shredded carrots and tasty dressing ($9), and you have a more reasonable dinner than entrées ranging around $25. Fish entrées are pre-pared with at least 4 flavors in the sauce and garnish, sometimes in combat rather than cooperation. One winner, however, is ahi luau ($25), fragrant with coconut. If you add a crab cocktail ($12), your dinner price increases to $35. Instead of an appetizer, you can request the smaller portion of delicious Maui onion soup ($5) instead of the full bowl ($9). Meateaters can choose baby back ribs ($16), prime rib ($18), or pastas ($14-$17).

At Wahoo's, you'll find generous portions, elegant and sometimes spectacular entrée presentations, some (but not all) at high prices. Choose carefully and consider having sauces served on the side.

Wailua. 733 Kuhio Hwy (Rt 56). 822-7833. Lunch 11:30am – 3pm; Dinner from 5:30 daily. Call about entertainment. Credit cards. Map 1

Wailua Marina Restaurant 822-4311

For more than 30 years, the Wailua Marina has been a local favorite for family dining, so an evening here is authentic 'Kauai.' The large dining room features an enormous mural of an underwater vista complete with stuffed fish and a turtle shell. Weather permitting, ask to sit outside on the large covered porch overlooking the Wailua River. Local ahi stuffed with crab is well seasoned and flavorful, and local ono is also tasty. Fried chicken ($14) may be more moist than teriyaki chicken, but kids love the teriyaki sauce for dipping, so order some on the side. Most entrées cost less than $18 and include rolls, rice or potato, a vegetable and salad bar. We prefer crispy french fries to fried rice, although even that's not too bad when flavored with the kitchen's justly famous teriyaki sauce.

To keep prices down, the Marina cuts a few corners, but they're the kind no one really misses if you catch the spirit of the place. Paper napkins and placemats are a small price to pay for the salad bar, which may lack imagination, but you can fill your plate with vegetables. Children can chose from ten dinners for about $3 less than adult prices. The dozen wines are not very exciting, but most cost less than $25, and you'll love the homemade pies.

Wailua River State Park, just south of the bridge on Kuhio Hwy. 822-4311. Lunch 10:30am - 2pm; Dinner 5pm - 9pm. Early Bird Special 5pm - 6pm. Closed Mondays. Credit cards. Maps 1, 3

Waipouli Deli & Restaurant 822-9311

Does this sound familiar? Your body clock is off. You're fully awake – and starving – 3 hours early. You'll never make it till lunch, but you want to spend the morning on the beach and not in some dark, air-conditioned restaurant with poky service. Well, the Waipouli Deli is for you. Generous portions of tasty food coupled with speedy delivery and unbeatable prices have made the Waipouli Deli a favorite spot on the eastside for local families and increasing numbers of tourists. It looks like formica city, so don't go expecting orchids on the table. But though short on atmosphere, it's got a 'breakfast special' ($6) deserving of the name – an egg, two slices of bacon, and two pancakes – perfect for hungry children, not to mention adults. Eggs are expertly cooked, side meats not overly fatty, and pancakes light.

On the lunch and dinner menus, you'll find bargains in American and Oriental food. Shrimp tempura ($8) includes rice and cabbage and 3 plump shrimp. Saimin is excellent ($4-$8). Service is fast, efficient, and friendly.

Wailpouli, Waipouli Town Center (behind McDonald's), Kuhio Hwy (Rt 56). 822-9311. Breakfast & Lunch 7am - 2pm (Tues - Sun). Dinner 5pm - 8:30pm (Wed - Sat). Credit cards. Map 1

Wasabi's 822-2700

Wasabi's looks like an under sea grotto, with a coral reef painted on the walls and fish painted all around you. It's a small grotto, but cozy, with only four tables (all of which may be taken when you arrive) and nine stools by a small sushi bar. Local folks like the reasonably priced sushi, Japanese à la carte items, and dinners from $13 (yakitori chicken dinner with two sushi rolls, miso soup, salad and rice). Everything is made with organic vegetables and no MSG. Service may be slow, so start with some delicious miso soup

($2.50). Bring in beer or wine from the ABC store across the street. This tiny storefront in central Kapaʻa is unpretentious and fun – sushi local style.

Kapaʻa, 1384 Kuhio Hwy (Rt 56). 822-2700. Dinner 5:30pm - 10:30pm. Closed Mondays. Call for lunch schedule. Credit cards. Maps 1, 4

Kauai in the Movies: *Golden Sand, Silver Screen*

Year	Title	Year	Title
2005	Band of Pirates	1980	Seven
	Komodo vs Cobra	1979	Last Flight of Noah's Ark
2003	Tears of the Sun	1978	Deathmoon
	Hilary Duff Birthday Bash		Acapulco Gold
2002	The Amazing Race 3	1977	Fantasy Island
	The Bachelor		Islands in the Stream
	The Time Machine	1976	King Kong
	Dragonfly	1974	Castaway Cowboy
2001	Jurassic Park III	1970	The Hawaiians
	Manhunt	1969	Lost Flight
	Moolah Beach	1968	Yoake No Futare
	The Time Machine		Lovers at Dawn
2000	War To End All Wars	1966	Lt. Robin Crusoe, U.S.N.
	Dinosaur	1965	Operation Attack
	The Testaments		None but the Brave
1998	Fantasy Island		Paradise Hawaiian Style
1997	Mighty Joe Young	1964	Gilligan's Island
	Six Days, Seven Nights	1963	Donovan's Reef
	The Lost World	1962	Diamond Head
1995	Outbreak		Sanga Ari
1994	North	1961	Blue Hawaii
1993	Jurassic Park		Seven Women from Hell
1992	Honeymoon in Vegas	1960	Wackiest Ship in the Army
1991	Hook	1959	Forbidden Island
1990	Flight of the Intruder	1958	South Pacific
	Lord of the Flies		She Gods of Shark Reef
1989	Millennium	1957	Jungle Heat
1988	Lady in White		Voodoo Island
1987	Throw Momma from the Train		Thunder Over Hawaii
1986	Islands of the Alive	1956	Between Heaven and Hell
1983	The Thorn Birds	1954	Beachhead
	Uncommon Valor		Hawaii Chindochu
	Body Heat	1953	Miss Sadie Thompson
1981	Behold Hawaii	1951	Bird of Paradise
	Raiders of the Lost Ark	1950	Pagan Love Song
		1934	White Heat

Vegetarian Adventures

Once upon a time, the best you could do on Kauai for vegetarian food was a salad bar, or in a pinch, some vegetable chow mein. Now that Kauai has entered a health-conscious age, vegetarian and natural food eateries are sprouting everywhere, including Kauai's best international 'fusion cuisine' and gourmet vegan restaurant, *Blossoming Lotus*, and Hanalei's favorite stop for gourmet organic cuisine, *Postcards Café*.

EASTSIDE: In Wailua, *Monico's* makes a sensational vegetable burrito, vegan if desired. Near Safeway, *Papaya's* (with another branch in Hanalei) offers organic groceries, fresh fruits and vegetables, and fresh prepared choices for breakfast, lunch, and dinner, including garden burgers, tempeh burgers, vegetarian sandwiches, pasta, salads, rice, and stir fry dishes. *Caffé Coco* offers tasty vegetarian/vegan dishes to take out or enjoy in its informal garden setting. In downtown Kapa'a, *Blossoming Lotus* is a must stop for wonderful vegan lunches and dinners. *Mermaids Café* has unbeatable tofu (or fish) wraps, curries, foccacia sandwiches, and organic salads for take-out. *Lotus Root* next door makes tasty vegan wraps and organic salads, organic juices, and the best chai banana frappe on Kauai. In Lihue, try *Kalapaki Beach Hut's* vegetarian sandwich, salads. Sample outstanding soups and sandwiches on fresh baked bread (Oriental sweet bread is famous) at *Deli & Bread Connection*, Kukui Grove Shopping Center (call ahead to avoid the line-up at lunch 245-7115).

NORTH SHORE, *Neidie's Salsa & Samba* turns out distinctive vegetable dishes with a Brazilian accent. Or try the soup/salad take out bar at *Papaya's* nearby. In Kilauea, try *Kilauea Farmer's Market* for soup, salads, and a great vegie sandwich. Across the street, *Kilauea Fish Market* has wonderful vegetarian wraps and salads, while around the corner, *Healthy Hut Natural Foods* has local produce, organic dairy products, dried fruits and nuts. Hungry for fruit or a smoothie? Try *Moloa'a Fruit Stand* (Rt 56 in Moloa'a) for vegetarian sushi, fresh island fruits, smoothies, frosties, and juices, including fresh sugar cane juice. *Banana Joe's* and *Mango Mama's* (Kilauea) have smoothies and local fruits, including a must-try, apple bananas.

WESTSIDE: *Hanapepe Café* serves vegetarian salads, sandwiches, and (occasionally) dinners. At *Wrangler's* in Waimea, try vegetarian sandwiches, pizzas, vegie wraps, & salads. *Grinds* has great sandwiches and salads.

PIZZERIAS are also catering to the health food crowd. *Pizza Hanalei* will make pizza with 'tofurella' cheese upon request, and a 'veggie special' pizza on whole wheat as well as white crust. In Kilauea, try *Pau Hana Pizza* for a whole variety of vegetable pizzas with excellent crust. *Brick Oven Pizza* in Kalaheo makes some of the best traditional cheese or vegetable pizza you'll ever find anywhere. In Koloa or Kapa'a, try *Pizzetta's* cheeseless vegetable pizza. In Wailua, try *Aloha Kauai Pizza* in Coconut Marketplace.

SALAD BARS: *Duke's Canoe Club* in Lihue; *Brennecke's Beach Broiler* in Poipu, *Wranglers* in Waimea; *CJ's Steak House* in Princeville. In Wailua, *The Bull Shed* and *Wailua Marina*.

Cheap Eats & 'Local Grinds'

EASTSIDE: LIHUE. *Barbecue Inn* has one of the largest, most reasonably-priced lunch and dinner menus, and it's air-conditioned. Try wonderful saimin at *Hamura's* on Kress St or *Okazu Hale* next to Ace Hardware on Rice St. *Tip Top* is a Kauai tradition for fast, hot, and filling breakfasts, and also lunches and sushi from *Sushi Katsu* inside Tip Top.

At Kukui Grove, *Deli & Bread Connection* has made delicious take-out sandwiches and tasty soups since 1988 (245-7115), or try *La Bamba* for inexpensive Mexican plates. *Quizno's* has made it to Kauai at Kukui Grove. Near Kalapaki Beach, *Kalapaki Beach Hut* makes great burgers, fresh fish sandwich, and salads. Call ahead to save the wait (246-6330). Across from Wal-Mart, *Fish Express* is a local favorite for excellent bentos, plate lunches, and poki (marinated local raw fish) (245-9918).

WAILUA: In Coconut Marketplace, *Aloha Kauai Pizza* is a family favorite, and *Fish Hut* makes great fresh fish sandwiches, tacos, wraps and dinner plates. Call ahead to save waiting time (822-1712). *Monico's* in Kinipopo Village has about the best Mexican food on Kauai (822-4300), and *Caffé Coco* (across the street) has bargain priced soups, salads, and fresh fish in a quaint garden setting.

KAPA'A now has a cluster of small eateries with real personality. *Mermaids Café* (821-2026) makes outstanding vegetarian/vegan dishes, and one of the best ahi wraps on Kauai, with a spinach tortilla, ginger infused rice and wasabi cream sauce, as well as burritos, stir fry, salads with tofu, chicken, or ahi. *Lotus Root* (823-6887) next door has tasty wraps, salads, unbeatable smoothies. *Pizetta* across the street has sandwiches, salads, and of course, pizza and calzones. *Java Kai* brews great coffee, with delicious mango cinnamon muffins, chai tea, bagels, smoothies, breakfast waffles and eggs. *Ono Family Restaurant* offers bargain-priced breakfast and lunches. Down the street, *Bubba's* serves up tasty hamburgers, fries, rings.

Further north in ANAHOLA is *Ono Char Burger*. While service can be pokey, the burgers, french fries, onion rings, and fried chicken will seem worth the wait. Call ahead (822-9181) for a beach picnic at Anahola Beach.

NORTH SHORE: KILAUEA: Near the Kong Lung Store, *Kilauea Bakery & Pau Hana Pizza* features fragrant breads, rolls, cookies and fresh baked pizza with local vegetable (828-2020). Try deli sandwiches, fresh local fruits, vegetables, and salads at *Kilauea Farmer's Market* next door (828-1512). Don't miss *Kilauea Fish Market* across the street for outstanding fresh fish sandwiches, wraps, plate lunches and dinners, and vegetarian specials (828-MAHI).

In HANALEI, *Tropical Taco* makes fresh fish burritos and other Mexican treats (827-8226; tropicaltaco.com). At *Hanalei Wake Up Café*, sample tasty home-cooked, inexpensive breakfasts and lunches daily (at times, also dinner; 826-5551). In the Ching Young Village, *Subways* turns out sandwiches from inside Big Save, and *Hanalei Mixed Plate* cook up a great ginger chicken combination plate for about $5. *Polynesia Café* has tasty Chinese/Polynesian lunch plates and wonderful ice cream. At *Pizza Hanalei* homemade crust is crispy and the cheese and toppings generous (826-9494).

Across the street, *Hanalei Gourmet* serves sandwiches on fresh-baked breads and rolls, *Bubba Burgers* fries up burgers within a reasonably short wait, and *Neidie's Salsa & Samba* makes wonderful Mexican lunches and dinners with a Brazilian accent. *Java Kai* serves hot and cold drinks, with fresh bagels, muffins, and snacks, and (pay) wireless.

On your drive to the end of the road, stop in at *Red Hot Mama's* walk-up window in Wainiha, next to the general store, for tasty, deftly seasoned Mexican treats made with local organic vegetables and beef (826-7266).

SOUTH SHORE: *Taqueria Nortenos* at Kukui'ula is a longtime local favorite for tasty, inexpensive Mexican delights (742-7222). *Pizzetta* in KOLOA will deliver excellent pizza, as well as inexpensive pastas and calzones (742-8881). Don't miss *Koloa Fish Market* (742-6199) for inexpensive, local-style plate lunches, great ahi sesame sashimi, and other (not necessarily fishy) treats. *Sueoka's* has wonderful plate lunches. In POIPU, try *Puka Dog's* 'Hawaiian style' hot dogs. A hole (*puka*) in the bun is filled with condiments, including relishes of star fruit, mango, banana, or papaya, then stuffed with your choice of sausage (742-6044; pukadog.com).

A few miles down Rt 50 in KALAHEO, *Camp House Grill* has great burgers, and for island's best pizza and delicious sandwiches, try *Brick Oven Pizza* (335-8561) nearby. *Kalaheo Coffee Company* makes deli treats and gourmet coffees (322-5868).

WESTSIDE: Check out *Grinds* in Ele'ele for coffees, breakfast, fresh-baked treats, and deli lunches (335-6027), or *Toi's Thai Kitchen* for saimin and hamburgers. In WAIMEA, it's *Wrangler's* for sandwiches, plate lunches, salad bar, hamburgers, as well as pizza and calzones (338-1218).

View from Bali Hai Restaurant

North Shore Restaurants

'favor...eats'

Perched on the ocean bluff, some restaurants in PRINCEVILLE have unforgettable ocean views. From *Bali Hai Restaurant*, you can watch the sun set over Hanalei Bay, and the view from the restaurants at the Princeville Hotel, *La Cascata* and *Café Hanalei*, is simply breathtaking. Try *Café Hanalei's* breakfast buffet, lunches, or sunset dinners, or come for tea or sunset cocktails at *The Living Room*, the hotel lounge overlooking the bay, and listen to Kauai's talented musicians play. Come early, enjoy the sunset, and bring your camera.

In nearby HANALEI, *Postcards Café* takes healthful, organic foods into a whole new dimension, with wonderful pastas and delicious fresh island fish. At *Neidie's Salsa & Samba*, tasty Mexican lunches and dinners have a Brazilian flair and unbelievable prices. A favorite lunch and dinner spot for fresh island fish is the *Hanalei Dolphin*.

Red Hot Mama's in Wainiha is a great stop for inexpensive carry out on your trip to the end of the road. In Hanalei's Ching Young Village, try *Hanalei Mixed Plate* for kalua pork many folks rave about, *Pizza Hanalei's* homemade whole wheat crust, or *Polynesia Café's* sandwiches. Across the street, *Bubba Burgers* offers hamburgers, and *Hanalei Gourmet* next door makes deli sandwiches. Down the street, *Tropical Taco* creates wonderful Mexican treats. After lunch, try shave ice at *Wishing Well* in the silver trailer near Kayak Kauai. Nearby, *Princeville Golf Course Restaurant* has salads and sandwiches in a beautiful, relaxed setting.

In KILAUEA, *Pau Hana Pizza* serves imaginative, home-baked pizza, soups, and bakery treats. Just around the corner, *Kilauea Farmers' Market* makes first-rate deli sandwiches, soups, and vegetarian delights. For some of the best local fresh fish (and vegetarian) wraps, sandwiches, burritos, as well as salads with home made dressings, you can't beat newcomer *Kilauea Fish Market*. Worth a postcard home! Map 5

Bali Hai 826-6522

Imagine dining as the sunset paints the sky all gold and orange above the magnificent angles of the dark and mysterious mountains, turning the ocean almost purple in Hanalei Bay. Sip a cocktail while the cool evening breeze, fragrant with tropical flowers, touches your skin like silk. At the Bali Hai Restaurant, you can find the Kauai of your imagination, the dream of an island paradise that haunts you in the dead of winter.

The dining experience could not be more relaxing, the food brought at a leisurely pace by polite waiters and served at large, elegantly appointed tables on china painted in colors of the sea. Open to the air on three sides, the dining room's tall ceilings and two-tiered arrangement of tables make the room spacious and, even when full, remarkably quiet

Bali Hai's Pacific Rim cuisine features fresh fish ($29-$32) in five styles: 'Ha'ena Hanapa'a' (with crab, cheese and portobello mushroom), 'Rock Jumping Fisherman' (Thai style, with coconut sauce), 'Pele Goddess of Fire' (blackened), 'Bali Hai Sunset' (sautéed with papaya ginger glaze), or 'Tropical Breeze' (grilled with fruit salsa). We prefer the fresh fish plainly grilled, though we enjoyed these sauces served on the side for a quick dip.

Entrées are expensive, from linguine with chicken ($22) to lobster pasta ($38) and are accompanied only by a vegetable and 'starch of the day.' Appetizers drive up the dinner price, though they are appealing, like blackened seared ahi with cabbage and wasabi cream, or crab cakes with curry corn sauce ($13).

Bali Hai has a wonderfully romantic ambiance and unmatched view. Before dinner, listen to some of Kauai's favorite musicians, like Norman Solomon, play nightly at *Happy Talk Lounge* next door (See *Kauai Music*,

128), or enjoy a pleasant evening stroll. Head towards the cliff along the sidewalk between the tennis courts. From path's end, you can look down at Hanalei Bay, sparkling with beads of light and turning deep purple as the sun descends. The dark craggy edges of the cliffs blend into soft purples and deep blues as the gold and orange sun sinks slowly towards the water, shining more brightly with each second, until flattened into a disk that shrinks to nothing before your eyes. A golden glow remains, burnishing the clouds, polishing the water, fading to a darkening dusk.

Princeville, Hanalei Bay Resort. Reservations: 826-6522. Breakfast 7am - 11am; Lunch 11:30am - 2pm; Dinner 5:30pm - 9:30pm. Children's menu. Enter Princeville at the main gate, take the third left onto Liholiho Rd, then turn right onto Hono'iki Rd. Credit cards. Map 5

Bar Acuda *826-1177*

Bar Acuda, a tapas-style restaurant in Hanalei, is a combination wine-bar and kitchen serving 'small plates.' This Hanalei location has yet to support a successful restaurant, perhaps because it has always been difficult, given inexpensive eateries nearby, to cover the cost of delivering fine ingredients to the north shore and a labor market which might just decide to head out when the next swell moves in.

Bar Acuda's small plates concept may be a workable compromise between high-end tasty food and the small portions which can be priced reasonably enough to attract visitors looking for an informal nite spot at the end of a hard day of vacationing. It is certainly pleasant to sit on the outer porch lit with lanterns, or inside the small dining room, and enjoy mellow music or jazz. If the mosquitoes start to view you as another small plate, ask for bug repellent.

The menu has a Mediterranean flavor, the creation of chef-owner Jim Moffatt. Try a small, tasty pizzetta ($11), tomato bruschetta with leeks and balsamic vinegar ($8). Consider Humbolt fog goat cheese served with Marshall Farm honeycomb and pear ($14), or a tasty beet and endive salad, more interesting than a rather bland Spanish tortilla ($8). A side of polenta ($6) which our vegetarian spotted on the menu with the braised beef short ribs, was also delicious. Hungrier diners can order full portion entrées from $21 (chicken) to $26 (whole roast pork loin).

Bar Acuda is a good choice for informal dining on those night your appetite is too tired to face a long, or a heavy, meal. It's interesting and fun.

Hanalei. 826-1177. Dinner from 6pm. Closed Mondays. restaurantbaracuda. com. Credit cards. Map 5

Bubba Burgers

Bubba's began life on Kauai on main street, Kapa'a, and is still there, though in larger quarters because the prices (most less than $7) and the burger menu have made Bubba's very poplar. The Hanalei Bubba's is also jammed. Kids will like the "frings" (fries topped off with a couple of onion rings). Burgers range from single to a triple patty (a half pound), to the 'Slopper' (with chili), or choose Budweiser chili or hot dogs. Looking for a healthy lunch? There are now tempeh burgers for vegetarians, who can also visit Papaya's soup and salad bar next door. Picnic tables available for all.

View from the Bali Hai Restaurant

Kapa'a and Hanalei. 823-0069. 10:30am - 6pm daily. Kapa'a location closed Sundays. Cash only. Maps 4 & 5

Café Hanalei, Princeville Resort . . . 826-9644

You could not imagine a more spectacular spot for breakfast than Café Hanalei, with its panoramic view of a bay that in any weather has the romantic beauty of a fairy tale. Even in the rain, you can watch the mountains peek out from veils of mist like shy princesses. Or watch as the sun's sorcery transforms the landscape from smoky greys into blazing colors – vivid greens and golds, brilliant blues, and on the mountains rising majestically above the bay, the shining silver ribbons of waterfalls. In this land of enchantment, each moment reveals a new mystery, and under the spell of such beauty, you could enjoy breakfast with only a chair!

The breakfast buffet will draw you indoors, a generous array of fruits, juices, and fresh baked pastries, blintzes with sour cream, even an omelette bar where your eggs can be whipped into a unique and tasty creation. The

View from the terrace, Princeville Hotel

breakfast buffet ($28 or $21 for a 'continental' buffet) combines an incomparable setting with delicious food and friendly, polite service. Where else could you find such radiance in the rain?

At dinner, the setting sun kindles the sky to flame in orange and turquoise behind the darkening cliffs. Visit the lounge, appropriately called the 'Living Room' first, and enjoy a cocktail while you relax on one of the plush couches in the elegant room. But who can stay inside at sunset? Outside, the terrace is enclosed by waist high panels of glass, so that you can enjoy the spectacular panorama of Hanalei Bay without a railing to obstruct your view. Boats glide silently; the only sound is the soft music of the waves. Mountains are shrouded in clouds, and the sky turns to gold as the sun slips slowly into the sea, while colors deepen the reflections in tall glass windowpanes. As Hanalei Bay recedes into the velvet darkness and the first stars appear, walk downstairs to Café Hanalei, where tall windows mirror dozens of dancing candle flames. Tables generously spaced are laid with elegant china and sparkling crystal and silver.

All this romance is expensive. Twelve entrées, priced above $33, reflect the flavors of the Pacific Rim. Try fresh island opakapaka presented like a stir fry, with shiitake mushrooms and Hawaiian sweet potatoes ($36), very moist and tasty. The least expensive entrée is chicken ($33). The price of dinner goes up quickly with appetizers like spinach salad with fresh shrimp and lobster ($13) or crispy crab cake ($15).

At lunch, we found fresh ahi sandwich ($12) to be generous and tasty with dill mayo, if somewhat overcooked. Tuna sandwich ($7.50) on wheat bread was a better choice. Both arrived with hot, crisp french fries. Clam chowder would have been better with more clams and fewer potatoes. But the view at lunch is wonderful. Special menus include the Friday night Seafood Buffet, an island tradition. Sunday Brunch is a sumptuous feast of hot and cold fish, chicken and meat dishes; egg dishes including omelettes; and tried and true favorites like pancakes, waffles, and blintzes. You'll find sushi and sashimi, as well as lots of fresh fruits, pastries, and desserts.

At Café Hanalei, the presentation is attractive, and the service friendly and professional. The best part of a wonderful dining experience remains the setting, which is spectacular enough to make dinner unforgettable. Walk around the hotel afterwards, take the elevator down to the beach and listen to the music of the waves and the melodies in the evening breezes.

Princeville, Princeville Resort Hotel. 826-9644. 6:30am - 9pm daily. Sunday Brunch ($53). Breakfast buffet ($28/$21 continental). Friday Seafood Buffet ($65). Children's buffet prices are calculated by age. Credit cards. Enter Princeville's main gate and stay on this road until it ends. Map 5

C J's Steak House. 826-6211

C J's Steak House replaces the popular Chuck's Steak House, giving it a fresher look while retaining the steak and salad bar menu that made Chuck's a local favorite. Dinners range from $23 (chicken breasts) to $30 (14oz prime rib), including rice, warm bread, and the salad bar. Request pacing the dinner, or your entrée may arrive when you've barely finished your salad. Dinners are reliably well-prepared. New York steak ($30/12 oz) has great flavor and is very tender (ask for teriyaki sauce). Fresh fish is moist and cleanly sautéed ($27). Wines are fairly priced.

Dinners at C J's will be reasonably priced and reasonably good. On the other hand, you don't get anything special either, in food or ambiance. C J's offers no views of Hanalei's magnificent mountains or valleys to paint a memory for dark winter evenings back home.

Princeville Center, Rt 56. 826-6211. Lunch 11:30am- 2:30pm (M-F); Dinner 6pm- 9:30pm daily. Keiki dinners from $10. Credit cards. Map 5

Hanalei Dolphin 826-6113

For years, the Dolphin has had the reputation of serving wonderful fresh fish in an informal setting. The menu hasn't changed much over the years, and neither has the no-reservations policy, which can start your meal off with an irritating wait. Service, though often friendly, can at time be harried, as the small restaurant is almost always crowded. Choose a weeknight and arrive before 7pm for your best shot at a quick seating. If there's a line, you can order wine and appetizers on the porch.

In the softly lit dining room, shutters are raised to let in evening breezes, and lanterns glow pleasantly on polished table tops. The menu features locally caught fresh fish with rice or hot, crispy steak fries. Depending on the season, you may find opah or moonfish, a sensationally light mon chung, as well the familiar ahi and ono.

Two and sometimes three chefs alternate during the week, and so the cooking inevitably varies – sometimes excellent, sometimes needing more (or less!) doneness. On our last visit, the mahi mahi ($26 for an 8 oz filet) was moist, tender, and flaky – cleanly broiled, with no taste of the grill. Ahi teriyaki ($26 for an 8 oz portion) is one of the most delicious fish dinners on Kauai – juicy, tender, and full of spark. Non-fishy eaters can try 'Hawaiian' chicken ($21) or NY steak ($26/12oz.).

Dinners include fresh hot bread, pasta, rice, or vegetable brochette, and Dolphin's signature 'family style salad,' a huge bowl of lettuce, cherry tomatoes, bean sprouts, and choice of oil and vinegar, or creamy garlic or Russian dressings (and you can request seconds).

Not so hungry? Several entrées are available in 'menehune' portion for about 40% discount, or you can choose from three 'light dinners' (like seafood chowder ($19) or broccoli casserole ($22) served with salad, rice or french fries, and bread.

The wine list offers good choices in the $25-$40 range, like a Kendall Jackson chardonnay. We were sad to discover that an old friend on the list – the bottle of Chateau Lafitte Rothschild, which had survived Hurricane 'Iwa in 1982 even when the roof did not – was no longer available for $200. Suddenly, we felt older.

You can try Dolphin's fresh fish for lunch – a terrific ono or ahi sandwich ($12), steak burgers, chicken and vegetable sandwiches, and wonderful fish & chips made with swordfish – light, crisp, and flaky ($11). Dine at picnic tables next to the Hanalei River, or stop in at the Dolphin's fish market tucked behind the restaurant and cook your filet at home.

The Dolphin has been a local favorite for years. The riverside setting can be pleasant. If mosquitoes tend to pick on you, bring Off and ask for a mosquito coil, for there are no screens. The fish is usually delicious, though warn the waiter that any overcooked fish will be thrown back, if not into the ocean, at least onto his tray!

Hanalei, on Rt 560, just past Princeville and the one-lane bridge over the river. 826-6113. No reservations. 11am - 10pm. Children's dinners: chicken, steak, or shrimp. hanaleidolphin.com. Credit cards. Map 5

The Hanalei Gourmet 826-2524

On your way to the beach at Hanalei, you need a first rate deli to pick up sandwiches for picnics on the sand. The Hanalei Gourmet in the old Hanalei schoolhouse features home-baked breads and pastries, deli meats and salads, fine cheeses, soups, and a selection of gourmet foods and wines. Insulated backpacks are available for picnics. Order a sandwich ($7- $9) at the deli counter, phone ahead, or take a table in the 'classroom' next door, converted into an attractive café cum bar for those who would prefer to avoid the sand altogether. In this 'tropical bar,' you'll find a large surprisingly large assortment of entrées ranging in price from $11 to $23, including pastas, salads, as well as chicken, fish, and steak. Try Big Tim's hamburger (1/3 pound for $9) or fresh ahi sandwich ($10). Early bird dinners are from 5:30pm - 6:30pm.

Hanalei Center. 826-2524. 8am – 10:30pm daily. Picnic baskets. Kauai's musical entertainers play nitely. Credit cards. hanaleigourmet.net. Map 5

Kalypso's 826-9700

Kalypso's is the new face of Zelo's, but offers pretty much the same menu of well-prepared meals at reasonable prices, with most sandwiches, burgers, and salads around $12 and most full sized entrées $17 - $25. A

Hanalei Valley's fields of taro

favorite from the Zelo's menu, specialty fish chowder ($8) is thick, creamy and tasty. Hamburgers (from $9) are excellent, served on a sesame seed bun with fries. Other choices include wraps, salads, fish tacos, and sandwiches. Fish & chips are made with fresh island catch, and fish tacos with ahi ($14). Dinners entrées range from pasta ($15) to NY steak ($24) and include only a small vegetable. To add a salad, like a 'lite' Caesar, will cost $6 more; a tasty waldorf salad with apples, blue cheese, and nuts adds $14. Macadamia crusted fresh mahi mahi is moist, tender, and flavorful with a lilikoi sauce and rice, reasonably priced at $20. With its full bar and espresso machine, Kalypso's is equipped to provide you with almost any beverage you desire.

The dining room is clean, cheerful, and comfortable, with the ceiling open to the rafters and doors open to the outside. Service is sometimes friendly and efficient, sometimes not. Given the reasonable prices and main street location, it's often crowded. Expect to wait on line if you come at peak mealtimes, so go early if you plan to take the kids.

Hanalei. 826-9700. 11am - 10:30pm daily. Entertainment some evenings. Credit cards. Map 5

Kilauea Bakery & Pau Hana Pizza 828-2020

The small bakery behind Kong Lung has tasty soups, delicious sand-wiches, and inspired pizzas, as well as crusty breads (Hanalei poi sourdough, sun dried tomato, or tasty molasses loaf), cookies (including wonderful macaroons), and macadamia nut sticky buns. Order pizza whole or by the slice; all are amazingly light and tasty. Try cheeseless vegetable calzones ($8) or wheat bread rolled in spinach and tomato spollenas ($8). Soups change daily. Mulligatawny is a tasty soup flavored with mango, coconut, and curry, bright without being sharp. Pizza may combine goat cheese, sun dried tomatoes, and eggplant, or perhaps be made with feta cheese (or even tofurella), olives, zucchini, fresh mushrooms, and tomato slices. Sometimes available, smoked fresh fish makes for a great combo with vegetables on the Billie Holiday pizza. Try organic coffee, chai lattes (powdered variety), and fruit smoothies. Eat at a half-dozen tables inside, or outside at patio tables with umbrellas to protect you from the sun as well as the sudden showers that can threaten to dampen your lunch.

Kilauea, Kong Lung Center, on the Lighthouse Road. 828-2020. 6:30am to 9pm; pizza from 11am. Credit cards. Order ahead to avoid the wait. Map 5

Kilauea Fish Market *828-MAHI*

On the back corner of the old plantation stone building, the Kilauea Fish Market is just large enough to fit a counter, a shining refrigerated case, and a lively cooking area behind it which houses the grill and stove, where four sauté pans may be sizzling merrily with fresh ahi, or mahi, or even opakapaka for the signature fat, juicy wraps. Local fishermen keep the chef-owner supplied with fresh snappers and tuna (even when most restaurants have to make do with ahi). She uses the freshest organic greens, bright red tomatoes and peppers, and orange sun dried tomato burritos for her wraps. Fresh fish wrap ($10) is bargain priced for the size, stuffed with fish, choice of brown or white rice, lots of vegetables, and one of her special sauces. Tip: Ask to have the sauce packaged in a separate container to keep the wrap dry on the way to the beach, and to have the halves wrapped separately.

Grilled mahi mahi sandwich or teriyaki sandwich are served on a round toasted roll with Maui onions, tomatoes, cilantro, scallions, organic greens, and a home-made creamy oriental dressing. The spicier fajita burrito blends pinto beans, brown rice, fresh tomato salsa, cheddar, sour cream, and organic greens with ahi or tofu. Vegetarians can choose a delicious wrap stuffed with tofu and vegetables, or an organic greens salad ($7 each).

best in local fish!

Looking for an inexpensive, tasty dinner? Try chicken and beef barbecue or teriyaki plates, kalbi beef ribs plate ($9) or the fresh fish filets, ahi poki, or even the corn fed beef steaks displayed temptingly in the case. The kids'

At sunset, an outrigger canoe glides silently across Hanalei Bay

menu is only $5. Eat outside at patio tables (kids can play and run around), or take your meal to your hotel. On Saturdays the Kilauea Farmer's Market is just down the road, so you can stop for lunch after you go marketing.

Everything is cooked to order, so be patient because Kilauea fish market is a must stop on the north shore.

Kilauea, 4270 Lighthouse Road, on the left almost opposite Kong Lung. 828-MAHI. 11am - 8pm. Closed Sundays. Credit cards. Map 5

La Cascata, Princeville Resort 826-9644

A sunset dinner at La Cascata can be one of your memorable island experiences. As you enter Princeville Hotel's spectacular lobby, where giant windows along the western wall appear seamless, you can see the spectacular colors of the cliffs beyond Hanalei Bay. In this wonderful spot is a beautiful lounge, called 'The Living Room,' where you can enjoy a glass of wine or a cocktail (or in the afternoons, afternoon tea and scones). Comfortable sofas invite you to relax with live music. Or step outside to the terrace and look out over Hanalei Bay, glistening in sunset's gold and orange.

One level below the Living Room is La Cascata, with an equally dramatic and panoramic view of Hanalei Bay. At sunset, you can watch the sky break in brilliant gold and orange waves across the mountains, so bring your camera. In the dining room, the soft golden terra cotta color of the walls blends with quarry tile floors to create an informal, comfortable ambiance. Tables widely spaced for privacy are set among arches, with picturesque looking chips in the plaster and water stains which are, we suspect, authentic souvenirs of Hurricane Iniki. Murals provide scenes of Italian landscapes. Candle lamps cast flickering golden light on the tables.

One chef and one kitchen serve both La Cascata and Café Hanalei, so you can order from either menu at either dining room at comparable prices. The menu features Italian specialities. Dinner can begin with a salad ($14) or fresh pastas (from $16). Entrées include at least two fresh island fish, perhaps pan sautéed snapper ($38) or beautifully grilled fresh ahi ($40). The chef prepared a very fresh special vegetable salad for our vegetarian. A prix fixe dinner ($65) includes 3 courses, coffee, cappuccino, or espresso. Service is polite, professional, and engaging. Do noodles leave your children cold? They may order a cheeseburger or grilled cheese sandwich from Café Hanalei. Not sure about a wine selection? You may be offered a taste before choosing from the extensive, and expensive, list.

At La Cascata, the food is not exceptional. But the setting truly is, and taken together, they can make a magical evening. When planning your dinner, try to set the time for sunset, when the dining experience is gilded with spectacular colors, particularly in summer when the angle of the sun allows it to sink right into the sea before your eyes. After dinner, stroll around the hotel and take the elevator down to the beach to watch moonlight sparkle on the waves.

Princeville, Princeville Resort Hotel. 826-9644. Dinner nightly 6pm - 9:30pm. Enter Princeville main gate and follow the road to the end. Reservations recommended. Credit cards. princevillehotelhawaii.com. Map 5

Lighthouse Bistro Restaurant . . 828-0480

Italian cuisine with local ingredients is the specialty here, served in an informal, open air setting. The attractive grey and white dining room has sliding glass doors that open to evening breezes, and a spare decor that, in candlelight, has its own charm. The menu features fresh fish ($26), steaks ($24-$35), chicken, and pasta (from $13) accompanied by rice, vegetable, and a small bread loaf. To add a green salad boosts your dinner cost ($7). In the past, we have found sauces to be on the strong side, and so we ordered our onaga plainly sautéed rather than ginger crusted. It arrived overcooked, a problem cheerfully remedied by the kitchen. The vegetarian dish, polenta tower, was also over-cooked. Really hungry? Try the all-you-can-eat pasta bar ($14); one visit (plus dinner salad) is only $16.

The 30 or so wines are mostly reasonably priced (Rosemount shiraz $21), though you might try a flavored martini ($7) like 'pineapple upside down cake' (vanilla and pineapple vodkas with fresh fruit juice). Delicious! Service is friendly and mostly efficient. Try excellent sandwiches ($7-$12).

Kilauea, Kong Lung Center, on the Lighthouse Road. 828-0480. Lunch & Dinner 11am - 9:30pm daily. Children's menu. Credit cards. Map 5

Mediterranean Gourmet. 826-9875

Mediterranean Gourmet serves a limited menu in a pleasant beachfront location in Ha'ena. Wood tables and comfortable rattan chairs face the ocean; fly fans encourage breezes and windows open to views of kite surfing on the breezy point. In this kitchen, garlic is a favorite. Hummus has a real bite, and we ended up sending ours back for a double portion of excellent tabbouleh ($13). Greek salad has lots of olives, feta, and tasty dressing; we ordered ours with a first rate piece of fresh ahi, cooked to perfect pinkness (ahi can also be seared) adding $8 to the salad price ($11). Service is pleasant and the setting relaxing. You can also order a take-out picnic lunch.

Ha'ena, Hanalei Colony Resort. 826-9875. Dinner 4pm - 8pm M - Sat; Lunch 11am - 4pm daily. Credit cards. Full bar. Map 5

Neidie's Salsa & Samba 826-1851

On a back porch in Hanalei, with only a tiny sign out front, you will find a slight woman cooking in a tiny kitchen just across a counter from a half dozen tables. Don't be fooled by appearances. Neidie makes magic in there, deftly blending Brazilian spices with Kauai's fresh vegetables and fruits. You may have to wait for one of these tables inside or on the porch outside. There are only ten, and they are usually full.

The reason is a combination of great food and great prices. Home-made chips and delicious fresh salsa start the meal, but save room for Neidie's wonderful Brazilian cooking. She weaves Kauai's fresh fruits, vegetables, and fish into recipes from her homeland. Local fish is cleanly grilled and tasty, with a delicious coconut milk sauce, served on a large platter with Brazilian rice and vegetable – at only $15, one of the best bargains on Kauai. Or try a vegetarian pancake with fresh pumpkin, tropical squash and whatever vegetables have tempted Neidie at the market ($9). Demand for Neidie's pumpkin pancake has shifted a neighboring farmer into hyperdrive to keep her supplied. Service may be on the slow side but for the right reason – Neidie cooks everything to order. Spicing is subtle rather than flashy, so if it's not hot enough for your taste, you can add as many chiles as you want. Prices are amazing considering the size of the portions. You can order some of her magic 'to go' and enjoy a picnic at the beach.

For delicious, carefully spiced and imaginative Brazilian dishes served with a pleasant, personal touch, don't miss Neidie's!

Hanalei. 826-1851. Lunch 11am - 3pm; Dinner 5pm - 9pm daily. Credit cards. Map 5

Postcards Café 826-1191

As you round the bend in the winding road into Hanalei, you'll see Postcards Café in the green Hanalei Museum. Despite its modest exterior, Postcards surprises you with a carefully crafted dining experience, an interesting, thoughtful cuisine served in a comfortably informal atmosphere. You enter Postcards from a small porch. Inside, you'll find an intimate dining room with open beamed ceilings and soft lighting that makes everything look at once clean and relaxing. Vintage Hawaiian postcards appear under glass table tops and in collages on the walls, along with black and white photographs of old Hanalei, even old-time ukuleles.

Dinner is café-style informal. Tables in this charming plantation cottage are set without linens, and windows, with the modern addition of screens, slide open for evening breezes, or close for occasional showers. The cuisine is exceptional, both in concept and execution, and everything is generous and fresh, prepared without meat, poultry, or chemicals. Taro fritters ($9) make a wonderful appetizer, the small patties deep-fried and served with a tangy home-made mango chutney. In salmon rockets ($10), tender slices of salmon are rolled in layers of lumpia and nori and quick fried. Summer rolls ($9) are delicious, as is homemade soup.

The dinner menu is small, only seven entrées featuring locally grown vegetables and fresh island fish. Least expensive are pasta primavera or a Chinese vegetable dish with roasted tofu and a tamari ginger sauce ($15). Fresh ono was cleanly cooked, moist, flavorful and flaky, and although we sampled all four sauces on the menu and enjoyed each unique flavor – particularly the coconut – we preferred the fish cleanly grilled. Of the three pasta choices, two vegetarian, we liked 'Seafood Sorrento,' a delicious combination of shrimp with medallions of all four fresh fish on the menu, gently seasoned in a sauce of mushrooms, tomatoes, bell peppers, and as requested, only light on garlic ($22). The portion was so generous that our son raved about the leftovers the next day. Children can choose pasta or quesadilla ($8). If you can't decide, the kitchen is ready to prepare your request, or you can opt for a beautiful local salad ($8 or $5).

deliciously healthy

Desserts, made without refined sugar, are elegant and delicious. Lilikoi mousse arrives in a lovely colored tumbler, and vegan chocolate silk is amazingly light for its dense chocolate flavor, or try coconut sorbet (all $7). The wine list is small, though well-selected, and includes some delicious organic wines, or you can try organic smoothies and juices ($5), or organic Kona coffee ($3).

Waitpersons are friendly, following the example of the owners who circulate among the guests, stopping to chat and give sound vacation advice to diners whom they treat as guests.

Postcards Café is a must stop on the north shore for an imaginative cuisine served in an attractive, comfortably informal dining room. If you aren't a vegetarian, Postcards might change your mind.

Hanalei. 826-1191. Dinner 6pm - 9pm daily. Reserve at least a day in advance. Credit cards. postcardscafe.com. Map 5

Princeville Restaurant *826-5050*

With a spectacular panoramic setting amid mountains, rolling fairways, and ocean, the clubhouse restaurant at the Prince Course is a great spot for a surprisingly inexpensive lunch or breakfast. The entry is all glass, and through enormous windows you can see all the way to the horizon as you walk downstairs, past the glass enclosed health club, to the dining room.

The menu is small, offering fewer than a dozen sandwiches and salads priced around $9, but portions are generous and the choices well-prepared. The vegetarian sandwich ($10) is stuffed with carrots, lettuce and sprouts, and accompanied by first-rate, crispy french fries.

Or try tangy Chinese chicken salad, filled with crunchy vegetables and a tender grilled chicken breast. Ask for homemade papaya seed dressing. Fresh ahi salad is moist, cleanly grilled, and generous ($12). There's a full bar, or try smoothies and juice mixes ($6).

Princeville Restaurant offers an incredible view, pleasant servers, and tasty and generous portions. For the price, it's hard to find a more reasonable slice of ocean on seven grain bread.

Just east of Princeville on Rt 56. 826-5050. Breakfast 7-11am; Lunch 11-3pm daily. Sushi menu M & F nites. Air-conditioned. Credit cards. Map 5

Red Hot Mama's 826-7266

Tucked up next to the Wainiha General Store is a tiny take out window which advertises the best Mex on the north shore (since Neidie's is Brazilian, we agree!). 'The Big Mama' is truly stuffed — brown or white rice, sour cream, beans, chicken or tofu, maybe even fresh fish, or sliced steak, all wrapped in a generous sun dried tomato burrito. Your choice can be small or 'big mamma' size. Kids can have a PBJ burrito. Owners Jason and Melissa want to support local organic farmers, so greens and herbs are always local and organic. They use brown rice and natural grass-fed beef. Fish tacos are in the works, as is breakfast. Each burrito and taco is made to order, so be prepared to be patient if someone is ahead of you on line. It's well worth the wait.

Wainiha. 826-7266. 11am - 5pm. Closed Sundays. Cash only. Map 5

Sushi & Blues 826-9701

On the second floor of Ching Young Village, Sushi & Blues is a happening place. The sushi bar takes up only a fraction of the space, and the signature elements are music (local musicians perform here) and camaraderie. For decor, Sushi & Blues aims for industrial chic, with a silver ventilation system on the black ceiling as part of the decor.

The menu features sushi and pupus, as well as a half dozen dinners (from $20 for teriyaki chicken) which include a first rate miso soup, stir-fry vegetables and either rice, wasabi potatoes, or half a California roll. Appetizers give guests a 'small plate' option, and a new chef is adding more variety, including a fresh fish dinner of the day. The sushi bar offers 22 specialty rolls. Prices are at the upper end of the island sushi scale, though hand rolls are generously thick. Live music at 9pm. Dancing on weekends.

Hanalei, Ching Young Village. 826-9701. Dinner from 5:30pm daily. Full bar. Call about entertainment. Credit cards. sushiandblues.com. Map 5

South Shore Restaurants

'favor..eats'

In Poipu, for a spectacular oceanfront setting, particularly at sunset, try the *Beach House Restaurant* near Spouting Horn. *Roy's Poipu Bar & Grill* features the signature Euro/Asian cuisine of Roy Yamaguchi in a busy-almost-frenetic bistro setting, with inventive dishes you will find nowhere else on the island. Roy's is a must stop for Pacific Rim cuisine. Next door at *Keoki's*, families and hearty eaters can enjoy generous steak and seafood dinners at reasonable prices. For pasta and fresh local fish in one of Kauai's most romantic garden settings, try *Plantation Gardens*. Or visit *Casablanca's* informal garden setting at the Kiahuna Tennis Club.

Wherever you dine, stroll through the beautiful *Grand Hyatt Resort* afterwards, a treat which can be yours for the modest cost of the tip for the valet who parks your car. Enjoy Hawaiian melodies at the Seaview Lounge overlooking the gardens and ocean, or stop in at Stevenson's Library for an after dinner drink or game of billiards, or simply stroll the hotel's lovely grounds. Dinner at *Tidepools*, while expensive, offers you excellent steak and fresh island fish.

On a budget? Try generous breakfasts and lunches at *Joe's on the Green* in the Kiahuna Golf Course clubhouse, and Mexican take-out from *Taqueria Nortenos*, Kukui'ula Center, on the road to Poipu. Don't miss the *Koloa Fish Market* for tasty plate lunches and some of the best ahi sesame you will find

– at bargain prices. But don't stay in Poipu. Take a short drive to Kalaheo for wonderful, reasonably priced restaurants – *Kalaheo Coffee Company* for deli treats, *Brick Oven Pizza*, a family favorite for the island's best pizza, or *Camp House Grill* for outstanding hamburgers, sandwiches, and the-real-thing milk shakes made in a gleaming milk shake machine. *Pomodoro*, an intimate, family-owned Italian restaurant, offers a carefully prepared cuisine and the professional service you'd expect at higher prices.

The Beach House Restaurant. . . 742-1424

A longtime favorite of both residents and visitors, the Beach House once perched on a sea wall only inches from the waves, a great spot to watch the sun set into the ocean and enjoy dinner in a relaxed and casual setting. In fact, the tables were so close to the waves that when Hurricane 'Iwa struck Kauai in 1982, the entire restaurant was swept out to sea – leaving only the concrete slab to mark the spot where so many evenings had passed so pleasantly. Rebuilt at a more respectful distance from the waves, Beach House was again destroyed by Hurricane Iniki, and then re-opened once more in the same location, clearly hoping the third time is the charm.

The two-tiered dining room has sweeping ocean views, and is beautifully detailed with paintings and elegant table dressings. The menu features flavors of the Pacific Rim. Appetizers arrive with a basket of delicious bread. Salad with fresh local asparagus, tomatoes, and goat cheese ($9) is tasty (though no longer made with Kauai's special white asparagus), as is wild mushroom gnocci served with organic greens and smoked salmon ($9). A small dinner salad of greens from nearby Omao is fresh and colorful with a light sesame and orange vinaigrette ($6). Entrées, particularly fresh local fish, are delicious, like fire roasted fresh ahi, both flaky and tender ($27), or macadamia nut mahi mahi served with a delicious citrus miso sauce and accompanied by stir fried vegetables. The menu also features steak, salmon, and rack of lamb ($29), as well as chicken ($23) and seafood, with entrée prices averaging $24, although two could make a light meal of several appetizers.

romantic spot for sunset dining!

The setting is truly lovely. Tables are well-separated, and sliding glass doors open to the evening air and spectacular views of surfers catching waves as the sun sets into the shimmering sea. It's beautiful even after dark, as the last light of sunset fades, and you can linger over coffee and watch the waves begin to glisten with moonlight. It's such a special spot that you might emphasize to your server to *slow* the dinner pace, so you can take time to enjoy nature's splendor. Servers have been known to try to hasten the departure of diners, so sit firm and hint at a large tip.

Poipu, on Spouting Horn Rd. 742-1424. Reserve at least a day in advance. Request a window table, but be prepared to wait (maybe a half hour) for it. Credit cards. 5:30pm - 10pm nightly. the-beach-house.com. Map 6

Brennecke's Beach Broiler *742-1424*

For almost twenty years, Brennecke's has served tasty, reasonably-priced dinners for the whole family, with a varied menu, a first-rate salad bar and friendly, efficient service. It's second-storey perch gives you a bird's eye

Kauai's cardinals can have red heads

view of Poipu Beach Park across the street, and in its informal open air dining room, you'll feel comfortable no matter what you're wearing. The decor looks very plain – a porch in soft grey and white tones – but everything is clean, the paint fresh looking, the chairs and grey formica tables immaculate, even the flowers in the window boxes bright and cheerful.

The food receives equal attention to detail. Clam chowder ($4/cup) is creamy rather than thick, generous with clams, and well seasoned. Tiger eye sushi, fresh ahi wrapped in rice and nori and quick fried, keeps the fish cool while the wrapper is hot ($13.50). Dinner entrées include fresh island fish (Brennecke's specialty), as well as beef, pasta, poultry, even prime rib in three sizes ($21-$29). Dinner entrées also include a visit to Brennecke's fresh, attractive salad bar.

Returning Brennecke's diners may notice that the signature kiawe wood grill has been replaced by a conventional gas stove, and that chef Ligea has retired after decades of kitchen magic, but we know that time does pass by. What doesn't change in owner Bob French's commitment to excellence.

A new chef and a new dining manager have revamped the menu to include a wonderful new combination option – 2 fresh fish filets of your choice on one plate – for only a dollar or so more than the regular portion ($28). Dinners include rice, sautéed fresh vegetables, and a visit to a first-rate salad bar – fresh, colorful, ripe, and appetizing. Instead of rice, try a huge baked potato ($2 extra). Not hungry enough for a full dinner? Brennecke's offers reasonably-priced burgers ($9 including a vegetarian variant) sandwiches, and small plates. Fresh fish sandwich is cleanly grilled and served on a soft bun. Vegetarians will enjoy vegetable stir fry or pasta dinners ($22) or the attractive salad bar ($9 by itself or $4 with a sandwich).

Though small, the wine list is fairly priced, with a Kendall Jackson chardonnay at about $25, or try an exotic drink from the full bar. The 'under-12's' have a great menu, including pizza ($8), fish sandwich ($9), or spaghetti, burger with fries, or soup & salad ($5).

The sandwich menu is served all day, and at lunch you can enjoy the view in full sunshine.

Poipu, on Ho'one Rd. 742-1424. Reservations suggested. 11am - 10pm daily. Happy hour 2pm - 5pm. For the menu, a surf report, or to order tee-shirts, Nukomoi surf wear: 888-384-8810; brenneckes.com. Maps 6, 7

Brick Oven Pizza. 332-8561

Ask just about any Kauai resident where to find the best pizza, and you'll probably hear, 'Brick Oven.' We agree. And we're not alone, for tourists, as well as local families, have made Brick Oven a favorite for years. The cheerful dining room has red–checked tablecloths and murals of pizza serendipity – a pizza shaped like the island of Kauai, for example, with a 'Garlic Grotto,' 'Mushroom Valley,' 'Grand Pizza Canyon,' and 'Port Anchovy.' Friendliness is in the air.

But good as all this is, the pizza is even better, as fine as you'll discover anywhere. The homemade dough – either white or whole wheat – is delicious, crunchy without being dry and with a fluted crust like a pie, shiny with garlic butter. The sauce, in the words of the teenage judges, has "awesome spice, cooked just right." There is lots of cheese, the Italian sausage is made right in the kitchen, and tomatoes are red, juicy and fresh. Portions are generous and quality unbeatable. You may also be tempted to try one of the outrageous special creations, like the 'super.' Or consider a delicious sandwich on fresh baked roll, or a salad. Wash it all down with a pitcher of ice cold beer or soda. Ice comes in

Kauai's best family pizza

the glasses, not in the pitcher. Kids love to watch the dough spin into pizza during that hard, hungry time of waiting, especially at peak hours when it's jammed.

At Brick Oven, you'll find a smile and pleasant word for short persons no matter how cranky. When one child spilled coke, our waitress not only wiped her dry but brought her a new glass filled to the very brim.

Each child can ask for a ball of pizza dough, which feels so good in the hands that it usually manages to stay out of the hair – all the way home.

Kalaheo, on Rt 50. 332-8561. 11am - 10pm. Closed Mondays. Credit cards. Map 6

Camp House Grill 332-9755

If you were able to find Kalaheo, a tiny blip on the line of Rt 50 going west from Poipu, you would probably decide Camp House Grill looks too much like a greasy spoon, and drive right on by. Once inside, however, you'd be pleasantly surprised by the crisp, clean decor: the woodgrain formica tables are well-spaced, blue window frames make a nice contrast with whitewashed walls, and even the green plants look healthy and well-fed. A cheerful waitress will seat you with a smile, no matter how much sand you bring in from the beach, or whether everyone in your party has managed to come up with an even number of shoes.

Though you cut some corners for such reasonable prices, paper place-mats and napkins, even paper cups, are a small price to pay for such tasty food and pleasant service. And the placemats with a drawing of a sugar plantation 'camp house' give hungry kids an opportunity to color, crayons courtesy of management. Another generous touch: sodas are served in a 'bottomless cup.' Camp House Grill makes kids feel welcome with a 'menehune special' cheeseburger, or a 'junior' quarter pound burger, fish, mac and cheese, or popcorn chicken with fries and drink.

Everything is cooked to order, so you might have to wait a bit, but it will all seem worth while once you start eating. Waimea Burger, a barbecue cheeseburger, is perfectly cooked medium-rare with tangy sauce and great cheese. In a Hanapepe Burger, broiled pineapple and teriyaki sauce make an ideal complement to the beef, Swiss cheese, lettuce, and tomato ($6.50). Barbecue 'Huli' chicken is a bit on the spicy side ($10.50). To cool it all off, there's beer, soft drinks, and wonderful milk shakes ($4.50).

Note: there is a different chef on the dinner shift, so consistency varies. Steak, ribs, or chicken dinner plates include soup or salad, potato or rice. Camp House Grill is cheerful and sincere. What you see is what you get –

and some extras, including wonderful home-baked pies. Try tasty and nourishing breakfasts. A deer head and a stuffed rooster look out through the window at what is passing by on Rt 50. Don't let that be you!

Kalaheo, on Rt 50. 332-9755 for take-out orders. Daily 6:30am- 9pm. Breakfast special till 8 am. Credit cards. Map 6

Casablanca *742-2929*

Imagine walking down a torch-lit path through the Kiahuna Golf and Tennis Club and finding a little slice of the Mediterranean. The open air setting, with wicker furniture and green plants, creates a comfortable, romantic atmosphere. And this restaurant has lofty ambitions: breakfast, lunch, dinner, tapas all day, as well as a full bar.

Somehow, Casablanca manages to pull this off, and at the same time transform local Kauai produce, fresh seafood, and Big Island beef into an interesting menu which varies seasonally. Dinner begins with fragrant, crusty bread still warm from the oven. 'Mozzarella Fresca' ($11) is served with a tasty port sauce over poached figs. 'Insalata Caprese' with roasted cherry tomatoes is a better choice than 'Panzella Salad,' a rather ordinary green salad with garlic dressing and croutons. Small plates are also tempting, featuring prawns, lamb, a house specialty lobster 'ceviche,' and crepes – plenty of choices to make up an interesting meal.

There's also a surprising variety of dinner entreés. Duck is seared, served with a balsamic sauce ($21), and roast pork is also excellent. The kitchen prefers to use natural juices and vegetables to enhance entrée flavors rather than overpower them. Even vegetable couscous, a tasty combination of roasted root vegetables over couscous, has distinctive individual flavors, and vegetarians have other options. Desserts are outstanding. Panna cotta is very light with a delicate boysenberry sauce. Blueberry noisetta, chunky with blueberries, is lighter than the ricotta cheese cake, and chocolate mousse with orange is deliciously creamy. At prices similar to Plantation Gardens or Casa di Amici, entrées average more than $20 and appetizers about $10. Keiki menu includes PBJ and grilled cheese.

All this makes Casablanca an excellent choice for dining in a casual yet romantic setting.

2290 Poipu Rd, Kiahuna Swim and Tennis Club. 742-2929. 7:30am until 10pm (M-Th) until 11pm (F-Sat); until 3pm (Sun). Keiki menu. Credit cards. Tapas, full bar, all day; Maps 6, 7

Casa di Amici 742-1555

Casa di Amici, once a Kilauea favorite, now resides in a space that used to be called the Aquarium, so named for the enormous aquarium which divided the dining room from the bar, whose fish population rose and fell with the restaurant's fortunes. The aquarium is still there, the fish are thriving, and Casa di Amici's updated dining room is spacious and at the same time intimate. Tables are well-separated, lit with candle lamps, and glass doors open to breezes.

Many of the entrées popular at the original Kilauea location are still on Casa di Amici's Poipu menu. A nice feature for those who prefer small portions, some entrées are priced as 'full' or 'light' portions, and include an impressive selection of veal and poultry, fresh fish, pastas, and some vegetable entrées.

Prices range from $20/light or $24/full for chicken or eggplant casserole, to $26 for 'Tournedos Rossini,' with medallions of beef, paté de foie gras and fluted mushroom caps (full portion). Appetizers range from $8 (salads) to $15, including 4 risotto dishes. The chef enjoys experimenting with flavors, and his spice and sauce combinations usually add zest to his creations, some more successful than others. Risotto Thai style, for example, resembled a curry served over rice more than a light risotto ($25).

Of the variety of appetizers on the menu, polenta served with mushroom beef marsala sauce ($13) was an enormous portion but on the heavy

Nature's disposable container

side. Salad of local greens is heaped with several lettuce varieties, with a delicious sesame ginger vinaigrette ($8). Fresh ahi ($26/ 9oz) is cleanly grilled and if you order it medium rare or seared rather than cooked through, it is tender and moist; we usually request sauce to be served on the side, and it is a good policy with fish here. The wine list offers a reasonable variety ($25 - $30). Baked Hawaiian made a spectacular appearance, though the flaming meringue sat in a congealed puddle of lillikoi still cool from the fridge.

Everyone is friendly, as is appropriate in a restaurant which calls itself Casa di Amici, from servers to the hostess who ask you how you enjoyed your dinner and reminds you to drive safely. The dinners are largely tasty, if you take the precaution of ordering plain rather than elaborate, and ask for all sauces served on the side. The lot is small; you may have better luck parking on the street.

Poipu, 2301 Nalo Rd. 742-1555. Credit cards. Dinner nightly from 6pm. Maps 6, 7

Dondero's, Grand Hyatt Resort 742-1234

Decorated in vibrant green and white, Dondero's elegant dining room is designed to capture the leisurely pace of the 1920's, before jet-set timetables pushed life into permanent fast-forward. Arranged on two levels, tables are comfortably spaced for privacy. Gracefully twining ivy vines painted on the walls complement jade green and white tiles, some designed with seashells, so that the room seems poised on the edge of a seaside garden, with large

Heliconia Parrot's Beak

windows and french doors opening to the terrace. China and silver are softly lit by the golden glow of crystal lamps.

More than a dozen à la carte entrées range from $27 to $41, as well as pastas from $17. For appetizers, try wild mushroom napoleon with cream sauce ($11.50), or a salad of tomato, fresh mozzarella, and fresh basil ($10.50). Among the entrées, fresh black cod is perfectly cooked, both moist and tender ($33). Chicken parmigiana served with fresh mozzarella was also tasty and tender ($27), and there are some interesting pasta creations. The Hyatt wine list is expensive, most above $50, but many vintage wines are available by the glass. You'll love the desserts – chocolate mousse, an outstanding tiramisu, and strawberry flambeau with vanilla ice cream.

At Dondero's, prices are expensive, with the cost per person well over $50, but the hotel comes with the meal. Consider your dinner as a single course in your entire evening. For an aperitif, walk around the hotel and listen to Kauai's musicians perform in the Seaview Lounge. After dinner, stroll the beautifully lit gardens and enjoy the breezes of evening.

Poipu, Grand Hyatt Resort. 240-6456 or conciergekauai@hyatt.com for reservations. Free valet parking. Children's menu. Credit cards. Maps 6, 7

Joe's on the Green 742-9696

The restaurant at the Kiahuna Golf Clubhouse has long been a favorite of local families for large portions at reasonable prices. Breakfast includes wonderful macadamia nut pancakes ($7) or 'make your own omelettes' ($9), and there's even an early bird special before 9am ($5). At lunch, sandwiches include Joe's Mama Burger; a quarter-pound 'Dog named Joe' with sauerkraut ($6); an excellent fresh fish sandwich ($10); and several salad options, including a 'build-your-own.' Soup with a half-sandwich or a salad is a tasty choice for $7.50. The dining room is open on three sides, with welcome breezes and mountain views. Two nights a week you can enjoy dinner with music by local Hawaiian entertainers. Call to check who's playing. For anyone looking for unpretentious food on large, rather than small plates, it's a great choice.

Poipu, Kiahuna Golf Course. 742-9696. Breakfast from 7am; Lunch till 2:30pm daily. Dinner W and Th 5:30pm – 8:30pm with live Hawaiian music. Happy hour 3pm – 5:30 with pu pus. Credit cards. Maps 6, 7

Kalaheo Coffee Company. 332-5858

Kalaheo Coffee Company has spacious new quarters across from Brick Oven Pizza in Kalaheo. Tall ceilings and fans keep the air moving inside, while outside, tables on the porch offer a view of what's going down Rt 50. Follow the 'House Rules': 'Grab a menu, Grab a table. Place your order.' Then wait at the table for the food to be delivered by runners.

You'll find specialty coffees as well as sandwiches, salads, or cold and hot plates prepared with high quality ingredients. The menu offers a variety of breakfast and lunch options. It's worth standing in line at the counter to order a tasty, inexpensive lunch on the way to the beach. Turkey burger is very fresh, tender, and moist ($8) served on fresh baked roll. Loyal customers rave about 'bagel benny,' toasted with ham, turkey or grilled veggies, topped with a poached egg and hollandaise sauce (with rice or potatoes), and served even at lunch. Try a croissant egg sandwich ($3.50), or a delicious wrap filled with tuna, bacon and melted cheddar and avocado. Don't miss the grilled vegetable sandwich (eggplant, zucchini, and lettuce and tomato), memorable for its unique spices, or grilled tofu and eggplant. On the children's menu, you'll find grilled cheese or PBJ ($3.50). For breakfast try delicious eggs, waffles, pancakes, bagel creations, and fresh pastries. For a beach picnic, call ahead. You can also buy Kauai coffee to take home.

Kalaheo, Rt 50. 332-5858. 6am - 4pm (M-F); 6:30am to 4pm (Sat); 7am - 2pm (Sun). Table service only at dinner Wed - Sat. Credit cards. kalaheo.com. Map 6

Kalaheo Steak House 332-9780

For more than ten years, the Kalaheo Steak House has been serving reasonably-priced steak dinners, a meat lover's delight. The cozy, knotty-pine interior is both pleasant and informal, with comfortable booths along the wall and roomy tables set with fresh flowers and candles.

The menu offers steaks, seafood, and poultry dinners which include rice or baked potato as well as salad. Our waitress recommended the New York steak ($20) and the fresh island opah (10 oz. $22), and we were pleased with both. The opah was flaky and tender, though you might have the butter sauce served on the side unless you love garlic. When the steak arrived too well done to be 'medium rare,' the replacement was perfectly cooked and accompanied by a freshly baked potato – well worth the wait. Prime rib ($27/12 oz or $30/26 oz) was both tender and tasty. Entrées are cooked with little salt, a nice feature.

The dinner salad is an attractive arrangement of ripe tomatoes, white beans and red onions, presented on a pretty glass plate. Choose a delicious papaya seed dressing or a home made blue cheese vinaigrette with real cheese, topped with fresh ground pepper.

Service is friendly and efficient, and prices are reasonable, with teriyaki chicken ($16) at the low end of the entrées. Kalaheo Steak House offers a good value, as two can dine in style for less than $70, including wine.

Kalaheo, 4444 Papalina Rd. 332-9780. Dinner nightly 6pm - 10pm. No reservations. Credit cards. Map 6

Keoki's Paradise 742-7534

At Keoki's you may feel as if you've wandered onto the set of a Tommy Bahama commercial. Tables on several levels surround a wandering stream, where taro grows among lava rocks, and a frog or two rest among the lily pads. Wooden tables are roomy and rattan chairs comfortably upholstered.

Ask to be seated outside, where dining is cooled by evening breezes and you can watch the sky turn luminous with stars. Should a passing shower threaten to douse the table, waiters will set the awnings. Keoki's offers reasonable prices as well as an atmosphere of South Pacific chic. In busy times, a line of hungry diners begins to form at 7pm.

To the right of the entrance is the bar, where you can eat pu pus, salads, hamburgers ($8), sandwiches (($9), and local style plates like grilled fresh fish ($13), or stir fry chicken ($10). Come early and sit at one of the half dozen tables near the bar and you can put together an inexpensive dinner.

Keoki's main dining room features a reasonably-priced, steak and seafood menu. Vegetarians don't have much of interest besides salad and a side of steamed vegetables ($5), but children have good choices.

Dinners include fresh baked rolls and bran muffins, white rice or rice pilaf, and Caesar salad (or romaine lettuce, oil and vinegar). Fresh fish ($23-$29) can be ordered in 5 styles, including 'simply healthy,' cleanly grilled with no butter or oil, and served simply with pineapple salsa. This is the preparation of choice, as we have found the sauces and marinades to be of varying quality, often too strong for the fish. Fresh-baked opakapaka was moist, generous, and cleanly grilled, a first rate piece of fish. Prime rib is tender, and though a bit bland, its appearance at 24 oz was a show stopper ($32). The small wine list offers a nice selection of California wines mostly in the $35 range. Don't miss 'hula pie' ($5 or look for the coupons often printed in the free magazines)

Keoki's reasonable prices and generous portions attract a large clientele. Service is friendly, and on some nights you can enjoy entertainment by Kauai's talented musicians. Call to see who's playing.

Poipu Shopping Village. Reservations for dinner are a must. Bar menu: 11am -11:30pm; Dinner 5pm - 10pm nightly. Credit cards. Maps 6, 7

Koloa Fish Market. *742-6199*

Do you want the best in plate lunches, the freshest poki (3 styles), the tastiest seared ahi? Look for this tiny store front on mainstreet Koloa for deli deals and fresh fish filets. Seared ahi is buttery smooth. Plate lunches (including pork ribs, chicken lau lau, and stir fry) are heaped. Good bets: summer rolls ($3.50), edamame ($3.50), and seaweed salad.

Local folks love it, so be prepared for a line-up at lunch time. The staff is fast and efficient, more than up to dealing with the lunchtime crowd, and you can't beat the prices.

Main street Koloa next to Big Save. 742-6199. 10am - 6pm (M-F); 10am - 5pm (Sat). Closed Sundays. Cash only. Maps 6, 7

Naniwa 742-1661

The Japanese restaurant in the Sheraton Poipu Resort, Naniwa won't whisk you away to an exotic world. The cuisine might be Japanese, but the restaurant was designed for western clientele, so you won't have to remove your shoes upon entering, and you won't be sitting on the floor.

Naniwa's dining room has been moved to the hotel's ocean side, which brings an advantage in location but the loss of much of its charm. Gone is the quiet room by the lagoon. Instead, you are seated in a room that can feel a bit like a cafeteria, surrounded by a sea of diners washed up from adjacent restaurants. You eat on paper place mats with disposable chopsticks at wooden tables at expensive prices.

Six entrées (chicken, seafood, striploin, tempura) can be ordered either à la carte ($28-$33) or as complete dinners including rice, Japanese pickled vegetables, and a delicately flavored miso soup (about $5 more). Sashimi ($11) and sushi ($12-$16) are prepared as you watch by the Japanese chef.

The dining room is attractive and comfortable, though you may find it noisier than you'd like because of its proximity to the main dining room.

Sheraton Kauai Resort, Poipu. 742-1661. 5:30pm - 9:30pm. Closed Sun & Mon. Credit cards. Map 6

Plantation Gardens *742-2121*

For more than 20 years, the lovely Moir Gardens have provided an especially romantic setting – a beautiful old plantation home, where you can dine outside on a veranda cooled by evening breezes fragrant with tropical flowers, and see water lilies glow in moonlit ponds like night-blooming stars. The newest resident of the old plantation home is by far the most elegant. China and crystal sparkle in candlelight on linen cloths. At the same time, the decor is understated, so that the gardens, lit with subtlety and flair, draw the eye to a landscape brushed with shades of darkness. The dining room glows softly yellow and pink in the evening, like a plumeria blossom.

Owned by Piatti, a successful chain of west coast Italian restaurants, Plantation Gardens presents an Italian cuisine Kauai style, incorporating island flavors, local vegetables, light sauces. Herbs, spices, greens, even eggplant, are grown in the restaurant's gardens. Crusty bread still warm from the oven arrives immediately, along with a dish of olive oil pesto. Though not distinguished, the wine list has some good choices at fair prices.

Water lilies bloom at night in Moir Gardens.

You'll find tasty home-baked pizzas from $12, salads and antipasti from $7-$14, and about 8 entrées ranging from lamb, veal, beef, pork, to chicken and seafood, pasta and risotto ($15 - $23). Many dishes feature local ingredients, like an appetizer of Kekaha shrimp ($10). Green salad with tomatoes ($8) was rather ordinary, less interesting than a delicious grilled chicken salad with local greens, almonds, feta, and lilikoi vinaigrette ($11).

Entrées are artfully arranged and on the whole well-prepared. If you prefer the pure taste of island fish, you might ask to have the sauce served on the side. Our fresh ahi, though moist and tender, was covered in a somewhat peppery sauce, as were the vegetables, while the fresh snapper, uku, was covered in a powerful soy-flavored sauce ($25). Pan roasted scallops arrived with a delicious edamame rice cake ($24). A favorite is 'Seafood Lau Lau,' with fresh fish, shrimp, and scallops steamed in their own juices inside a ti leaf, a dramatic and tasty presentation ($25). Try a stir fry of fresh fish, shrimp, and Asian vegetables ($19), or teriyaki grilled eggplant with mushrooms and baby bok choy, a vegetarian option ($19).

If you are looking for a romantic dinner with quiet conversation, Plantation Gardens is a good choice. You won't be hurried, and the setting, almost more than the menu, is a gorgeous centerpiece to your meal. Dine on the veranda, or if you prefer a more informal experience, on the porch near the bar, and see the gardens by candle light.

In Kiahuna Resort, Poipu. 742-2121. Request the veranda. 5:30pm 10pm daily. Take-out. FAX 742-1570. Credit cards. pgrestaurant.com. Maps 6, 7

Poipu Beach Broiler

The Poipu Beach Broiler is decorated in a kind of coconut frond motif, like early Hawaiian church. Tables have a sponge painted top, and fly fans move cooling breezes from the open rafters. A focal point is the bar, where local people enjoy pu pus during happy hour.

The dinner menu offerings are reasonably priced, including chicken ($16), prime rib ($22/14 oz), steak ($20), and fresh fish ($17) which can be prepared blackened, spiced southwestern style, sautéed with macadamia nuts, or grilled. Our fresh ahi, described as "seared" arrived almost ocean-cold, and worse, the grilled ono tasted bitter from the grill. With a modest salad, each dinner was close to $30 for a fairly ordinary meal.

Service is friendly, and the no reservations policy ensures that you come to know the reception staff well by the time you are seated. The manager comes around to ask how you are enjoying your dinner and your wine. He is very proud of the list, which has some excellent choices at good prices, particularly among the reds, like a La Crema pinot noir ($36).

1941 Poipu Rd. 742-6433. 11am – 3pm; 5 - 10pm. Credit cards. Maps 6, 7

Pomodoro 332-5945

Once upon a time, two hardworking brothers from Italy arrived on Kauai via New York City (where one found a wife) and opened the island's first Italian restaurant. Over the years, as Casa Italiana grew into a successful restaurant, they imported the island's first pasta machine from Italy. As time went by, other restaurants, including the specialty restaurants in the big hotels, began to order their pasta, and so they sold Casa Italiana and became full-time purveyors of fine noodle creations.

Kahili ginger

But long hours with eggs and flour were just not as interesting as working with people. A true New Yorker, Gerry missed all those midnight hours in the restaurant, the seven-day workweeks, the temperamental customers and frazzled servers. So the family sold the pasta company, opened Pomodoro Restaurant, and Gerry is once more in her element, bustling from table to table keeping her diners happy.

Pomodoro is both attractive and small, only ten tables. The dining room, filled with leafy green plants, is clean, comfortable, and informal, with a second room for small parties. Everything is prepared to order, with pastas from $12 and the most expensive dishes, the veal specialties, at $22. Add salad or soup, and the price goes up about $6. Children can eat spaghetti, ravioli, or small portions of some entrées.

What comes to the table is fresh, light, and tasty. Dinner begins with homemade foccacia served with extra virgin olive oil and balsamic vinegar instead of butter. Mixed greens ($6) look beautiful with purple and green spinach as well as various fresh organic lettuces. Minestrone arrives in a large bowl generous with noodles, beans, and still crunchy vegetables.

Pomodoro's sauces are light and flavorful without being overpowering, for example in pasta primavera, where the vegetable-based sauce perfectly complements fresh zucchini, carrots, tomatoes, green onions. Traditional pastas are more robust, like delicious manicotti, thin crepes generously stuffed with cheeses, or cannelloni stuffed with meat and spinach. Or try ravioli filled with ground beef or riccotta cheese, and even served with tasty meatballs, or a delicious lasagne.

There's no fresh fish on the regular menu, but you'll find meatless choices like chicken cacciatore or eggplant parmigiana. There's a full bar (try an excellent chi chi) as well as reasonably priced wines.

At Pomodoro, two can enjoy a first rate dinner for about $55. For excellent Italian cuisine and professional service at reasonable prices, Pomodoro is well worth the short drive from Poipu to Kalaheo.

Kalaheo, Rainbow Shopping Center. 332-5945. Dinner nightly. 5:30pm - 9:30pm. Closed Sundays. Credit cards. Children's menu (under 12). Map 6

Roy's Poipu Bar & Grill 742-5000

Roy's is 'dining theater.' From the time you arrive (and you'll probably have to wait, even with a reservation), you're part of a performance. No matter where you stand, you'll feel like you're in the action, as waiters whoosh by, leaning like skiers into the turns in the pathways between tables, steaming plates in hand. Given Roy's long, narrow layout (it occupies several converted souvenir stores along one arm of the Kiahuna Shopping Center), each step, each turn counts, as servers maneuver through an obstacle course of patrons and supply stations.

The kitchen takes up a long slice of the restaurant, or it could be equally accurate to say that the dining room takes up a long slice of the kitchen. For at Roy's, the cookery is the main act, and the kitchen is center stage, just behind a wall of glass from the nearest tables. Chefs and servers hustle and bustle as if performing in a silent movie starring Charlie Chaplin. Watch one chef adorn plates with colorful greens and vegetables, another ladle steaming sauce, and a third flame pasta dishes. In a constant stream, servers enter the in-door, scoot along a narrow pathway picking up plates, and emerge from the out-door, while the executive chef surveys it all, smilingly serene.

At Roy's, what emerges from the kitchen is, for the most part, carefully crafted and delicious. Most entrées can be ordered in appetizer portions for about half the price, so you can

lively Pacific Rim dining

sample a variety of dishes. Try blackened ahi, high-grade, flash fried and outstanding. Even a salad becomes an event when granny smith apples are paired with cheese, walnuts, and sesame miso. 'Hibachi salmon' is as tender and moist as fish can be. Most entrées range from $19-$30. You can try as many as 7 varieties of fresh local fish in memorable preparations ($30-$36), like thyme seared monchong with grilled asparagus and polenta. Vegetarians can have kiawe grilled mushrooms and vegetables.

Roy's is organized for volume, with one person taking your order, another serving bread and water, and food delivered by runners. This system works well for the most part but is not foolproof, as some parts of our order have arrived late, one never appeared at all, and sometimes dishes come so fast that there is no time to appreciate the presentation. Entrées have on occasion arrived at room temperature, or with undercooked accompaniments. Once, the kitchen was out of five items by 8:30, and custom ordering, we were told, always requires prior consent of the chef.

The first Roy's opened in 1988 on Oahu and now has ten branches in Hawaii, Guam, Tokyo, and Pebble Beach, California. All feature the same Pacific Rim cuisine, the same dining style. If you were to imagine the finest in dining, you might envision your table as a peaceful island, where discrete waitpersons present each course unobtrusively, and the only sound you hear is the delicate tinkle of silverware and china.

Well, not at Roy's. You won't find a quiet table, and you are never alone, for the plan, in the words of our waiter, is to 'attack the table' with a barrage of attention – serving and clearing, offering fresh baked rolls or ice-water, sweeping away crumbs from the granite-topped table, or just asking how you are enjoying your meal. It's interactive dining. You're part of the performance, and everyone on the staff seems to be enjoying the show.

This almost electric energy, as well truly delicious food, makes Roy's a unique dining experience on Kauai.

Poipu Shopping Village. 742-5000. Reservations. Nightly 5:30pm - 9:30pm. Credit cards. roysrestaurants.com (menus, recipes). Maps 6, 7

Shells, Sheraton Poipu Beach .. 742-1661

The main restaurant of the Sheraton Kauai Resort Hotel, Shells offers sweeping views of Poipu Beach in a large, comfortable dining room with a relaxed ambiance. Tables are spacious, and tall ceilings keep temperatures cool.

However, a recent design decision has located all three hotel restaurants side by side, more like a dining court than separate dining spaces. Next door,

Amore serves Italian cuisine for slightly lower prices than Shells, though the kitchen is the same for both restaurants.

Shells offers à la carte entrées from $29 to $45 (Kona lobster tail). Appetizers quickly increase your dinner cost, with the least expensive a green salad ($9). Families have a great deal – one '12 & under' dines free with each adult.

Sheraton Kauai Resort. 742-1661. 7am - 11:30am; 11:30am - 2pm; 5:30pm -9:30pm. Sunday Brunch. Credit cards. Map 6

Taqueria Nortenos 742-7222

When you drive by the Kukui'ula Center in Poipu, you often see a jammed parking lot and a small cluster of people on the sidewalk waiting for some of the best, most sensibly priced Mexican food on Kauai. You'll have to wait on the take-out line by the tiny kitchen. (For those in a rush, there's an 'express window') and while you're being driven crazy by the wonderful aromas, you can calculate the price of your selections.

The menu offers meat or vegetarian burritos, tacos, and tostadas at modest prices ($4-$5) with fillings and toppings priced separately, so you can skip the sour cream, say, and not pay for it. Beans, rice, and sauce come free, and extras like tomatoes or onions will be cooked inside your burrito or taco. Nachos have lots of cheese, and fresh corn and flour chips. Guacamole is chunky with avocados. Beef burrito is filled with chunks of tender, tasty shredded beef, covered with cheese, in a large portion. Spices are mild, with hot sauce available.

Poipu, Kukui'ula Shopping Center. 742-7222. 11am – 9pm. Closed Wednesdays. Cash only. Maps 6, 7

Tidepools, Grand Hyatt Resort

Nestled at the bottom of the cliff in the center of the lovely Hyatt Regency Hotel, Tidepools combines an elegant ambiance with expertly prepared dinners, particularly fresh island fish. To get to Tidepools, you walk down from the hotel lobby, a spectacular marble perch built into the cliff and overlooking the sea. At the bottom, clustered near the edge of the hotel's wandering waterways, is the restaurant, laid out like a 'village' of connected Polynesian style huts.

The dining room is comfortable, spacious, and attractive. Parquet tables with cloths of Hawaiian tapa design are well spaced for privacy (there's really not a bad table in this restaurant). Candle lamps glow golden in the evening light, reflected in dark blue glassware.

Tidepools Restaurant, Hyatt Regency Resort Hotel

Tidepools features steak and seafood, some choices in contemporary versions of Hawaiian recipes flavored with local spices and ingredients. On the appetizer menu, mango lobster and crab cake is wonderful ($15), and you'll find several salads from $9. Entrée choices include prime rib, chicken ($29), and fresh island fish, which can be steamed, sautéed, grilled, or even blackened. Try grilled ahi ($34), Hawaiian opah (moon fish), or onaga, our favorite snapper ($34). We like the unique flavor of the fish, and so usually we order all sauces served on the side. Or you can choose lamb, chicken, prime rib, or steak, while vegetarians have options, too. Beef tenderloin ($38) is excellent, crisp on the outside, moist and tender inside. Children have a great menu – chicken nuggets, grilled cheese, fish, pasta, or hot dog.

At Tidepools, portions are reasonably generous, presentation attractive, service polite and unhurried. Prices are high, but the hotel comes with the meal. Explore the lovely grounds after dinner; walk along the ocean and find a hammock, lie back, listen to the waves, and look up into the bowl of stars.

Poipu, Grand Hyatt Hotel. 240-6456 or conciergekauai@hyatt.com for reservations. Dinner nightly 6 - 10pm. Credit cards. Valet parking. Maps 6, 7

Tomkats Grill 742-8887

In a covered veranda at the rear of Koloa's historic Kawamoto Building, Tomkats offers informal, open-air dining at reasonable prices. About a dozen tables with cushioned rattan chairs cluster on the plank floor, and just beyond the railing is a small quiet garden, fringed with red ginger. Fly fans encourage breezes, and even in a sudden shower, this sheltered spot is peaceful, the rain beating a muffled tattoo on the tin roof.

Tomkats courts families and features a special 'kittens' menu with hamburger or grilled cheese. The all-day menu offers a wide range of sandwiches, burgers, salads and complete dinners (from $11 for 1/4 rotisserie chicken). Sandwiches are carefully prepared and attractively served in baskets piled high with french fries. Turkey club on rye with avocado ($1.25 extra) was first rate, as was Cobb Salad. Portions are generous, service friendly, and the hours make Tomkats a convenient stop after the beach, when some of your party may be hissing with hunger.

Central Koloa. 742-8887. 7am -10pm daily. Take-out. A full bar is adjacent, though not intrusive. Credit cards. Maps 6, 7

Yum Cha Asian Eatery 742-1515

The setting is wonderful, a comfortable, air-conditioned dining room with spectacular views. This Poipu Bay Golf Course restaurant has gone through transformations over the years – at one time a terrific soup, sandwich, and salad bar for self-serve, speedy lunches. Now it is a Chinese eatery (actually, this would be the second time) with a chef who has trained in Beijing and Bankok. Try delicious lychee-pomegranate martinis – a house speciality ($10) and pu pus like wok seared edamame with garlic hoisin sauce ($5), piping hot and tasty. Crispy kalua pork spring rolls lined with seaweed nori on the inside, were also delicious. Poached spinach salad ($6) with sesame dressing pleased our vegetarian – and the rest of the table.

Most entrées cost less than $20, a welcome relief from hotel prices. Our vegetarian loved her stir-fried soba noodles with Asian vegetables and tofu ($12). Whole Asian snapper was on the dry side but delicately flavored. Tempura fried banana desert ($7) was shared so quickly that an observer who blinked might not have known it was even on the table. The décor is simple, with a few folding screens separating the small bar area from the rest of the restaurant.

Yum Cha ("to drink tea") offers an extensive variety of teas, as well as Sake, Asian beer, wine, alcoholic beverages, and special fruit concoctions for the entire family. Sadly the dining room is not open for lunch, when you could take full advantage of the view overlooking the rolling fairways of the golf course, studded with palm trees, though you can visit the bar for pu pus and cocktails in the afternoon.

Poipu, Golf Course Clubhouse, Grand Hyatt Resort. 742-1515. Dinner 5:30 - 9:30pm (Tuesday - Sat); Pu pus 3pm - 5pm. Credit cards. Maps 6,7

Na Pali Coast

Westside Restaurants

'favor...eats'

In Hanapepe, *Hanapepe Café & Espresso* serves wonderful vegetarian dishes, as well sandwiches and coffee drinks for lunch, and occasionally dinners. After lunch (or before) visit beautiful Salt Pond Beach Park, a great spot for family picnics. In nearby Ele'ele, try *Toi's Thai Kitchen* for inexpensive, delicious Thai food, and *Grinds* for tasty, generous sandwiches on home-baked bread.

Visiting Koke'e or the westside beaches? In Waimea, stop in at *Wrangler's Steakhouse* for excellent hamburgers and a salad bar; next-door a smaller dining room serves great pizza, calzones, and first-rate sandwiches. *Waimea Brew Pub* has a terrific fresh fish sandwich and wonderful salads.

After the beach, stop in at *Jo Jo's Shave Ice* in 'downtown' Waimea for an ice-cold treat.

Hanapepe Café & Bakery 335-5011

The sign to Hanapepe announces 'Kauai's Biggest Little Town,' and Hanapepe Café & Espresso is a major attraction for vegetarian cuisine with an island flair. You'll find scones flavored with passion fruit, as well as a changing menu reflecting what's up with the chef and what's fresh at the local farmers' market. A half-dozen tables, with fresh flowers and leafy green plants surround the gleaming tiled counter, a remake of the 1940's curved lunch counter of the Igawa Drugstore.

Though this legendary spot has changed hands, the main attraction remains, a healthful, reasonably priced menu (lunches start at $6.50). Garden burger is made from oats, carrots, cottage and mozzarella cheeses. It's served on a cracked wheat roll with bright red local tomatoes, lettuce, and a tasty spinach spread, accompanied by an excellent potato salad. Vegetable fritatta is stuffed with red and green peppers, zucchini, squash, mushrooms, mozzarella – and topped with fresh local tomatoes. 'Healthnut' sandwich is spread with homemade hummus and served open faced with tomatoes, lettuce, sunflower sprouts, cucumbers, and onions. Pasta can feature local vegetables with a light, delicious creamy tomato sauce.

Dinner is served on Fridays (when it's Art Night in Hanapepe), but call ahead to check. The dining room turns Cinderella-like into a lovely black and white café, with soft lighting and music. Entreés (from $16) can include vegan lasagne, pasta with mushrooms, eggplant parmesan, as well as salads, soups, and appetizers.

Afterwards, stroll the main street – it won't take you very long. You can try out the swinging bridge, visit Banana Patch Studio, and sample some taro chips made at the Taro-Ka 'factory,' just around the corner. You'll love those chips!

Hanapepe, 3830 Hanapepe Road. 335-5011. 11am - 3pm (M-Th). 11am - 2pm (Fridays). Dinner on Fridays 6pm -9 pm (call). Credit cards. Map 8

Toi's Thai Kitchen 335-3111

You can't get more underground that Toi's Thai Kitchen! It's original home was a carport semi-attached to a bar called 'Traveler's Den' in sleepy Kekaha, with a half dozen formica dinette sets, some with card table chairs. Now you'll find Toi's in a shopping center in almost-as-sleepy Ele'ele, or you'll try to find it, huddled under the arm of Big Save. Painted cinderblock walls are decorated by white lace curtains and plants, while fresh anthuriums brighten up the dozen formica tables. What comes out of the kitchen is

On Kauai, poinsettia bloom along the road, and glisten in rain showers.

much more special. Toi's has developed a loyal clientele who have spread the word, attracting newcomers who can't believe their eyes when they arrive – and are smiling when they leave.

We came in for lunch one afternoon, hungry and sandy from the beach. We loved Toi's saimin, Thai style – fresh white flat noodles float in a gently spiced broth colorful with vegetables, several varieties of bean sprouts and because the fishermen had been lucky, fresh and delicious ono. Rich and flavorful tofu soup was also terrific. Crispy spring rolls are served with fresh lettuce, mint leaves, and a zesty peanut sauce. The hot yellow curry pleased Jeremy, our spice enthusiast. Everyone loved Thai fried rice, so colorful and tasty that it was devoured to the last grain. Those who prefer American food can try hot, crisp french fries, sandwiches, or burgers.

Dinners include green papaya salad, dessert, and brown, jasmine, or sticky rice. Try Pad Thai, the tender chicken and fresh Thai noodles sweetened with coconut milk and fresh basil. Fresh eggplant sautéed with tofu and huge fresh mushrooms offers a marvelous contrast, both pungent and spicy. Be sure to try Toi's Temptation, a sweet curry made with your choice of chicken, beef, pork, or fish simmered in coconut milk and flavored with lemon grass, lemon, and basil leaves, and served with either potatoes or pineapples. Dinners include green papaya salad, rice, and dessert.

Ele'ele Shopping Center, Rt 50. 335-3111. Lunch 10:30am - 2pm; Dinner 5:30pm - 9:30pm (M-Sat). Credit cards. Map 8

Waimea Brew Pub. 338-9733

Waimea Brew Pub serves a modest menu for lunch and dinner in the living room and on the porch of a restored planation house in Waimea. You can order sandwiches, burgers, salads, or pu pus. At dinner, try steak, fish, or chicken. Best is the fresh fish sandwich ($11), which is juicy, tasty, attractively served in a basket with fries and spicy peanut cole slaw, one of the great lunches on Kauai. Or try your local fish in a salad. As for home brew, four beers are typically on tap, two ales, a porter, a stout, and a wheat.

The comfortable old planation house has wonderful wide verandas. An adjacent museum and gift shop has wonderful, reasonably priced stitchery, including beautiful patchwork and island style pillows made by 'Gramsy.'

Just west of Waimea Town, 9400 Kaumuali'i Hwy. 11am - 9pm daily. 338-9733. wbcbrew.com. Credit cards. Map 8

Wrangler's Steakhouse. 328-1218

Wrangler's dining room retains the outlines of its historic building, where you expect to see Butch Cassidy amble in and take a chair. Ceilings are open to the rafters, fly fans keep the air moving, tables are arranged on two levels for quiet and privacy, with a veranda for open air dining. The decor has a plantation flavor – saddles and tools from the Hawaiian cowboys, the paniolos. On the lower level, you can try calzones, a terrific turkey wrap, home baked pizza with crispy crust, and deli sandwiches.

With most lunches ($8 - $12), Wrangler's offers a salad bar, with fresh greens, tasty pasta salad, even home made chips and salsa. Sandwiches and plate lunches include a 'plantation worker special' with beef teriyaki and tempura served in a traditional three tiered 'kau kau' pot. 'Wrangler Burger' is a juicy half-pounder on a sesame seed roll, with bacon, mushrooms and cheese, served with crispy, piping hot steak fries. Fresh ono sandwich is also first rate.

Service is friendly, prices reasonable, and Wrangler's gift shop features lovely items from local artists, including Hawaiian quilts, dolls, and stuffed animals. Deborah Tuzon of Waimea weaves placemats and jewelry of lauhala; Caz creates wonderful sunflower barrettes and headbands of colorful woven plaid paniolo cloth, and you can try Dennis Okihara's local grown 'Black Mountain' coffee. On your way to Koke'e or to Polihale, you'd be hard pressed to find a better spot.

Downtown Waimea, on Rt 50. 328-1218. Lunch 11am - 4 pm (M-F); Dinner 4pm - 8:30pm (M-Sat). Closed Sundays. Credit cards. Map 8

Index

Kauai Underground Guide
'Campaign for Kids'

The profit from each book sold benefits these outstanding non-profit agencies helping Kauai's children. Our donated dollars help individual children whose needs could not be met within the regular budget. Every dollar goes a long way, and there are no administrative costs.

- **The YWCA Family Violence Shelter** needs money for books, toys, clothes, writing materials and art supplies and child car seats. "We have almost no money in our regular budget for the special needs of individual children." 3904 Elua St, Lihue HI 96766 (808-245-6362).

- **Friends of the Children's Justice Center** helps young victims of abuse and neglect. 4473 Pahee St, Suite M. Lihue HI 96766 (808-245-6214).

- **Hale 'Opio** helps children referred by the Family Court. After- school learning programs include literacy, computer skills, photography, and special tutoring. 2959 Umi St, Lihue HI 96766 (808-245-2873).

- **Kauai Children's Discovery Museum** brings hands-on educational activities to Kauai's children, involving science, computer studies, photography, art. 6458 B Kahuna Rd, Kapa'a HI 96746 (808-823-8222).

- **Ambassadors of Aloha** provides scholarship aid for children gifted in the arts. 5151 Nounou St, Kapa'a, HI 96746.

Tax-deductible contributions can be sent directly to these fine agencies.

Na Mele O Kauai

A perfect companion for exploring Kauai! Just pop this CD into your rental car's stereo and enjoy all-time favorite Kauai songs like 'Hanalei Moon' and 'Beautiful Kauai.' Album sales support Kauai's schools, particularly music education. Talented singer composer Norman Ka'awa Solomon and partner Jon Scott have a great idea – and a great album! Order from *songsoftheislands.com* or buy in music stores on the island.

Start planning your own Kauai Adventure today!

Name
_____

Address
_____

City _____ State _____ Zip code _____

e-mail address

$14.95 includes our exclusive CD of beautiful Hawaiian music by Keali'i Reichel.

Book profits will be donated to the organizations helping Kauai's children, listed at left.

_____ Number of copies @ $14.95

_____ Shipping ($4/priority)
bookrate shipping is free

_____ Total enclosed by check or money order

Papaloa Press

362 Selby Lane
Atherton CA 94027
(650) 369-9994
(650) 364-3252 FAX
papaloa@pacbell.net

Mahalo!
Lenore & Mirah

Keep Up-to-Date on Kauai!
For the latest updates, visit our web site

explorekauai.com

Papaloa Press & Punahele Productions present

KEALI'I REICHEL

and the *Kauai Underground Guide*
exclusive CD Sampler of songs from
some of his hit albums.

KAWAIPUNAHELE

Keali'i's first – the top selling album
of all Hawaiian music – now the first
Gold Record for a predominantly
Hawaiian language album.

Hawaii's foremost entertainer

LEI HALI'A

Keali'i's 1995 award-winning album

E O MAI

Keali'i's acclaimed 1997 album

MELELANA

Winner of 6 Hoku awards, 2000 – a universal favorite

KE'ALAOKAMAILE

Winner of 7 Hoku awards, 2004 – a tribute to family

KAMAHIWA

The Keali'i's collection – a CD of beautiful songs and a CD
of Hawaiian chants, 2005

MAHULIA

The Christmas Album, 2006

Many Hoku Awards since 1994:

Best New Artist, Best Album of the Year, Best New Song,
Best Male Vocalist, Most Popular Hawaiian Artist,
Favorite Entertainer of the Year

To order these albums visit: mele.com

ke.liireichel.com